Ding Dong! Avon Calling!

The Women and Men of Avon Products, Incorporated

KATINA MANKO

OXFORD

UNIVERSITY PRESS

OXFORD
UNIVERSITY PRESS

Oxford University Press is a department of the University of Oxford. It furthers
the University's objective of excellence in research, scholarship, and education
by publishing worldwide. Oxford is a registered trade mark of Oxford University
Press in the UK and certain other countries.

Published in the United States of America by Oxford University Press
198 Madison Avenue, New York, NY 10016, United States of America.

© Oxford University Press 2021

Portions of chapter 4 have previously been published in Katina L. Manko, "A Depression-Proof
Business Strategy: The California Perfume Company's Motivational Literature," in *Beauty and
Business: Commerce, Gender, and Culture in Modern America* edited by Philip Scranton
© 2001 Routledge, pgs. 142–168. Reproduced by permission of
Taylor and Francis Group, LLC, a division of Informa, plc.

Library of Congress Cataloging-in-Publication Data
Names: Manko, Katina, author.
Title: Ding dong! Avon calling! : the women and men of Avon Products,
Incorporated / Katina Manko.
Description: New York, NY : Oxford University Press, [2021] |
Includes bibliographical references and index.
Identifiers: LCCN 2020058276 (print) | LCCN 2020058277 (ebook) |
ISBN 9780190499822 (hardback) | ISBN 9780190499846 (epub) |
ISBN 9780190499853
Subjects: LCSH: Avon Products, Inc. | Cosmetics industry—United States—History. |
Selling—Cosmetics—United States—History. | Direct selling—United States—History. |
Women sales personnel—United States—History.
Classification: LCC HD9970.5.C674 A9563 2021 (print) | LCC HD9970.5.C674
(ebook) | DDC 381/.456685506573—dc23
LC record available at https://lccn.loc.gov/2020058276
LC ebook record available at https://lccn.loc.gov/2020058277

DOI: 10.1093/oso/9780190499822.001.0001

1 3 5 7 9 8 6 4 2

Printed by Sheridan Books, Inc., United States of America

For Gary, Sylvia, and Juliet

Contents

Acknowledgments   ix

Introduction: Avon and the Direct Selling Industry   1

1. The California Perfume Company: A Formula for Sales,
   Motivation, and Female Entrepreneurship   12

2. "Now You Are in Business for Yourself": Representatives,
   Gender, and Business, 1900–1929   41

3. Agents and Agency: The Work and Business Culture of
   California Perfume Company Traveling Agents, 1890s–1930s   75

4. "The Dawn of a New Era": Introducing Avon Products and a
   Depression-Proof Business Strategy   106

5. The Men and Women of Avon: City Sales and the Gender
   Division of Management   133

6. "Ding Dong! Avon Calling!" Selling Women's Economic
   Personality in the Era of *The Feminine Mystique*   163

7. Women of Enterprise: Avon and the Women Who Wanted
   It All   209

   Epilogue   237

Notes   241
Index   273

Acknowledgments

This book began as a dissertation at the University of Delaware, where I had received a generous and long-standing fellowship from the Hagley Museum and Library to study history, business, and technology. Thank you to Arwen Mohun, Roger Horowitz, Anne Boylan, Phil Scranton, and Kathy Peiss, all of whom served on my committee.

I owe enormous thanks to the Avon Corporation. When I decided to write about Avon, I knew I would have to access their corporate archives. I called their headquarters on and off for months to ask about historical records, only to be told that none were available, and usually received only a public relations packet in the mail. But one day I asked the receptionist if I could speak to the Avon archivist, and to my utter delight she said, "We don't have archives anymore." Taking a closer look at the Avon board of directors, I focused on Cecily Selby, listed as a professor of Science Education at New York University, and wrote to her directly, as a fellow academic, explaining my interest in writing a history of the company. She forwarded my information to Jim Preston, Avon's CEO. And twenty-four hours after that, I got a call from Preston's secretary to make an appointment to visit them New York City. I was shown to the back of a mail room where about fifty boxes of archival material had been kept, including a complete run of color catalogs dating from the early 1900s, and was given an office on the twenty-second floor where I worked for several months. As a Hagley Fellow, and knowing Hagley's interest in business manuscripts and their love of beautiful trade catalogs, I asked Michael Nash, the late director of the Hagley Archives, to see the collection. One year later, the Avon archive was moved to Wilmington, Delaware, and to my great good fortune, I was hired as an archival assistant to process the records in it. (To anyone who uses the manuscript collection, that's my handwriting on all those folders.) I owe enormous thanks to the late Lynn Catanese and Michael Nash for securing this incredible collection and supporting my research, and to Roger Horowitz at the Hagley Center for the History of Business, Technology and Society, who has always ensured that I've had access to Hagley's intellectual, financial, and staff support. Thank you to Kevin Martin who created the digital images and secured permission from Avon to use them. And to Carol Lockman, who continues to make every single visit to Hagley a happy adventure.

To my friends from graduate school who made it all bearable—Jan Davidson, Connie Anderton, Gary Ralph, Christine Sears, John Davies, Katie Leonard, and Alan Meyer—thank you from the bottom of my heart. And thanks to my colleagues at the Business History Conference—Jeff Hornstein, Kevin Reilly, Tracey Deutsch, Sharon Murphy, and Stephanie Dyer—as well as the impressive number of people who made valuable and kind comments on my papers, especially Maura Doherty, Mary Yeager, Susan Yohn, Wendy Gamber, Mary Yates, Geoff Jones, and Angel Kwolek-Folland. Debra Michals at Merrimack College has been my generous friend, supporter, and confidant for many years, and I value every step we have made together toward writing our books.

I am grateful to Niko Pfund at Oxford University Press for doggedly sending me email inquiries when this project on Avon Ladies was still young and for remembering me when I finally answered years later. I am especially thankful to him for forwarding my manuscript to Susan Ferber, the most patient, professional, and encouraging editor a reluctant writer like me could ask for. The valuable comments of three anonymous reviewers helped to reshape several chapters and expanded the scope of the book for the better.

Finally, this book would have never been finished without the fervent support and constant, unrelenting, and unbounded exasperation and pleading of my husband, Gary Mitchell. Gary read every word of this manuscript a dozen times. He helped edit every page and spent long days at the table outside this past summer inputting revisions. A writer himself, he actually thinks this has been fun and is already offering to help write the next book, but I forgive him. I hope that our amazing children, Sylvia and Juliet, will develop their voices and their art with as much grit and determination. They will have all the loving support our family can muster.

Ding Dong! Avon Calling!

Introduction

Avon and the Direct Selling Industry

"Ding Dong! Avon Calling!" A whole generation of Americans can sing those words to the tune of a two-chime doorbell. The Avon Lady was made famous in the 1950s by the legion of suburban women who rang doorbells and gave away tiny lipstick samples shaped like bullets. Some would know the Avon Lady through a stack of catalogs left in a staff lounge or on a counter at the beauty shop. Today, the Avon Lady most likely appears as an e-representative through a webpage who, if requested, will personally deliver beauty and cosmetics products right to your door.

The Avon Lady is a company representative who sells lipsticks and lotions, eye shadows and mascara, shampoo and perfume. She is an independent contractor, so she keeps a portion of her sales as commission and can build her business as big or as small as she wants. A woman in business, the Avon Lady serves as a model to test assumptions about what business is, what an entrepreneur does, how managers work, and what economic independence looks like. This book is a women's business history about a company that promoted women as entrepreneurs, not merely consumers. While Avon, known as the California Perfume Company during the first fifty years of its history, sold cosmetics and beauty products, this book is not about the products themselves. It instead focuses on the hundreds of thousands of women who owned their own businesses selling those products.

Founded in 1886, Avon was the only company of its kind to hire women exclusively as its representatives. At a time when Yankee peddlers and itinerant salesmen crisscrossed the country selling pots and pans, cutlery and medicines, furniture, tools, dishes, lightning rods, and all types of sundries, Avon recruited women to sell soaps, perfumes, and household supplies to their neighbors, paid them on commission, and managed the company through the mail. The company took on the name "Avon" in 1939, adopting the brand name of its line of face powder and lipstick introduced in 1929. The number of representatives increased, from about 10,000 before World War

I, to nearly 40,000 at the start of World War II. The size of the representative sales force grew exponentially in the postwar era as women looked for ways to supplement their household income. In the 1960s, Avon had entered a dozen countries, and by the 1980s it had contracted with about a half million American women who were joined by nearly four million representatives in seventy countries worldwide.

Avon was a manufacturer, producing all of its cosmetics, toiletries, and household products in its own factories, and a distributor, publishing sales catalogs, developing marketing strategies, and creating national advertising campaigns. Women worked for Avon in one of two ways in a complex and unconventional corporate structure unique in American business history. Women could work directly for Avon as salaried employees at the level of corporate headquarters, in regional sales and distribution centers, or in manufacturing. Avon hired women as secretaries, marketing specialists, sales managers, or distribution center workers, in packaging, data entry, and correspondence, or as receptionists, to name just a few positions. This history looks closely at those women and the strategies Avon used to promote women into management positions. Avon also contracted with women to generate sales in their neighborhoods, and these company representatives, or "beauty consultants," were the iconic Avon Ladies who knocked on doors, took orders, and delivered products to customers. Representatives were not employees of Avon, but independent contractors, a legal status defined in 1936 that made them independent business owners. They were compensated solely by commissions ranging from 30 to 40 percent of their sales, and they were eligible to earn prizes for achieving tiered sales levels or highest sales in a region. The direct-sales business model—in which a company sells its products to representatives, who in turn sell them directly to customers through home demonstrations—set the stage on which Avon developed a business ethos uniquely for women.

Just as Avon employed women in two very different ways, it also sold and advertised two distinct products. As a cosmetics company, Avon manufactured, advertised, and distributed its line of toiletries, perfume, skin care, cosmetics, beauty, and household products. As a direct sales company, Avon also sold a business opportunity; its advertisements and recruiting scripts promised women financial independence. The women who became Avon Ladies were in the most technical sense Avon's only customer. The Avon Lady bought products from Avon and then acted as a distributor. For more than 100 years, Avon had no other outlet for its products. The company did not sell to wholesalers or retail stores. If a customer wrote directly to Avon headquarters to request an item, the company would redirect her to a local representative. Until the 1980s Avon offered its representatives exclusive territories in its sales contracts and taught women to build independent businesses in their homes. The distribution system was highly personalized but remarkably inefficient, especially because the company sent tens of thousands of small orders to individuals instead of supplying retailers in bulk. Yet direct selling was phenomenally successful for introducing certain types of products to consumers.

Avon is the oldest and largest continually operating direct-sales company in the world. Its rivals were both other cosmetics companies such as Revlon and Max Factor, against whom Avon fought for market share, and also other direct sales companies such as Fuller Brush, Tupperware, and Mary Kay, with whom Avon competed for personnel. As a leader in the direct sales industry, Avon played a powerful role in shaping the language of women and business ownership.

Direct sales, the door-to-door interactions between a representative and the customer, has a long history in the United States and was a method used to sell everything from vacuums, brushes, and Bibles to encyclopedias, vitamins, and cosmetics.[1] Avon's roots in "Yankee peddlers" hawking goods to those who lived in small towns had sustained this model across decades. For the first seventy years of its existence, the California Perfume Company was led by just three different men who gave it a steady and cohesive corporate vision: the founder, David McConnell, who served from 1890 to 1937; his son, David McConnell Jr., who served as president from 1937 to 1944; and John Ewald, who started with the company as a sales clerk in Kansas City and became president and CEO from 1944 to 1967. David McConnell Sr. had sold books door-to-door in the 1880s and was surprised that the samples of perfume he used as an enticement were more popular than the books he hawked. His innovation of developing an all-female corps of representatives distinguished his direct sales business from those of his competitors. Few other companies did so, including those that sold household products, such as the Fuller Brush Company, founded in Hartford, Connecticut in 1904 by Alfred Fuller. Fuller had invented a machine to twist wire into bristles allowing him to make many different shapes and designs of brushes, which he sold himself door-to-door. Soon his wife Evelyn also began selling brushes door-to-door. "Being naturally a saleswoman," Fuller wrote, "she borrowed my samples one day and tried her luck. She outsold me the first day, and almost every day thereafter for two years." He said her selling was "an art," that she was skillful and savvy. "It is odd, come to think of it," Fuller later wrote, "that after Evelyn's great success, I did not recruit women for sales work. In 1908 it was not done."[2]

Alfred Fuller could not have been more wrong. By 1908, the California Perfume Company (CPC) in New York claimed a representative force of nearly 7,500 women who generated more than $750,000 in annual sales. Other direct sales companies founded in the early twentieth century, such as Real Silk (stockings) and Wearever Aluminum (cookware), also recruited women to sell. But to most American businessmen, female door-to-door sales representatives worked in the shadows close to the kitchen or parlor and hidden out of sight from modern retail, which was quickly moving away from itinerant peddlers and toward department store emporiums. While many companies sought to enter city markets, David McConnell kept his sights on a distinctly rural market, and like many direct sales companies, he found it more lucrative to introduce new products in rural markets through a personalized approach.

A demographic profile of the salesforce mined from sales statistics, recruiting and motivational literature, and the 1910 and 1920 census shows that the vast majority of California Perfume Company representatives lived in small, rural towns of fewer than 500 people. They were recruited by CPC's traveling agents, a proto-managerial group of women who toured the countryside to monitor the door-to-door sales representatives and were the first group of women to take on the roles of management within the corporate structure. These traveling agents crisscrossed their large territories, consisting of four to eight states, mostly by train. Usually older and often widowed, they were the backbone of the organization, and their pay and status within the company reflected this; but even then they had to assume various expenses. True parity with their male counterparts at corporate headquarters was unthinkable. Yet the traveling agents' independence and sterling personal reputations attracted many dedicated women to their ranks. Traveling agents ascribed meaning to business that drew on an older, evangelical tradition that equated work with a calling. This concept of a "calling" to become a representative is evident in the rhetoric these traveler agents used to describe the ways they "bestowed" a business "opportunity" on "needy" and "worthy" women throughout the country. Traveling agents taught the local representatives to rely on their social networks to build up business and to incorporate transactions into their daily lives.

While the California Perfume Company sold a wide array of products, including laundry soaps, cleaning products, tooth powder, and toiletries sets for babies, it benefitted from women's evolving attitudes toward cosmetics in the post–World War I era. The corporate hand-picked representatives and the representatives' selection of customers from within their own neighborhood and acquaintance circles ensured that the business opportunity would remain in an arena of the white rural class. Rejecting the association of make-up with "painted ladies" or loose morals, the California Perfume Company representatives privately and personally offered a small array of beautifully packaged face creams, perfumes, rouge, eye liner, and lipstick to their neighbors. Packages featuring the "American Ideal" label rested on the white cultural ideal of pale skin and blushing cheeks. The CPC never purchased any national advertising before 1936, and relied only on the exceptionally beautiful color plate catalog and the product samples that representatives carried.

When the Depression came in the 1930s, many direct sales companies either failed or changed direction, some converting to retail sales while others innovated and expanded their market. Under the new leadership of David McConnell's son, the California Perfume Company became Avon, named after a new line of cosmetics packaged in a sleek blue and silver art deco design.

Avon started to expand into city markets just before World War II, but most of its businesswomen continued using door-to-door methods. Neighbors calling on neighbors, however, was impractical in the crowded and impersonal city markets, which posed a number of problems for nearly all direct sales companies. Alfred Fuller, for example, struggled to establish his business in New York City, a place he characterized as having "vast potential with complicated problems. Apartment houses, anti-peddling ordinances, a floating population, much discourtesy and a fetish of privacy."[3] Although door-to-door methods would never be successful in dense urban areas, the growing suburbs surrounding them offered extraordinary potential. One of Fuller's sales managers, Frank Stanley Beveridge, had already broken off from Fuller Brush in order to start a new company, Stanley Home Products, with a new sales formula designed for suburban sales: the home party. Beveridge urged housewives who liked his products to invite several friends and neighbors over for a sales demonstration and party in exchange for discounts and free prizes. Beveridge's goal was efficiency. Potential customers, handpicked by current customers and urged on by friendly competition to buy, quickly increased sales. Like the Wearever cookware company, Beveridge recruited husband and wife teams as sales agents, the men offering the sales pitch in the living room while the women cooked up meals in the kitchen with the new pots and pans.

Avon's move to establish city markets was bolstered by the war effort in the 1940s. While the size of the sales force shrank during the war, its efficiency soared. Avon's long-standing corporate hierarchy between the "Men of Avon" (the executive staff) and the "Women of Avon" (both among the new sales managers and door-to-door representatives) evolved in important ways during the immediate postwar era. The women who would finally occupy meaningful and influential managerial positions in the company played a crucial role in ensuring the company's success during this period. Avon consciously created a separate middle-management career ladder for women, complete with a corporate glass ceiling, while simultaneously promising independent business control to its representatives. Yet Avon faced problems retooling manufacturing when the war ended. Under the affiliated brand "Allied Products," Avon had provided toiletries kits, deodorant, powder, toothpaste, shampoo, and soaps to US soldiers, and when these lucrative wartime contracts had come to an end, the company needed to rebuild its door-to-door sales force. Avon settled its traveling agents into city and regional sales offices, where they created wholly new management systems in their offices. They recruited hundreds of thousands of women nationwide. Most were married, and most were white. The vast majority worked part time, staying active for fewer than three months, especially before the winter holidays. Most made modest sales and then disappeared from the Avon ranks. Despite such a vast turnover, Avon survived and even thrived. The company experienced phenomenal growth in the 1950s and rose within the cosmetics and direct selling industries to control a substantial portion of the cosmetics and toiletries market, rivaling traditional retail competitors such as Max Factor and Elizabeth Arden. Historian Kathy Peiss notes that "by 1948, 80 to 90 percent of adult American women used lipstick, about two-thirds used rouge, and one in four wore eye makeup."[4]

During this period of growth the direct sales industry changed around Avon, but the company chose to follow none of the new postwar trends. Avon never regarded its most important competitors or the new sales systems they developed as a threat, and instead it played the role of paternalistic advisor to small companies through the Direct Sales Association, creating a set of rules and regulations that could both keep competition in check and ensure the reputation of the direct sales industry. Against the backdrop of

Avon's success in the 1950s, the home party system started by Stanley Home Products was recreated by Tupperware, and a new multi-level marketing compensation structure that was developed first by Amway, a direct sales company selling household cleaners. Among Stanley Home Products' most successful sales agents were single women. Brownie Wise, the mastermind of the Tupperware sales force, began her career with Stanley, as did Mary Kay Ash of Mary Kay Cosmetics and Mary Crowley of Home Interiors and Gifts. Wise, Ash, and Crowley all founded their direct sales companies in the 1950s and 1960s, targeting a huge pool of consumers in a "veritable picnic ground" on the crabgrass frontier of America's postwar suburbs.[5]

Suburban recruiters found a ready and accessible market for new representatives, who in turn found customers lined up in neat little rows, newly redesigned and reorganized in convenient, prefabricated neighborhood blocks, presided over by female homemakers.[6] Tupperware home parties, and the like, fit the needs and structure of new suburban communities, and direct sales companies offered a means to bring together new neighbors who could bond through the process of consumption.[7] The structure of home parties built on and created new suburban traditions and manners, while making extensive use of women's rituals and social networks. A woman would agree to "hostess" by providing the selling space, refreshments, and entertainment, and would reach out to find other consumers. Ideally, the hostess would actively encourage some of her attendees to become hostesses themselves and thereby perpetuate the selling process.[8] Home parties allowed a representative to work more efficiently; she sold to several customers at once, and the social setting assisted her sales pitch. By the very nature of being "guests" women felt a social obligation to at least act interested in the products and maybe even to make a small obligatory purchase.[9] A very large percentage of new direct sales companies adopted this sales model. Meanwhile Avon resisted home parties, largely because its own door-to-door methods continued to be so lucrative in the postwar era.

In some new companies home parties went hand-in-hand with multi-level marketing: a new bureaucratic structure, commission plan, recruiting mechanism, and selling scheme. Under this type of marketing system, sales representatives recruit new representatives from among the customers who attend their sales parties. They are paid commissions from their personal sales and take a slice of the sales made by representatives they recruited, as well as those representatives' recruits. In the business, this is known as establishing a "downline." Paying commissions on multi-level sales was relatively new, first used by the Nutrilite Company in 1945. Two Nutrilite distributors, Jay Van Andel and Richard DeVos, founded and spun off Amway from Nutrilite in 1959 to escape FDA lawsuits about the false advertising claims it made about its vitamins. Multi-level marketing companies use a tiered commission schedule by which recruiters could earn 4, 8, or 13 percent of their recruits' wholesale purchases, depending on the group's activity during a financial quarter.

Another of Avon's future rivals, Mary Kay Cosmetics, started fairly inconspicuously in 1963 as a multi-level marketing company. The Mary Kay cosmetics line included just a fraction of the products that Avon carried, but the multi-level commission structure added a new dimension to women's economic potential. Avon always maintained a dual-marketing formula, which limited representatives' earnings to the commissions on their personal sales. At Mary Kay, however, when a representative had recruited three women into the company, she earned 4 percent of their wholesale purchases, provided each had submitted a minimum wholesale order. The more women a representative recruited to her downline, the greater would be her financial incentive to motivate them to sell. Within just ten years, a dozen top-earning Mary Kay representatives each claimed more than $1 million in commissions every year.

Like the sales structure, Mary Kay's recruiting philosophy relied on developing women's social networks. And its recruiting rhetoric self-consciously linked family and business. Mary Kay Ash believed that multi-level commissions were better for the representative and used it to build her sales staff. In her personal experience, dual marketing commissions did not pay enough to allow a representative to become independent, nor did a corporate sales management position provide stability or fairness. Mary Kay had served as a district sales manager for the World Gift Corporation, for which she had to travel more than eight months of the year, recruiting, training managers, attending conventions, and delivering motivational speeches. Her sales unit was in World Gift's top five for more than fifteen years. In 1962, she approached her boss with the idea to make audio-video training tapes. He assigned her a male assistant who one year later was promoted above Mary Kay at nearly twice her salary. This wasn't the first time that she had experienced sexism at the company, but this time she quit and started her own. "Those men didn't believe a woman had brain matter at all," she said. "I learned back then that as long as men didn't believe women could do anything, women were never going to have a chance."

The biggest changes in direct sales industry corporate structure and marketing strategy were accompanied by the formation of distinctly charismatic styles of new direct sales companies in the 1950s, '60s, and '70s. The powerful and successful emotional management techniques developed concurrently by women such as Brownie Wise at Tupperware, Mary Crowley of Home Interiors and Gifts, and Mary Kay Richards Ash of Mary Kay Cosmetics blended an overtly Christian moral code with a politically conservative rhetoric that worshipped the myth of the self-made man. Thousands of direct sales companies copied and expanded this approach to create unique corporate images in the postwar period. Industry giants such as Amway, Shaklee, A. L. Williams Life Insurance, and Princess House created the most recognizable corporate cultures and, in the process, cemented a public vision of direct selling with charismatic religious organizations and a management style many generously identified as brainwashing for profit.

The history of direct selling in the postwar era was marked by feminization of the industry. Women came to dominate the industry sales force, the cultural status of direct selling declined dramatically, and more companies were created and managed with strategies that recognized, mirrored, and exploited women's social networks.[10] More than 5,000 direct sales companies existed in 1965, at least two-thirds of which had started between 1950 and 1960. As more companies adopted home parties and multi-level marketing, the gender makeup of the sales force shifted industry-wide. Women represented less than 15 percent of all direct sales agents in the United States in the 1930s, but by 1980, they made up more than 80 percent of direct sales representatives industry-wide.[11] Even established door-to-door companies such as Fuller Brush admitted in 1965 that 60 percent of Fuller Brush Men were women.[12]

In sharp contrast to the start-up direct sales companies, Avon's corporate culture built on its reputation in the late twentieth century as a modern, multinational, billion dollar company, a major player in the mainstream cosmetics industry. Given its sheer size and reputation, Avon was neither intimidated by other upstart direct sales companies nor pressured to adapt any of their marketing or compensation schemes. Instead, Avon developed a sales philosophy that was mirrored in advertising campaigns in more than a dozen magazines. Avon expanded into new international markets, having first entered Cuba in 1953, and Puerto Rico and Venezuela in 1954. Its president, John Ewald, rang the bell at the New York Stock Exchange, selling its stock publicly for the first time, in 1964. Contrary to doomsayers in business magazines who declared direct sales dead, Avon continued to add more diverse and dedicated salespeople to its staff in the decades following the war. It relied on volume to make a profit, and the new suburban sales force produced results. The ingrained corporate ethos at Avon allowed it to disregard any competitor, and its size allowed it to dismiss the wide number of innovations in the direct sales industry. Steadfast adherence to its door-to-door system precluded any consideration of challenges or modernization of its methods. This tendency would prove to be both Avon's strength and its weakness.

Avon was considerably challenged by the changing corporate and cultural movements that shaped America during the 1960s. Its place in the popular culture remained strongly aligned with the white, middle-class women who still responded to the doorbell at home. Moving outside this demographic, both for marketing and recruiting purposes, proved nearly impossible for Avon. Nevertheless, while executives were sometimes slow to react, Avon maintained a significant role in American women's business history as the company rode the wave of the civil rights and the women's movement through the 1970s and '80s, and began developing a forward-thinking, purpose-driven corporate philosophy. The Avon Foundation added a new mission to Avon marketing, raising millions of dollars for breast cancer research and the prevention of domestic violence.

During the 1980s, Avon's corporate staff entered into a robust conversation with both the feminist movement and antifeminists. Helen Gurley Brown, former editor of *Cosmopolitan*, had written a book called *Having It All*, a phrase women across the spectrum wielded as both a goal and a bludgeon. Soon, conversations about "having it all" were joined by examination of the "glass ceiling" and the "mommy track." The company wrote new recruiting literature that positioned the entrepreneurial role of the Avon representative in relation to the wave of women working full time. Believing it could play a productive role in understanding the role of women in the corporation and in independent business, Avon joined with the US Chamber of Commerce to bestow the Women of Enterprise Award, intended to shine a light on both women business owners and the value of the Avon representative's direct sales business opportunity. The award applications form the basis of an analysis of businesswomen, including those at Avon who sought to "lean in" to small business ownership.

"More than a beauty company," the Avon slogan of the 1990s said, "Avon is a company of women, and for women." Executives focused a lot of their energy on forging a woman-positive and feminist identity when most other companies, especially in the 1970s and 1980s, were only beginning to grapple with concerns about structural and cultural restrictions put on women in business. Avon corporate offices made remarkable efforts, winning nominations throughout the 1990s on lists of "the Best Companies for Women to Work For" by offering on-site child care, providing for flexible work schedules, and making measurable efforts to promote women into management. Despite its success, the company only slowly welcomed women into the highest ranks of corporate management and protected the male preserve of the executive suite. Avon made headlines in 1999 when it finally named Canadian-born cosmetics executive Andrea Jung as CEO, fully 113 years into its history.

At that point, Avon was already on a downward trajectory. Only a few years earlier, Avon had survived hostile takeover bids from both Amway and Mary Kay Cosmetics. Representatives had mounted letter writing campaigns to resist both companies, fearing that they would soon have to adapt to multilevel marketing, recruiting, and commission structures. But Avon could not ignore the appeal of more lucrative opportunities and soon started trying all options to see what would work. In the 1990s, some representatives could choose a modified multi-line recruiting and commission program, regional meetings ramped up a charismatic motivational style, and a new line of Mark cosmetics were rolled out to target younger and trendier women as Brand Ambassadors. Andrea Jung also expanded Avon's marketing reach into brick and mortar stores with an eye toward competing with luxury brands. But Avon, reaffirming its commitment to direct sales through independent representatives at every turn, could never quite solve the twenty-first-century challenges presented by internet marketing and nearly instantaneous delivery of products.

1

The California Perfume Company

A Formula for Sales, Motivation, and Female Entrepreneurship

In 1877, nineteen-year-old David McConnell left his father's farm in Ithaca, New York, to work for a small firm in Manhattan called the Union Publishing Company, where his first job was to hawk magazines, greeting cards, and book sets door-to-door.[1] Union Publishing, like many book companies in the post–Civil War era, sold products directly to the home, and like many itinerant peddlers before and after, McConnell took up sales work as a means to pay for his adventure. He traveled alone and earned a straight commission on the products he sold. "I traveled in nearly every state east of the Rocky Mountains and this gave me valuable experience . . . and good insight into human nature," he later wrote. "The one thing I learned successfully was how to sell goods to the consumer." [2] McConnell's supervisor, Mr. Snyder, soon promoted him to general agent, which meant that in addition to selling, he also recruited and trained men and women to sell Union Publishing products in their hometowns. McConnell monitored his recruits' sales records and frequently wrote them letters of inquiry, motivation, and product updates.

McConnell traveled the eastern United States coast for nine years and managed temporary sales offices in Maine, Chicago, New York, and Atlanta, earning $40 per month plus commissions and expenses. Then in 1886, he purchased half of Union Publishing for $500 when Snyder moved to California to seek his fortune.[3] McConnell continued to deal in books and paper but expanded the product line to include items such as furniture polish and silverware, which were common stock in the peddling trade. "The book business was not congenial to me, although I was, in every sense, successful in it," he later explained.[4]

Ultimately, he wanted a more profitable line than books, and according to company folklore (which he himself likely originated), he offered perfume samples to prospective customers as gifts if they would listen to his selling spiel. McConnell's mostly female clientele enjoyed the samples more than the books. He learned to mix perfume himself, and the first line included popular scents (or, as he called them, "odors") of violet, white rose, heliotrope, lily-of-the-valley, and hyacinth. He also added flavoring extracts to the line, which he manufactured using the same process as perfumes, including favorites such as vanilla, peppermint, and almond. "My ambition," he wrote, "was to manufacture a line of goods superior to any other, to put the moneyed value into the goods themselves, and just enough money in the package to make them respectable, and . . . take these goods through canvassing agents direct from the factory to the consumer."[5] Perfumes and extracts proved so popular that he soon phased out the books altogether. In 1892, McConnell's business partner, who was living in California when he launched the perfume business, suggested "I call [it] California Perfume Company [CPC], because of the great profusion of flowers in California," even though the California Perfume Company was neither based in California nor limited to the manufacture of perfume.[6] He chose "California" he said, because it seemed exotic both to him and to the hundreds of rural women who made up his sales force and consumer base.

McConnell turned first to the sales force already working for Union Publishing when he purchased his share of the company in 1886 and introduced his new scheme for selling extracts and perfumes, offering them a flat 30 percent commission on every product sold.[7] "Dear Friends," he wrote in 1892, "We have decided to place these goods on the market after our own peculiar method, and will necessarily have to make confidants of a large number of worthy and enterprising people in order that we may carry out this system perfectly."[8] McConnell's "peculiar method" was a variation of peddling; he wanted women agents to sell his products in the communities where they lived rather than traveling from town to town. By 1899, nearly 5,000 CPC representatives sold perfumes, extracts, vegetable colorings, tooth cleaning tablets, shampoo creams, witch hazel and almond balm creams, baking powder, olive oil, and a variety of other household products in every state in the Union.[9] McConnell's two innovations—recruiting women to sell directly to other women, and offering them a venue of economic possibility and empowerment—formed the basis of his uniquely profitable enterprise. They were elements found in no other turn of the century business venture.

At the turn of the century, the California Perfume Company entered a fluid and unstructured consumer market. When David McConnell began his company, the cultural history and traditions of Yankee peddlers and commercial travelers had a significant impact on the way he organized and

Figure 1.1. David H. McConnell, founder and president of the California Perfume Company, 1908. (Courtesy of Hagley Museum and Library.)

marketed his products and business.[10] Direct selling was an alternative merchandising method promoted at the same time that an increasingly competitive and complex marketplace—composed of mail-order houses, branded products, and corporate-sponsored selling organizations—had transformed a nineteenth-century style of mercantile economy.[11] In order to compete with the new and growing pool of mass production and distribution firms, some of the smallest companies established a foothold in the retail sector by introducing their products through a direct sales representative force selling door-to-door. Given that products would be delivered in person, companies tended to manufacture and distribute products they could produce in small batches and deliver easily and cheaply.

During the first third of the twentieth century, door-to-door sales competed with mass merchandising through department and country stores, as well as and mail-order catalogs, such as the Sears and Roebuck, which sold thousands of new products to consumers in rural communities and cities across the United States. Perhaps as many as 2,000 direct sales companies existed in 1910, although they are difficult to count because they are not categorized as such in the census, and they did not utilize advertising, or claim retail shelf space.[12] Direct selling, or house-to-house canvassing, allowed small companies to enter the marketplace using commissioned sales agents. The system had the advantage of building direct relationships to consumers and was much cheaper than retail, as many companies at the turn of the twentieth century made substantial investments in advertising, brand development, shop space, and distribution. Consumers in rural markets purchased an array of branded and unbranded soaps and toiletries through a variety of venues, including direct sales.[13] But while a direct sales company allowed smaller and poorer manufacturers a relatively cheap way to place their goods on the market, but there were obvious disadvantages. Most companies operated on a small scale and incurred high distribution costs. Market coverage was very inefficient, and while these smaller manufacturers might have wanted to exert some control over their sales force, they lacked the means to organize, train, and monitor their performance. As a result, the vast majority of direct sales companies survived only a few years, then either folded in the face of competitors' centralized corporate marketing or joined in and converted their sales operations to regular retail venues once their products or services became popular.[14]

Itinerant salesmen, though, became embedded in the new commercial culture. Tens of thousands of sales agents had introduced the vast majority of novel products, such as sewing machines and farm equipment, and new branded products like Ivory soap, Crisco, and canned foods, especially in rural areas. Salesmen's behavior on and off the job quickly became a part of popular folklore. Their reputations and theatrics entertained consumers in general stores and informed shopkeepers about the latest merchandizing trends. Salesmen were know for their ability to spin tales, to speak in the latest slant, and to tell the latest joke. They packed and repacked their sample cases and trunks in hotel lobbies and in rooms created specially to accommodate the traveling trades. Many assumed that traveling salesmen were familiar with illicit sexual behavior simply because they spent most of their time in hotels and witnessed liaisons between "solid citizens" and "tempting women." The Gideons, a commercial travelers association, formed just to counter this behavior, hoping that the Bibles they placed in every hotel room would reform wayward men.[15]

But more important than the culture, the inefficiency within the sales system drained corporate profits that brought salesmen to heel; independent salesmen had a difficult time maintaining inventories, could not extend credit to customers, and returned payments late to the central office. Companies blamed the "live wires," the salesmen who were unaffiliated with a single company, as a source of uncertain and uncontrollable activity. Eventually, independent agents were replaced with salaried salesmen and uniform policies for sales, accounting, and credit. Most distributors, wholesalers, and manufacturers eventually folded independent salesmen into a corporate structure in order to protect their company's public image and improve efficiency within growing bureaucracies.[16]

Salesmen connected both manufacturers to retailers, and consumers to the company and its products. They worked in a variety of locations and with a wide range of responsibilities and latitude; some salesmen worked as jobbers for large warehouses that bought and sold unbranded goods in mass quantities, while others specialized in a particular manufacturers' products. By the 1910s, many manufacturers of branded products relied on their own salesmen as liaisons between proprietors and the company: monitoring stock, setting up displays, distributing premiums and consumer advertising literature. As troubleshooters, they handled loss and damage claims and credit problems, and acted as housekeepers, replacing dirty and faded displays, and spiffing up products on the shelf. By reaching out to consumers outside urban retail centers, salesmen paved the way for mass merchandizing throughout the twentieth century.[17]

The California Perfume Company made its mark by remaining dedicated to direct selling and house-to-house canvassing. McConnell remained focused on developing a rural market where he used women's social networks to sell his goods. Rural markets were also home to a seemingly unlimited pool of women who had few job opportunities and whom the company consciously recruited as sales agents.[18] McConnell did not try to compete directly with similar products on the market or to place CPC products on retail shelves. As other retailers surpassed his company at an astonishing rate, McConnell only slowly adjusted to modern distribution and marketing techniques. Had he been in competition with a company like Sears, established by R.W. Sears the very same year that McConnell began the CPC, he would have lost on many counts. For a short period of time, the two companies followed similar paths. Both met the challenges of marketing to the rural consumer by offering money-back guarantees and building name recognition and trust. Both relied on improved distribution systems and the national infrastructure of railroads, telegraphs, and post offices to transport their goods directly to thousands of homes and bring their products to rural Americans.[19]

However, their techniques for serving this rapidly expanding market were vastly different, as were their results. The Sears catalogue, introduced in 1895, transformed retailing history. McConnell, on the other hand, eschewed depersonalized mail-order sales and continued to rely on a comparatively small corps of women who solicited house-by-house to sell his products. The vast disparity between their results is impressive. Sears filled 19,000 orders for sewing machines in October, 1897 alone; McConnell and his small staff celebrated wildly when they received orders totaling just five hundred dollars in one day that same month. Sears reached $2,000,000 in annual sales in 1908, but it would take McConnell until 1926 to achieve that same mark. Whereas Sears was willing to experiment with selling methods and expand his supply line and distribution system, McConnell continued to manufacture his own goods and towed a conservative line in terms of business practices. In fact, he insisted on continuing business and management methods that, in light of modern retailing organization procedures, seemed categorically old-fashioned and illogical.

To be successful, CPC had to overcome a significant public distrust of direct sales and salesmen. Distinguishing his method from peddling was important not only for building a strong consumer base but also for recruiting women to sell the CPC line. "One thing we want you to bear in mind distinctly," he told his recruiters in the 1899 traveling agent's manual, "[is] that [CPC work] is not peddling or anything of that kind."[20] In an era when middle-class women sacrificed some of their social respectability by working, McConnell walked a thin line between offering employment and avoiding association with a seedy profession. He upended the idea that women were merely housewives in need of pin-money, and instead created sales and recruiting manuals that justified women's need for money and emphasized the respectability of women participating in business. McConnell also hoped that women's reputations and networks would help him avoid some real legal issues. Protests throughout the United States against traveling salesmen led many communities to pass local ordinances banning unsolicited sales. As many towns denied permission to salesmen to practice outright, even legitimate companies created crafty techniques to circumvent such ordinances. Fuller Brush, for example, claimed their salesmen only left its catalog with a housewife on his first visit and on the second only wanted to pick it up. But if, in the course of conversation, the "lady of the house" mentioned she would like to order a few items, then the salesman could take an order at her request. Local intolerance of traveling salesmen continued well into the 1920s and 1930s, and CPC representatives and recruiters wrote many stories in sales manuals and journals detailing how they dealt with signs on doors of homes, train stations, and post offices announcing "solicitation not welcome."[21] McConnell believed that hiring women who built customer bases on pre-existing kin, friendship, and community networks would mean that their selling activities would provoke few, if any, complaints or lawsuits. Overcoming the public's distrust of sales was solved by developing women's social networks, which led to an original management formula that promoted women's sense of economic possibility and empowerment.

Women served as one of two types of California Perfume Company agents: door-to-door sales representatives and traveling agents. One group sold products to consumers, the other sold "business opportunity" to women they hoped would become representatives. Those who agreed to sell CPC products door-to-door were originally called "Depot Agents," because they often lived in towns adjacent to railroad lines.[22] They followed the same practices that McConnell had as a Union Publishing agent. CPC door-to-door representatives sold only in restricted territories, usually their own hometowns, and did not travel. The traveling agents, on the other hand, were the elite in the CPC sales organization, and their position was comparable to middle management. They had the power to choose and hire women as representatives, and they received privileged information from the company about sales strategies and the value of business their recruits generated. To qualify as a traveling agent, the CPC required each candidate to have previously worked as a door-to-door representative and in that capacity to have made at least $250 in wholesale orders, as proof that she knew "the business." By 1900, McConnell employed forty-eight traveling agents who recruited and trained more than 6,500 door-to-door CPC sales representatives throughout rural America. In 1910 the numbers grew to 100 traveling agents and nearly 15,000 representatives; in 1920 there were more than 150 travelers and 20,000 representatives. McConnell had now put into action his singular idea that he was not merely selling toiletries and cosmetics, but he was offering women something unique, a business of their own.

McConnell highlighted the singular contributions of one traveling agent in his 1903 company history: Mrs. Persus Foster Eames Albee from Winchester,

New Hampshire. McConnell may have recruited Albee, the president of the Winchester Literary Guild, into Union Publishing in the 1880s while he worked as an agent in the Maine office.[23] Albee was, according to McConnell, "one of the most successful General Agents I had in the book work, and it was in her hands I placed the first [perfume] sample case, or outfit."[24] McConnell charged Albee with recruiting and training other women to sell the new perfumes in the early 1890s; according to his history, she was his only general agent, or recruiter, "in that line" for six months. "It is, therefore, only befitting that we give her the honorary title of Mother of the California Perfume Company," McConnell wrote, "for the system that we now use for distributing our goods is the system that was put in practical operation by Mrs. Albee."[25] McConnell seemed highly aware that women's perspectives and unique social position were especially important. He rhetorically balanced his own patriarchal authority with Albee's maternal practicality and granted women authority over sales and service in his company.[26]

McConnell's praise and gratitude to Albee for developing the CPC sales system, however, is the only evidence of Albee's contribution, for nothing else in the historical record bears her name. It is unlikely that she wrote the sales or recruiting manuals, for, according to McConnell's Union Publishing Company correspondence files, McConnell established a successful sales system through which agents recruited, trained, and motivated sales representatives—and it closely mirrored the system CPC agents used later. Albee's name never appeared in sales records, traveling agent accounts, newsletters, or company correspondence before McConnell wrote his company history in 1903.[27] Not until 1978, when the first "Albee" porcelain figurine was awarded to the top representative in sales in each district was she re-dubbed (somewhat misleadingly) Avon's first sales representative and the "mother" of the company.[28] Despite the incomplete details about the extent of Mrs. Albee's singular contributions to the company's sales and recruiting methods, McConnell's focus on Albee illustrates the importance of class and gender in creating a respectable business strategy. Albee's stature in the Winchester community as a lawyer's wife and literary club member brought an element of middle-class decorum to a culturally suspect peddler's system.[29] CPC literature reflected McConnell's class-conscious emphasis on the importance of cultivating a positive business image.

Nothing in Avon's extant records directly reveals McConnell's personal reasons for hiring women. In the 1920s, when he was fond of printing self-congratulatory pieces about the company, McConnell claimed that he had felt sorry for women who had no means of earning a livelihood. Actually, he seemed to have stumbled into recruiting a female sales force somewhat by chance or, more accurately, in his search for profit. It seems likely that the success of Mrs. Albee in New Hampshire and of other travelers throughout the United States was what convinced McConnell of the value of hiring women to peddle his wares. Much in the same way that he did not attempt to sell his goods in large cities because of the difficulty of organizing sales, he may initially have chosen to hire women because they had not been part of a customary male traveling tradition. Women's more settled life in small towns allowed McConnell to exploit his business plan for providing steady service to consumers on a continual basis.

Regardless of his original intent, three trends resulted from having a predominantly female sales corps. First, even though McConnell and his staff recognized that they wanted women to sell CPC products, they stopped short of altering their motivational and business literature to accommodate the specific needs and desires of women. Instead, CPC literature combined language that clearly spoke to women but that also drew from a literature addressed to a broader audience of male business writers, owners, and managers. Second, McConnell created a profitable system that did not rely on traditional full-time sales representatives or the work patterns that men usually fashioned. Despite constantly encouraging women to make sales their full-time occupation, McConnell knew that representatives worked just five to ten hours a week. Yet, as long as they worked consistently, he could profit from their labor. Instead of relying on large and continuous business from a smaller corps of full-time salaried workers, McConnell compensated for women's short-term, occasional labor by basing his sales strategy on attaining a high volume of small orders from a large corps of representatives. On paper, it did not matter whether men or women sold CPC products, so long as overhead expenses remained low and orders could cover his costs.

Third, McConnell relied on representatives who worked independently within their communities and from their homes, a strategy that substantially reduced expenses. He did not have to provide regular salary and office space for the vast majority of his workers, and he eliminated the expense of retail space. Unlike mass retailers who spent hundreds of thousands of dollars on building their selling emporiums, the CPC representative and her customer—not the company—created the selling space in private parlors and kitchens. However, McConnell risked losing control of his workforce, for there was no way CPC managers could regulate the quality or frequency of representatives' work. Also, although it cost CPC very little to maintain distributors' contracts beyond the cost of the paper and stamps to communicate with them, this approach relinquished the leverage employers had on salespeople to help ensure that the company would profit. McConnell's solution, ironically, combined a sophisticated information and mapping system with a decentralized management structure. Women, therefore, had an extraordinary amount of freedom to shape the public perception of the CPC, its values, and its mission. The California Perfume Company thus represented an alternative form of business organization, one that women made viable.

A female sales force also led the California Perfume Company's entry into cosmetics and beauty products that were widely promoted by women's magazines such as *Godey's Lady's Book* in the latter part of the 1800s. The gradual acceptance of cosmetics and beauty products provided peddlers with a small but growing market, although adoption of daily routines of "painting" one's face were relatively rare, and cultural bias against "painted ladies" still held sway. By 1900, the demand for creams, lotions, perfumes, and eventually lipstick and rouge increased dramatically. Rural women, living in remote areas underserved by the burgeoning retail markets of the city, became a good bet for enterprising salespeople who brought perfume and toiletries into their small towns, which meant that the CPC was well positioned to expand along with this cultural shift in the widespread use of cosmetics and women's shifting attitudes toward using them. McConnell purposely avoided growing urban markets in favor of courting rural consumers. In fact, more than 85 percent of CPC representatives worked in rural towns with populations of fewer than 2,500 even into the 1920s.

McConnell's goal of serving rural women did not extend to African American women and families, going so far as to instruct agents to avoid African American neighborhoods. It was a missed opportunity, both for recruiting and sales. As historian Lu Ann Jones notes, southern women welcomed the rolling stores brought by peddlers that provided both access to wares and a venue of entertainment. Whereas country stores catered to the needs and customs of men, African American communities and women found that the personalized home visit by the peddler allowed them to barter and trade independent of lines of credit that might be needed in town.[30] McConnell ignored the African American markets believing that he had solved problems identified with peddling: the public perception of selling as disreputable and the need for consistent and reliable service. But in reality, his solution to create trust was supported within a racially conscious policy. McConnell's all-female sales force assured their customers that they were not like other itinerant peddlers who quickly moved through towns and rarely could be located once products arrived at consumers' homes. His all-white sales force ensured that CPC products would be sold only in white communities.

Other companies stepped in where McConnell would not. One standout example of the early direct sales era was Madame C. J. Walker's Manufacturing Company, known for its hair care products and salons specifically catering to the needs of African American women. Born Sarah Breedlove in 1867, CJ Walker was a commissioned sales agent for Annie Turnbo Malone's multimillion dollar company, Poro, that specialized in door-to-door sales of cosmetics and hair care products. When the two women split following a disagreement, Walker adapted Malone's methods and pioneered the "Walker Method" of hair care and sold her services in both salons and through direct sales. Between 1906 and 1917, Walker established shops and offices in Denver, Indianapolis, Philadelphia, and New York. She trained "beauty culturalists" and instructed women on sales, recordkeeping, and product use. More than 20,000 women served as Walker agents between 1911 and 1917, rivaling the size of the CPC sales force and providing opportunities for entrepreneurship and commerce to black women and their families in a racially segregated market. Both Malone and Walker pioneered a version of multi-level marketing that encouraged representatives to recruit others and built modern franchise methods for hair salons.[31] Each used sales agents to open isolated consumer markets and rewarded their agents with cash and prizes. Like many African American businesswomen of the Progressive Era, Walker organized her representatives into state clubs, modeled on the National Association of Colored Women. She and Malone were renowned for contributions to charities and educational institutions that supported the African American community; both women were recognized for their work with the National Association for the Advancement of Colored People (NAACP). The focus on community uplift that characterized black entrepreneurship was rarely shared by white-owned businesses. Whether through outright bias or disregard, McConnell consciously avoided the lucrative and underserved African American market for decades.

Sales and Motivation: "The CPC Way"

CPC grew from a one-room operation with fewer than ten employees to a complicated, bureaucratic organization. From 1892 to 1895, McConnell oversaw most of the operations and maintained all company records from his Manhattan office at 126 Chambers Street, where he claimed he manufactured, bottled, packaged, and shipped his perfumes to his representatives. In 1895, he built a separate manufacturing facility thirty-five miles away in Suffern, New York, where he employed eighteen workers. He also expanded the Chambers Street building to fill six floors for billing, correspondence, and sales management offices.[32] Representatives canvassed their neighborhoods with catalogs and a CPC sample case, then sent their orders to the central offices; from there, the order form went through billing and representative accounting. All orders were collected and tallied in Manhattan, then sent to the Suffern plant by late morning. By early afternoon Suffern employees loaded up a train car to bring products back to Manhattan, where representatives' orders were boxed and shipped that same day via an express service. (After 1908, products were shipped to representatives directly from Suffern.) The door-to-door representatives delivered the products to their customers who, ideally, paid the representative and gave her another order. Thus completed and started again the cycle of CPC manufacturing, sales, and distribution.[33]

Very early in CPC history, McConnell had relied on managers in regional sales offices he had inherited as part of Union Publishing, in Kansas City, Kansas; Davenport, Iowa; San Francisco, California; and Dallas, Texas. Each regional office maintained sales performance records and correspondence files for representatives in those regions.[34] After the Davenport and Dallas offices closed around 1912, the New York office assumed responsibility for maintaining representative contracts in the East, while the Kansas City office handled all contracts west of the Mississippi River. CPC's single manufacturing plant in Suffern managed all production and shipped products to representatives in the eastern United States by train. CPC also built a warehouse and distribution center in Kansas City in 1909, to fill western representatives' orders.

Initially, McConnell sought to put his money "into the products themselves," but he soon realized that his original scheme to distribute quality merchandise in plain, economical packaging was overly cautious. "Women were very willing to pay more for products in pretty packages," he recorded.[35] His first 1896 catalog (fifteen pages long and measuring three by

Figure 1.2. Bottling perfumes, California Perfume Company, Suffern Lab, New York, 1902. (Courtesy of Hagley Museum and Library.)

five inches) featured textual descriptions of the thirty products in the CPC line. In 1902, McConnell split his product line into two catalogs, one for beauty products and the other for basic toiletries and household products. The beauty catalog, called the "The CP Book: A comprehensive and authoritative guide to the intelligent selection and use of Milady's Toilet Articles and other Household Necessities," contained descriptions of more than twenty products and thirty "odors," including three French perfumes. It also included black and white illustrations of several items, including the CP Manicuring Set, CP Hygienic Face Powder, CP Face Lotion and Massage Cream, CP Talcum and Sachet Powders, CP Shaving Soap, and a variety of scented soaps, perfumes, and toilet waters. The more commonplace products, like CP Bandoline (hair styling oil), tooth powder, and lavender salts, as well as more urbane and perhaps controversial products, including liquid rouge, "Lait Virginal" (milk bath to whiten skin), and CP theatrical rouge, received only narrative description. Reflecting McConnell's discovery of the profitability of pretty packaging, the production division wrapped most products in ribbons, developed colorful labels, and hand-colored boxed presentations.[36] A separate catalog, "For Beauty, Health, and Home," featured standard toiletries, such as shampoos, tooth washes, cold creams, and household articles such as flavoring extracts, baking powder, and cleaners like "Carpet Renovator."[37]

Both catalogs featured the company guaranteeing that products would be "pure, harmless, and exactly as represented" and entitled customers to their money back if not satisfied. "It is a significant fact that no other manufacturer of toilet articles offers to its customers a guarantee like this," it claimed.[38] They also included a recruiting pitch, in case the catalog came to a customer who had lost her representative. "If this book should fall into the hands of any one who would like to make money by acting as our local representative, application should be made to our nearest office," it said, "unless we already have an active local representative."[39]

The catalogs, which CPC provided to representatives to leave at customers' homes, were the company's only printed promotional material. Ideally a representative would go through the catalog with her customers to explain certain items. She also carried a sample case of the more popular items, flaconettes of four or five perfumes, a shaker of violet powder, or a bottle of face lotion, which she invited her patrons to try. After a representative had taken an order and delivered it (preferably on a regular, four-week cycle) she might take along a second "outfit," or sample case, filled with another fourteen items in the "For Beauty, Health, and Home" catalog.[40] The representative's "Manual of Instruction" offered very specific advice on how to present both the catalog and the product so that it would lead to a "good order." The catalog and the representative's selling spiel acted as the only venues for CPC advertising and marketing.

William Scheele, McConnell's treasurer, began lobbying in 1910 to produce a large, color plate catalog that would feature every product in full size and color. The production costs for the initial run of color plate catalogs would run over $10,000. First, McConnell balked at this amount of money, but he eventually agreed. In addition to advertising, the color plate catalog would serve a practical function for representatives. As the number of products increased, it had become impossible for sales representatives to carry full-size samples of all the products in their sales outfits. Some representatives quit because the heavy sample case had become impossible for them to carry, and the company worried that its expanding line would reduce the pool of potential recruits for sales. As a 1915 instruction manual explained to traveling agents, the new color plate catalog "enables you to appoint [as salespeople] frail, delicate people, even those who are semi-invalids" as they would not be burdened with carrying cumbersome

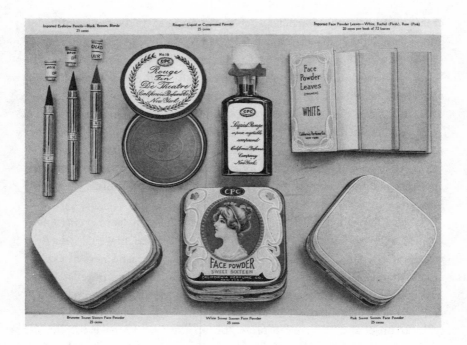

Figure 1.3 and Figure 1.4. American Beauty soaps and an assortment of CPC flavoring extracts, food colors, baking powder and oil, from the California Perfume Company's 1915 color plate catalog. (Courtesy of Hagley Museum and Library.)

samples.[41] Representatives supplemented the images on the pages by carrying one full-size sample of whatever product the company suggested as a "product leader," such as talcum powders in the summer, hand creams in the winter, and perfumes during the holiday seasons. Scheele claimed that the color plate catalog had "made scientific salesmanship possible" for CPC representatives.[42]

To cover the costs of recruiting and outfitting representatives with catalogs, order forms, manuals, product information pamphlets, and sample cases, McConnell required new representatives to invest some money in their business. Representatives paid a deposit on the sample case that varied from a high of $6.00 in 1896, to a low of $3.95 in 1917, and finally settled at $5.00 from 1918 to 1925. The deposit covered the cost of the products in the case, generally estimated at approximately $3 retail, or $1.35 wholesale (in 1922), and surely less than that in terms of actual costs to the CPC.[43] Representatives could recover their deposit money once they submitted $200.00 in wholesale orders. They also received CPC's monthly magazines, *CPC Outlook* and *Bulletin*. For the company, however, the cost of appointing a representative was barely covered by what it received in a deposit, since the CPC also incurred the expenses of the traveling agent, including her salary and transportation expenses. Agents generally recruited twenty to twenty-five representatives a month; a conservative estimate puts the cost of recruiting a new representative at about $4 each, which was only just offset by the deposit.

Once on board, a representative's smallest order yielded a profit because McConnell covered the increased expenses of shipping small orders by charging graduated shipping rates. Sales representatives earned a straight 40 percent commission on orders of $30 or more, and the company shipped their orders free of charge. Representatives who submitted orders of between $20 and $30 paid a flat shipping fee and earned a reduced commission of only 30 percent. On orders of less than $20, representatives incurred the full cost of shipping and earned only a 20 percent commission. Shipping and mailing have historically been the direct selling industry's largest overhead expenses. Unlike mass manufacturers who shipped in bulk, CPC guaranteed express delivery to all its representatives to ensure quick service to customers. In order to not lose money, McConnell required his representatives to pay the shipping costs on small orders.[44] Individual accounts referenced each representative's financial status, including whether she had a "letter of credit" on file which allowed her the benefit of receiving an express package. The company allowed the representative four weeks to collect payments from customers, at which point she likely would collect and submit a second order, along with payment for the first. Representatives without a letter of credit received freight shipments that required cash on delivery, requiring them to pay in advance. Company records of these accounts no longer exist, making it impossible to analyze patterns among representatives with and without letters of credit.

Personal profiles of representatives were created on a complex Kardex indexing system that recorded every order, sales report, and bit of correspondence to track each representative's progress.[45] This system allowed the CPC to employ the innovation of "scientific management" to their operations. Traveling agents filled out a Kardex card for every representative she appointed in the field, noted personal and household information, including her name and address, as well as husband's and children's names, number of boarders or other relatives residing at the house, and the names and addresses of credit references. Traveling agents also noted the size of the town and major industries, as well as the new representative's business plan: when she intended to start work, the size of her first order, and the date she would mail it to the company. The central sales offices collected the Kardex cards and a clerk noted every single order, inquiry, business mailing (such as sales manuals, contract amendments, reward notification, and sales updates), and personal letter to or from a representative on her Kardex file card. The billing department tracked monthly, quarterly, and yearly sales on Kardex using ink color codes to indicate various sales levels or prize categories. Representatives' cards were also flagged by the month of the last order to measure consistency and regulate company response.

Letters of encouragement and, eventually, of warning could be sent to representatives who failed to submit orders on a regular basis. For example, a representative who had not submitted an order after two months received a letter from the division manager requesting information on her business plans and offering motivation, along with sales and product-trend information. Representatives who let more than three months lapse without an order were then sent letters reminding them of their contractual obligations to their customers and warning them that a traveler was on the way to reassign her territory to another representative.

A representative's sales results were also cross-referenced to the accounts and performance records of the traveling agent who appointed her, allowing the CPC to use Kardex to monitor the performance of individual agents, including the number of monthly appointments and the business her representatives produced. An agent was then issued detailed monthly reports on how many new appointees had sent in orders and the size of their orders, which the payroll department used to calculate the agent's bonus and commission statements. Many monthly reports also included representatives' biographical data, such as occupation, age, and family situation, so agents could determine who their best (and worst) producers were. CPC managers based their approach to managing the sales force on their analysis of data and trends of the representative corps, which they took from the Kardex system on a monthly and annual basis. Having instituted the first of his goals, subverting the gender and composition of his salesforce, and having created a dynamic data-driven system, McConnell turned his attention to self-help.

Motivation

Increasing sales involved more than distributing color plate catalogs and creating sophisticated marketing techniques; it required motivating sales representatives. With the exception of one two-inch text-only advertisement in the back of *Good Housekeeping* in 1906, the CPC did not advertise its products in national magazines before 1936, nor did it engage in any mass-advertising campaigns, offer premiums, or distribute samples. The sole means of marketing CPC goods before World War II took place in face-to-face meetings between the CPC representatives and their customers. The success of this plan depended on one key element: the representative's initiative. Without it, McConnell had no way of moving his products. But rather than overcompensating for his absentee management system by investing in direct supervision, McConnell chose to bombard his representatives with incentives for positive thinking and appeal to their social conscience as women.

McConnell's management system mimicked the one he had worked under as a traveling sales agent for Union Publishing in the 1880s which used extensive correspondence to keep in touch with representatives. Very early in the CPC's history, McConnell wrote personalized letters to representatives about once a month offering instruction and encouragement. These letters emphasized the loyalty shown by the company they represented and the quality of products they sold. The correspondence department, one of the first and most important departments that McConnell created, handled, tracked, and responded to all communications from representatives. His writing style remained paternalistic and personal, and even "form" letters appeared tailored to individuals. CPC secretary William Scheele introduced many modern business correspondence techniques, including the use of "boiler plates" and standard sentences and paragraphs, to compose letters for specific business purposes. Scheele standardized acknowledgments for reports, orders, and remittances as well as acceptance and termination of contracts. Scheele also understood the need to avoid completely standardized correspondence. "We do not wish to depart from our long established custom of adding a personal note *always* to such form acknowledgments," he said. It was important, he said, to add a personalized message that applied only to the specific sales representative, sending good wishes for improved health or congratulations on a new purchase or a "well done" for finding new customers. "Do not neglect this important sales opportunity to cement your worker to the CPC and increase the goodwill and friendship of such Sales [Representative] by adding the *personal note* to every form letter."[46]

McConnell's letters all included a direct appeal to representatives to start canvassing immediately and to write back about their work plans and sales goals. Although each representative could operate her business according to her own needs, the CPC retained the right to revoke her selling privileges if her sales performance was not up to par, which occasionally became a threat to women who did not send in regular orders. "We want to say right here, that every day we receive applications for additional territory from Agents who have pretty well covered their own and want to increase their field," McConnell wrote to an inactive representative. "To preserve your territory, let us hear from you promptly."[47] And he expected representatives to comply with his requests. "On looking over our contracts," one form letter began, "we notice you did not answer our last communication. This we regret as we especially asked you to do so and let us know if you could start in at this time. . . . If we do not hear from you in reply to this, we will feel at liberty to place the territory on our General [Traveling] Agent's list and put another worker there."[48]

McConnell needed to know each representative's situation and work plans because he took the number of working sales representatives into account when he calculated his inventory. The CPC's strict policies committed staff to filling and shipping orders on the same day they were received, which necessitated cooperation from the Manhattan office staff, the Suffern manufacturing facility, and the representative. Correctly estimating how much product to manufacture, especially for seasonal items, hinged on knowing how many representatives were active.

Even if representatives did not regularly submit orders, McConnell offered them many opportunities to explain their lack of activity. He wrote gentle inquiries, asking if the representative had become ill or if something had prevented her from starting work. Bad weather, rain, heat, and cold were always acceptable explanations for why someone was not out selling, as were family emergencies. "In case you feel that you cannot continue the work at the present time, if you want the territory reserved for you, drop us a line promptly."[49] Nevertheless, giving representatives the benefit of the doubt could quickly turn sour, and McConnell frequently resorted to good old-fashioned guilt trips. He reminded each delinquent representative of the "privilege" of being entrusted with "protected territory" and her promise to work that territory.

> Then how about the responsibility that goes with this privilege? Does it not obligate you to take care of our interests in your territory? Is it not fair for us to ask you to be sure you are not losing a single order in the field over which you have been selected to reign? If we keep faith by removing and keeping out competition of every description, do you not owe it to us to see that we do not lose a penny's worth of business that can possibly be secured? Surely this is no more than fair. . . . [I]t doesn't seem possible that anyone would be so neglectful of their responsibility, especially when we pay them so generously for their work.[50]

Ultimately, McConnell asserted, the success of the representative and of the CPC were mutually dependent.

McConnell sought to create a relationship where representatives would feel morally, if not legally, bound to the company.[51] The emotional appeal was both necessary and effective. Stern words were used as a last resort, for McConnell also believed that women responded better to positive reinforcement. He used successful representatives' sales reports to motivate his sales force. The *CPC Outlook*, a monthly newsletter that replaced McConnell's wordy letters to representatives in 1905, featured columns listing representatives' names, home states, and orders from across the country. Typically, *Outlook* printed monthly sales reports from thirty to fifty women who worked about twenty hours per week, made about three sales calls per hour, received orders from about 75 percent of the homes visited, and averaged $1 or $2 per order. To head off a representative who claimed that her territory was not large enough to support such a strong sales report, *Outlook* invariably featured an outstanding order from a representative working a particularly isolated territory of only 300 people. In one example, Mrs. William Guest of Brownsville Junction, Maine (population 500), started work as a sales representative in September 1924. Her total business through April 1926 amounted to $1,133.77 retail.[52] "This is particularly noteworthy," sales manager Mark Taylor wrote, "in view of the northern location of her field. Conditions apparently don't mean a thing to Mrs. Guest. We have no reason to suppose that the field is any different in business possibilities than hundreds of other districts of its type, and better. . . . It isn't the territory that's different—it's the Representative."[53]

Weekly sales reports printed in the monthly newsletters for representatives were flanked with maxims about work, self-discipline, enthusiasm, and success—such as these: "The work habit is the sieve that separates the dreamer from the doer," or "Far and away the best prize that life offers is the chance to work hard at work worth doing."[54] *Outlook* featured sales reports for wholesale orders over $30, the level CPC encouraged representatives to sell every month. It was impossible for most representatives to know how unusual the published sales figures were since they worked independently and could not correspond with each other or share experiences personally. Regardless of how skewed the published figures might have been, the CPC printed the sales reports to inspire and empower representatives: "Having determined what can be done, enter upon your work joyously, without fear, and push for the result desired. Give no place to 'I can't' but plenty of room to 'I CAN.' Think it, be it, live it, and you not only can but WILL succeed."[55]

McConnell also invested in an ever-larger array of material incentives to encourage higher sales. Most prizes were awarded to representatives who met a certain sales quota, such as a Rochester Coffee percolator for selling seventy-five packages of furniture polish and carpet renovator, or an Alca vacuum cleaner for a wholesale order of $60. Twice a year *Outlook* announced luxury prizes, such as bed and table linens, curtains, silverware sets, lamps, phonographs, aluminum cookware, ironing boards, watches and jewelry, and cleaning equipment.

Other prizes were useful for business, such as traveling bags, umbrellas, raincoats, clocks, and stationery sets and elegant fountain pens for writing orders. Although suitable for both men and women, the array of prizes were those items women would have procured for their households, extras that they might have bought using their CPC earnings during good economic times. For example, in January and February 1917, *Outlook* featured

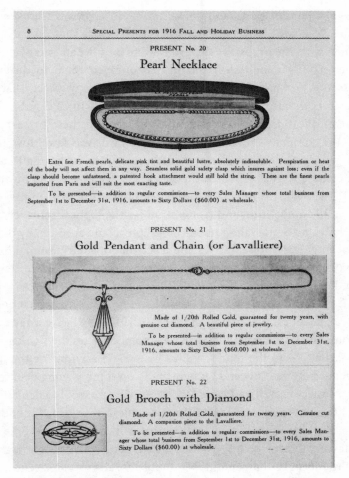

8   SPECIAL PRESENTS FOR 1916 FALL AND HOLIDAY BUSINESS

PRESENT No. 20

Pearl Necklace

Extra fine French pearls, delicate pink tint and beautiful lustre, absolutely indissoluble. Perspiration or heat of the body will not affect them in any way. Seamless solid gold safety clasp which insures against loss; even if the clasp should become unfastened, a patented hook attachment would still hold the string. These are the finest pearls imported from Paris and will suit the most exacting taste.

To be presented—in addition to regular commissions—to every Sales Manager whose total business from September 1st to December 31st, 1916, amounts to Sixty Dollars ($60.00) at wholesale.

PRESENT No. 21

Gold Pendant and Chain (or Lavalliere)

Made of 1/20th Rolled Gold, guaranteed for twenty years, with genuine cut diamond. A beautiful piece of jewelry.

To be presented—in addition to regular commissions—to every Sales Manager whose total business from September 1st to December 31st, 1916, amounts to Sixty Dollars ($60.00) at wholesale.

PRESENT No. 22

Gold Brooch with Diamond

Made of 1/20th Rolled Gold, guaranteed for twenty years. Genuine cut diamond. A companion piece to the Lavalliere.

To be presented—in addition to regular commissions—to every Sales Manager whose total business from September 1st to December 31st, 1916, amounts to Sixty Dollars ($60.00) at wholesale.

Figure 1.5. CPC offered representatives a variety of prizes for Fall sales including gold and silver jewelry. *CPC Outlook*, September 1916. (Courtesy of Hagley Museum and Library.)

cut glass sugar and creamer sets, powder-puff jars, and hair receiver jars as prizes for wholesale orders of $50 or more. Other contests allowed representatives to collect wholesale orders over a period of three months; in 1915, for example, McConnell offered silver serving sets for accumulated orders of between $60 and $100 collected between September 1 and December 31. In some campaigns he gave $5, $10, and $15 in gold to the top three representatives each quarter. Representatives earned these prizes in addition to their regular commissions, and only those representatives who submitted orders in excess of $250 were offered cash bonuses on a sliding scale.

Women used the prizes for themselves and as gifts, and many reported that their family members frequently encouraged them to do enough business to earn more. Despite the amount of copy space that prize photographs, descriptions, and contest rules took up in CPC publications, fewer than one-third of all representatives received these prizes, and in general the company's investment in such rewards was fairly low. In fact, McConnell partially owned or managed companies, including the H. M. Rogers Company, that provided the silver sets, tableware, and most other prizes.[56] The company intended the contests to be fun, to be motivational, and to build competition and recognition for the highest achievers, especially when a bit of the salesperson's biography could accompany the prize announcements. Representatives could see that ordinary women in small markets could achieve large orders, demonstrating that size of territory did not determine business success.

The CPC set the bar high and became the first direct sales company to offer a car, a contest presented just twice. In 1911, CPC gave away a Brush Runabout, one of the most inexpensive automobiles on the market—but a car nevertheless—to the representative who could accumulate the highest sales record between July and December. To level the playing field for representatives from small and large territories, CPC based its calculations on every "1,000 of white population." "In this contest it isn't the size of the district, but the 'size' of the Representative that will count most."[57] Effie Miller from Stayton, Oregon sold $1,088.43 of CPC goods and was photographed sitting proudly in her new automobile.[58] Miller's sales would have earned her a total of $435 in commissions and $25 in bonus plan money, or about $75 per month, and several other prizes. The number of hours she worked during the six months, however, is unknown. Later, in September 1916, *Outlook* announced the second auto contest, won by Mrs. Amy Linnell of Bisbee, Arizona.[59]

Such extraordinary contests served a psychological business purpose. Prize pages in *Outlook* and the *CPC Bulletin* established various sales goals and encouragements for individual representatives to increase their order sizes. They were also a tangible benefit of CPC work, although certainly not a family-sustaining form of compensation. Rather, offering prizes as compensation for labor harkened back to an older form of barter and exchange

Figure 1.6. Sales Representative Effie Miller of Stayton, Oregon, (population less than 500) won a Brush Runabout for selling $1,835 wholesale orders, the highest sales in the nation during the Fall 1911 sales campaigns. (Courtesy of Hagley Museum and Library.)

of products and materials in lieu of cash—a payment system that, although subsumed by the wage system, had never completely disappeared, especially within women's informal economic networks. Of all the prizes offered, the vast majority were available to any representative who had achieved a particular sales level, which made the system less competitive, although McConnell's system favored representatives who responded positively to competition. However, for most representatives, who did not look to the CPC to provide an income to sustain their households, the prize system reinforced the purpose of CPC work as part-time intended to help them procure "extras." After all, at a 40 percent commission rate, a $60 wholesale order equaled $40 in commissions to the representative; it was hardly enough for a representative to support herself, but could earn her a pretty new Empress percolator coffee pot.

Positive Thinking and the Success Ethic

Remember that the fact of you having aspired to such a position is in-dicative of your ability to do that which is your highest aspiration.... All success lies within one's self and not in external conditions. It is a fixed law that the view we take of the world is but a reflection of the one we hold ourselves, and the estimate we place upon our ability is the estimate that is reflected upon the world. ... So if you have built air-castles from the realms of vivid imagination and you have the energy, the motor power beneath them, be assured that if you will launch out courageously you will attain the full realization of your aspirations. No person ever achieved that which was worth doing until some fixed ambition led him or her to use with con-fidence the requisite means, and the only assistance that can ever be given is that which inspires and strengthens us in the use of the talents which we possess.[60]

— "Instructions for General Agents" (1915)

Positive thinking, goal setting, and evangelical spirit—characteristics of modern business, progressives, and religious philosophy—were rarely ap-plied so specifically to women. But in the world of direct selling, the mention of goals, prizes, and the success ethic was more than a rhetorical trope; it was the central feature of a business strategy. Developing "positive thinking" ideas and techniques was integral to the economic success of the individual and to McConnell.

The California Perfume Company was exceptional in that its managers ap-plied these qualities to women. They assumed that women, as well as men, could succeed in business. Suggesting that success "lies within one self and not in external conditions" empowered women by suggesting that they could overcome obstacles through the strength of their character. Instructing them to use their imaginations to envision "air castles" and find "fixed ambition" to achieve economic independence taught them to create specific goals, which were later held out as both incentives and rewards. Finding "that which inspires and strengthens us" encouraged women, sustained by their faith, to place themselves at the center of economic exchange. In *Outlook* and all company correspondence, McConnell constantly reminded his agents, rep-resentatives, and recruits that for those who wanted to work, rewards were limitless. Hard work equals success. "The rewards of CPC General Agency are limited only by the ambition and enthusiasm of the Traveler," one recruiting booklet stated. "Anyone with ordinary ability, but with the qualities of earnestness and perseverance and the capacity for honest work is assured of a high degree of success, physically, mentally and financially."[61]

> The pleasant people best succeed on life's journey. . . . [A] sunny disposition . . . and a pleasant smile is a passport to all hearts. . . . If you have unconsciously permitted unpleasant thoughts and discouragements to efface the more attractive lines from your countenance, set about at once to see the brighter side of life, and try pretending to be happy, and almost before you are aware life will bear for you a different and more desirable aspect.[62]

The business strategy of direct selling in part demanded this constant barrage of "positive thinking"-style literature because workers were so isolated. Without traditional, on-site disciplinary supervision, representatives or agents could just have easily chosen not to work. By presenting the potential rewards of CPC work in such personalized form, the distant and unseen company was made to seem tangible and present.

The language in CPC literature—instruction manuals, daily Chats, and early CPC *Outlooks*—included an odd mix of gendered and racialized messages. On the one hand, CPC writers were aware that their audience was predominantly women. They consistently used female pronouns when talking about both representatives and customers: "*She* dashes up to you . . ." " Congratulate *her* . . . " "Get your prospect to voice *her* consent. . . ." "He" and "his" were rarely used to denote a "generic" population of representatives. The company knew it was hiring white women. But there is also an odd use of "male" anecdotes and situations in advice columns and motivational literature. CPC managers frequently treated their female representatives and traveling agents as "one of the boys." They included stories about fishing, for example, to emphasize patience and the need to stick to one area until an agent found her representative. To encourage agents to search for prospects, one writer told a long tale of a fisherman at Lake Tahoe who was stymied by "trout swimming saucily" ignoring his grasshopper bait "making motions at him with their tails, just as though they knew he was no fisherman." Despite many attempts using various methods, the fisherman finally watched long enough to realize that the fish wanted to eat the grasshoppers on top of the water, not those weighed down. Everyone thought his theory foolish and believed that "these fish have been canvassed so many times that they were wary." So the fisherman decided to stay where he was and study his prospects (the fish, that is), see where they lived, and learn how they conducted their business. "He remembered the advice of the old negro: 'when youse wants to ketch fish, honey, stay whar the fishes is.'" The article continued for three pages, until finally the moral of the story was clear: that towns where previous agents had canvassed unsuccessfully were not impossible. "When you work it in your own individual way, making your arguments fit the case in each instance, you will 'catch' your 'Representative' or 'Sales Manager' where others have failed."[63]

Wars and battles also figured prominently in CPC motivational literature. The First Punic War was discussed at length in the 1915 General Agents' manual to illustrate "the power of determined resolution and energy, plus courage and confidence." "Take along mental grappling irons," the manual suggested, to earn the "supreme confidence of victory and success as did those Romans of old, and fight to win. Don't let your prospect drift away by irrelevant remarks and gossip; don't be put off till to-morrow or the next week, month, or season; . . . Fight it out then and there."[64] Gunpowder, carpentry, mining, gaming, horse racing, boxing, hunting, governmental diplomacy, Greek mythology, shrewd business deals by business titans such as Carnegie and Ford, and even bees frequently served as metaphors for constantly working, searching out, convincing, and appointing prospects. One CPC Chat memo told travelers: "Babe Ruth never hit a homer sitting on the bench. Dempsey never knocked out a man in the dressing room. De Paulo never won an Automobile Race resting in the pits. You, too, must keep going."[65]

While many traveling agents probably had a good understanding of these activities, it is interesting that CPC managers assumed that women knew enough about these "male" preserves to identify with and be motivated by them. CPC writers took many of their motivational ideas, even entire articles, from sales management trade literature. Much of the instructional advice—everything from anecdotes highlighting clever responses regular salesmen made to customers' objections to the sage advice offered by leading business tycoons—was frequently copied straight from salesmen's magazines, such as *Success, Sales Management,* and *The Sample Case,* and reprinted in the CPC *Outlook* and *Bulletin.*

Despite the rhetoric created and parroted by both the company and the representatives about independence and control, the company maintained crucial control of the representative's business. The fine print on the back of the CPC contract, devoid of the rhetoric that dressed up and sold the business as entrepreneurship, made clear the relationship between the saleswoman and the company. The CPC exposed itself as the partner who held the power. According to the rules that governed the operations of representatives, "the California Perfume Company, Inc. has only one method of doing business and Sales Representatives must conform to this method." As an authorized agent, "the Sales Representatives does not buy the goods and resell them, but merely acts as our Representative in taking orders and delivering goods for the Company"; their authority is "strictly limited to taking and forwarding orders on our account, subject to our approval, and assisting us in delivery of the goods from the factory to the consumer, and in the remittance of the funds from the customer to us."[66] Stripped of positive thinking and self-help language, the CPC representative was just an order taker.

The most remarkable aspect of the CPC's strategy is how little it changed between 1892 and 1929. Sales and recruiting manuals featured the same instructions in nearly every edition. Entire chapters appeared in the 1924 version exactly as they had in the first 1899 edition. The 1915 recruiting manual expanded on the 1899 one only by incorporating advice columns and letters that the CPC had distributed to its agents and representatives in prior years. Although by 1924 the manual had become shorter, the catalogs more sophisticated, and the sample cases and prize brochures filled with more goods, McConnell still remained dedicated to his basic distribution formula. Despite the problems of high turnover and low individual sales, McConnell had learned to manage his company so that he could profit from even the smallest sale. Building a broad sales base gave him the leeway to profitably retain those women who consistently submitted orders, regardless of size. The CPC's mastery of the direct selling format, in place for nearly forty-five years when the worst of the Depression hit, gave the company a distinct competitive advantage.

Year after year McConnell battled high turnover among the representative staff, incurred high distribution costs, lacked control over product presentation, and over-extended credit to representatives, all problems that seemed directly related to absentee management of representatives that many other companies had corrected with bureaucratic control. However, the advantages of direct sales as a form of long-term capitalist enterprise, while perhaps not immediately apparent in terms of profits and sales, allowed McConnell to carve out a niche in rural markets, tap a seemingly unlimited labor force, and introduce rural consumers to skin care and beauty products previously una-vailable to them. By the 1930s, McConnell had created a corporate structure with a representative management team of women, along with the propa-ganda of self-help, motivational correspondence and literature, that would dominate his business model in the future.

2

"Now You Are in Business for Yourself"

Representatives, Gender, and Business, 1900–1929

Dear Gentlemen: It was just a year yesterday that I signed the contract and commenced work the same day. During this time I have sent you thirteen orders and have never been sorry that I began work for the CP Co.; in fact, am surprised to have done so well. I have sold over $770.00 worth of goods besides doing my own housework, and being home in time to get three meals a day; in fact, do all my own work. Am thankful for all the kindness you have shown me.

Mrs. Mabel Feiler, New York district E-360, 1922

The women who worked as representatives of the California Perfume Company wrote many letters like this to David McConnell. Mrs. Feiler was responding to his letter congratulating her on a one-year anniversary with the company.[1] She was proud of her success, but emphasized that business had not forced her to sacrifice her domestic responsibilities. In between laundry and cooking, she managed to canvass her territory with her color plate catalog and sample case in hand and to gather orders from friends and neighbors: $770 retail sales brought Feiler $308 in commissions, or nearly $25 a month. The California Perfume Company contract allowed her to accommodate her interest in both making money and maintaining her family obligations; Feiler's priorities clearly lay with the latter.

Other women wrote to the CPC to express their gratitude for the company's help in a time of need: "Through sudden financial losses and the failure of my husband's health, I found that I must be the bread-winner for my family of six," wrote Mrs. R. W. Agnew of Missouri. "I began working . . . the first of February 1914 and I have been able to keep my living expenses, keep my two girls in school besides giving them music lessons and I am now contracting for a home"—all from her earnings as a CPC representative.[2] Mrs. R. J. Franklin experienced similar financial success in district F-24 in Tennessee. "Gentlemen," she wrote, "My last order completed my first year's work for the CP Co. In that time I have taken in orders for $660.10 worth of goods, and I may say I am not ashamed of the results." Indeed, she had earned well as a CPC representative; orders amounting to $660 wholesale equaled $440 in commissions for Mrs. Franklin's pocketbook, or about $36 per month. If she were single and a schoolteacher, she probably would have earned about the same monthly salary (although for eight months of nearly full-time work each year); few married women could claim similar incomes. Franklin's annual sales figure also put her in the top 10 percent of sales representatives ranked by earnings in the company, although she probably did not know that. Franklin earned her commissions solely by her own volition and labor, but still she insisted, perhaps for the sake of propriety, on thanking the company for its encouragement. "But I must also acknowledge that your encouraging letters have been a great incentive to me in the accomplishment of this work," she wrote, "for which I extend to you my sincerest thanks. The work has been a pleasure to me, and my health has been greatly benefited. Not only that, but it has been profitable as well."[3] Representing the CPC was a pleasurable and healthful occupation, and that she earned money at it appeared almost as an afterthought in her letter.

In its newsletters, recruiting pamphlets, and manuals, the CPC presented an image of representatives that was designed to motivate and build women's confidence in their selling ability. It favored the representative who had succeeded in sending in large orders; if she had also overcome hardship the way Mrs. Agnew had, so much the better. The corporate literature set a standard that managers hoped all representatives would strive to achieve. In doing so, it created a business culture that celebrated women's success, personal responsibility, and individual achievement. At the same time, some of women's letters and attitudes showed strain and disappointment. They show an awareness of their subordinate responsibility in "corporate domesticity." The businesses they "owned" did not free them, but rather still tethered them to domestic duties. So, while CPC literature and motivational material tried to reverse the stigma for women of earning money and owning a business, some representatives had a more nuanced or even limited view of their work and did not wholeheartedly embrace CPC sales as a vocation.

Corporate sales manuals, contracts, recruiting pamphlets, and letters and stories CPC representatives wrote for publication in *Outlook* illustrate the meaning and consequences of business in the lives of representatives and their customers.[4] By virtue of the products that they sold and the service they provided to other women and families, CPC representatives functioned as both directors of and participants in consumption; they both distributed and used the toiletries and household products, and as such integrated business and domesticity.[5] Company rhetoric, created by executives and representatives alike, defended women's right and obligation to engage in business, and these remained virtually unchanged from 1900 to 1928.

Was this truly effective or did the domestic ties of most representatives overshadow their entrepreneurial spirit? The letters, of course, are selected by the company for the express purpose of motivation. The domestic realm that women occupied allowed them to invite other women into their households, but for most representatives, selling in their community or social groups did not necessarily translate to a sense of true ownership over their "business".

The CPC representative corps can be broken down into three categories. Women like Franklin, Agnew, and Feiler were among an elite group of CPC representatives: they were the high achievers who consistently sent in orders over the course of a year or more. These three women were among the top third of the annual representative corps; as such, the company catered to them, encouraged them, and held them up as examples for all to follow. Below them were the mass of average representatives who sent in a few orders over a period of three to six months, who occasionally responded to company correspondence, and who, for a variety of reasons, discontinued their contracts with CPC within a year. Their relationship with the company was unproblematic, from the perspective of company management, because the large profit margin on products allowed enough leeway to accommodate average orders. Average representatives most likely spent fewer than five hours a week canvassing, and their economic lives were not devastated once they gave up the extra $15 a month they occasionally earned in commissions. Finally, the below-average representatives were the canvassing disasters. These women never sent in an order or might have requested just a few products. They cost the company in correspondence expenses, catalog and brochure stock, recordkeeping space, and ultimately in the cost of sending a traveling agent to find replacements for them. While company literature favored the top third of sales achievers, it is possible to read through the lines to discern the sales and business strategies of representatives who occupied the average and below-average rungs.

Census research shows that the demographic profiles of successful representatives varied according to age, family status, and location. It was impossible to predict from these criteria at the outset into which category of earnings any one new recruit might fall; representatives were young and old, married, single, divorced, and widowed. Many had young children and/or elderly parents at home. They lived in large towns and small. The typical representative was married, about forty-seven years old, and lived in a town with a population under 2,500. Still, the reasons that some women succeeded in direct selling and others did not ultimately rests on how individual women experienced and judged their opportunities as representatives. A woman's personality and perspective helped determine the meaning she found in her work.

"'Tis a small, narrow mind, indeed, that would accord no place to women in the business world." Instructions for General Agents, 1915

Company managers faced an uphill battle in persuading women to envision themselves as active economic agents. In the business world at large, there were very few examples of visibly successful, independent businesswomen in the early twentieth century, and most of those came from finance or retailing centered in large urban areas. Although there was a culture of support for women who inherited money, middle-class women rarely celebrated other women who earned money in business. Nevertheless, some women in the early twentieth century were well versed in money; they collected it and used it within non-profit structures for social reform, especially through churches and charities. Although many Progressive Era women celebrated corporate organization of modern institutions, most women were expected to remain non-profit-oriented.[6]

Exceptional women who earned money for personal gain, and not for social good, violated accepted gendered stereotypes.[7] Contemporaries speculated that the severe Quaker upbringing of stockbroker Hetty Green, the "Witch of Wall Street" who earned hundreds of millions of dollars trading stock and property in New York City, Chicago, and Western railroads during the Gilded Age, had somehow "steeled" her for the brutal world of high finance.[8] Money became a subject of contention in women's lives, so people's attitudes about it differentiated good and bad, proper and improper economic behavior in gendered and class terms. Entrepreneurial women became coded by words like "witch," "vamp," and "gambler," whereas women who raised money for progressive causes were described using words such as mother, beauty, and guarded. The popular press portrayed women as economically cautious, "unable" to invest or trade in stocks, and naturally "risk averse." Indeed, women in the late nineteenth and early twentieth century who made claims to money experienced a backlash against their financial performance. More commonly, both the non-profit sector and financial institutions like banks and insurance companies taught women to give money and to invest it in projects that were socially responsible rather than personally profitable, testaments to their selflessness. Some city banks sponsored separate "ladies departments," waiting rooms, and customer service areas that coddled women and advised them to keep their inherited money in property and bonds, testaments to their social dependence.[9] One traveling agent said, "CPC really means Clean Piles of Coin," echoing the common description of women's social fundraising activities as merely "collecting pennies." Small amounts of money, therefore, were not so dirty that average women would not want them.

Given this image of women in business, the California Perfume Company's aggressive insistence that women had the right to access money, should be encouraged to accumulate big incomes, and could develop their ability to learn, understand, and manipulate business is notable. CPC provided a forum that allowed women to express an economic personality characterized by efficiency, hard work, and cleverness, and it offered them money that neither resulted in social disgrace nor turned them into business pariahs. Most advice de-emphasized the implications of greed, noting the smaller scale of money that sales representatives earned, exposing the apparent limitation that while women were empowered to accrue an independent income, they would not disregard domestic obligations or wish to break free of traditional gender roles. According to CPC literature, women's earning power worked for the benefit of both the family and the individual herself, mutually reinforcing home and economy. Managers and recruiters, therefore, avoided social misgivings about women's earning and potential economic independence by describing CPC work in domestic terms.

Respect for women's ability to earn and control money shaped the way CPC editors talked to and about women in its literature. At no point did they present women as weak, emotional, hysterical, or demure, as did other prescriptive literature of the time. Nor did the company ever suggest that women who achieved extraordinary success in their careers were radical, feminist, revolutionary, dangerous, or threatening to the male order.

Whereas many contemporary reformers, politicians, and business and labor leaders claimed that women's paid employment would devalue traditional domestic situations by pulling women away from their family responsibilities, CPC promoted the notion that women's individual economic success would serve their families and society in general. The concept of business and financial success for women did not automatically muster up images of mothers abandoning their households and family responsibilities.[10]

Just as CPC literature remained silent about the disadvantages to society of women working outside the home, the company remained neutral about other women's issues from women's rights to fashion and style, except, of course, when it came to beauty. Only in 1922 did the *Outlook* mention women's suffrage, saying that women were "required" to use their political power with the vote, and therefore they should also take the opportunity to use their economic power with their business. As traveling agent Mrs. Pedrick claimed in one of her recruiting pitches to a woman on the fence about accepting a CPC contract, "God gave you just as good a mind as he gave one man, some late authorities say better, and now the laws of this U.S.A. say *use* it."[11]

The CPC may have chosen to challenge popular perceptions about money and the "women's sphere" in part because of the nature of the representative's work and in part because of class-based expectations of women. Representatives were not asked to make choices between work and family, or paid employment and domesticity, and the company never suggested that women would give up their domestic responsibilities in order to canvass their neighborhoods and take orders. Thus they created what can be described as a "corporate domesticity." Although company literature emphasized that women needed to learn to budget their time and plan their duties to make more time available for selling, it also supported the assumption that women were ultimately responsible for their households. It spoke to a relatively class-specific audience, or at least one that recognized that women's work—paid, unpaid, and bartered—functioned as part of a family economy.[12]

The CPC did not write directly in its literature about contemporary debates over women's changing roles in society, but the company could not avoid the issue of paid work on a practical level. When traveling agents approached prospects about taking up canvassing work, men and women alike frequently resisted the idea of women working, saying that woman's place was in the home. The CPC offered material for meeting these objections and hoped that traveling agents would not be swayed by "their wrong ideas on the subject."

The 1924 recruiting manual, for example, included sections titled "Women Are in Every Profession" and "All Honest Work Is Honorable" that described how they might handle such an encounter.[13] "Oftentimes you report meeting so-called sensible women who believe that work is beneath them" began the section titled "Women in Business."[14] "If these persons' ideas in this connection are not too warped and too set, they could easily realize that the whole world was involved in business. Every man, woman, and child who was taking products from the soil, mine, forest, sea or air, carrying products 'hither and thither' every one who collects or pays money for them, is in business." To be "in business" was not ignorant or degrading, for everyone was either "actually engaged in it or dependent upon those who are."[15] The argument would have been familiar to anyone who had debated a woman's place in politics: many argued that the political sphere, like the economic one, was inherently polluted. Depending on one's point of view, women could clean it up and bring it dignity by their very presence there, or it served as grounds for women to stay out. But business, according to the CPC rationale, unlike politics, was already "noble" and therefore women's social status was not endangered if she engaged in it.

McConnell and his executives set out to create a respectable image for the California Perfume Company by emphasizing the value of combining home and business. By positioning the company in a nurturing and guiding role, McConnell and his CPC managers bridged the gap between economy and home. Even the nearly constant references in company literature to "this house" suggested that the CPC was familiar and caring, not a hostile masculine market. "Corporate domesticity" feminized and personalized business service.[16] The CPC effectively created a domesticated business that incorporated the best of private and public spheres and defended merging home and commerce.[17]

Gendered notions about appropriate women's behavior, grounding them as domestic creatures and not as market directors, both justified their CPC business activity and camouflaged it. When a woman joined the CPC, McConnell encouraged her to make her business an integral part of her personal life by incorporating her family, friends, and even her church into her selling activities. In short, McConnell asked his representatives to make their social networks serve his business and theirs simultaneously.[18] To consumers, a CPC representative's visit was supposed to resemble a social call. McConnell expected them to have frank discussions about household needs and personal care with their neighbors, which required a degree of familiarity that some women may have been reluctant to develop with itinerant male representatives. The CPC representative's business did not prevail over life in the home; rather, domestic life served and subsumed business and consumption. Representatives did not need to travel to a factory, office, store, or other workplace and meet other workers or supervisors where women were sequestered for long periods of time. Sales transactions took place in the privacy of customers' drawing rooms and kitchens; business literature and equipment were stored in the representative's home. Unlike shop owners, CPC representatives chose their customers; as retailers, their doors were not open to the entire community.

Profiles of CPC Representatives

The typical representative, according to McConnell's propaganda in *Outlook* and recruiting pamphlets, worked hard and never let weather or misfortune discourage her. Indeed, some women did use the CPC as a vehicle for spectacular opportunity and their experiences drove the company's recruiting and motivation, two central components of the direct sales industry management philosophy. Also emerging from the cursory profiles in CPC literature is another type of business experience, one in which women fell short of the goals a CPC contract offered them and gave up. Company literature attempted to pre-empt those women with negative exhortation in a tone typical of Progressive Era moralizing: "Don't drop out." "Don't walk away when they say no once, go back a second and third time." "Don't leave the house with a dirty sample case or your clothes looking tired and worn." "Don't sell only to your friends across the street, knock on new doors every month." These "don't" statements probably characterized the sales experience of far more women than the success stories. And for these women who walked away, whose sample cases were worn, and who were afraid to approach unfamiliar houses, lackluster effort frequently resulted in failure.

It's easy to assume that some women never intended to do the work that the CPC had encouraged them to try. Understanding the place this business had in their everyday lives is more difficult. Even among the women who built more conventional and active businesses, very few worked for more than twenty hours a week. What accounted for their success? Were they "gifted" somehow in the "art of salesmanship," or were they simply more driven? The answers to these questions lie in information mined from representative profiles printed in the monthly newsletters, which show clear patterns among those women the company sought to honor and hold up as examples to the entire representative staff.

There are several limitations to describing the CPC representative sales corps. The company did not keep their sales records or the situation reports on their towns, nor did it systematically collect information about representatives' ages, how many children they had, or their average family income. Neither the sales contracts nor the credit forms printed places for this information. Occasionally, for human-interest stories, *Outlook* might have a feature on the "oldest representative" by age or tenure. The company clearly had an archetype in mind when it wrote *Outlook* and sales manuals, but this does not necessarily reveal what the representative corps actually looked like. Census searches are of limited use and impractical to perform. Historically, sales representatives, traveling and local, have been under-counted in the national census.[19] Census takers frequently missed traveling agents, for example, simply because they were not at home. Furthermore, the ten-year

A Sales Manager who is not afraid to get out on a winter's day.—Miss Fannie Hunter, Contract E 857, New York.

Figure 2.1. Miss Fannie Hunter, New York, carrying her color plate catalog. *CPC Outlook*, March 1917. (Courtesy of Hagley Museum and Library.)

gap between censuses might as well be a lifetime, given that CPC sales representatives worked, on average, for less than six months. And it is practically impossible to find any woman in the 1910 census if either her husband
or father's first name is unavailable, as is the case for the majority of CPC
representatives.

The CPC's earliest records listed the names and hometowns of top representatives who submitted wholesale orders of $30 or more in the *CPC
Outlook*. It was part reward, for many women felt proud to see their names
in print in the company magazine, and part motivational maneuvering, for
all women could see that the $30 goal was indeed achievable. After 1912,
CPC stopped publishing the names of representatives' place of residence
in order to protect them, the editors said, from being pestered by other direct sales concerns that subsequently might try to recruit them. "It has been
our custom in the past to give the full post-office address with each Field
Note, but we have received so many complaints from our Representatives
that they are being constantly annoyed with circulars and unwelcome propositions from houses who get their names from our papers, that we have been
compelled to discontinue giving addresses."[20] Between 1903 and 1912, more
than 2,000 women's names appeared in *Outlook*. Even though 60–80 percent
of representatives canceled their CPC contracts before their first year had
ended, those whose names appeared in *Outlook* still represent a fairly large
cross-section of the company's door-to-door sales force.

From 1906 to 1910, the *Outlook* listed 786 women who were identified by
their hometowns as prize and award winners and who came from forty-seven
states, the District of Columbia, and the Indian Territories (later Oklahoma).
While there were no women listed from Wyoming, Alaska, or Hawaii, thirty-
four states each claimed fewer than twenty representatives. Washington, DC,
Delaware, Arizona, Montana, and Idaho only contributed two published
prizewinners each. The top four states, which together accounted for 23 percent of the names on the list, included Georgia (fifty-five names), New York
(forty-six names), Michigan (forty-one names), and Illinois (forty names).

Significantly, only 115 names (15 percent) appeared more than once over
the five-year period. Of these multiple listings, eighty-five representatives
appeared twice, eleven appeared three times, and nineteen appeared four or
more times. In the pool of multiple listings, some representatives submitted
prize-winning orders just months apart; others were active over the entire
five-year period. While this trend may have resulted from a managerial decision that favored listing only new names each month (and certainly the

CPC did have the capacity to track whether a representative's name had already appeared in publication), these statistics also correspond closely with the tenure rates. The average representative stayed for fewer than six months and submitted fewer than three orders. Only 15 percent of representatives remained with the company for one to three years. Over a five-year period, fewer than 20 percent of all representatives would have the opportunity to appear in multiple listings. Therefore, it is unlikely that CPC editors purposefully decided to track and limit the number of times any one representative's name might appear in *Outlook*; more likely, the low percentage of multiple listings reflects the tenure trends that characterized the company throughout its history.

The list also provides a clearer breakdown of the ratio of men to women and the percentages of married and unmarried women in the CPC representative workforce. Of the 786 names, 62 percent (489) of women's names used the title Mrs., and 18 percent (140) used the title Miss; 4 percent (31) used the title Mr.,[21] and 16 percent (126) did not indicate a title or used only initials, making it impossible to know their gender identity. CPC managers strongly advocated recruiting married women, and clearly agents were successful at it. Given that so few jobs and professions allowed married women to work, this characteristic, that two-thirds of the CPC sales force were married or once-married women, is by far the most unusual and important for understanding the success of the company throughout the twentieth century.

CPC agents deliberately recruited women in rural towns. The company's managers classified towns based on their population, which determined both the number of workers an agent might assign there, and the number of orders the company expected a representative to submit. A representative in a class one town with a population of 2,500 would submit at least one order per month; class two towns, between 1,000 and 2,500 population, supported an order every two months; once every three months in class three towns, with populations between 500 and 1,000; and an order every four months for class four towns with populations fewer than 500.[22] It is significant that the CPC did not create a classification for towns with populations larger than 2,500. City markets were simply not in the company's lexicon before the Depression era. There were also X class towns, also with populations of fewer than 500; how they were different from class 4 towns is unclear, except that they may have been nothing more than a population at a crossroads as in northern Minnesota, for example, or in the West, and not an incorporated town. The company frequently assigned X class towns to representatives who had done good business in their own towns and who requested extra territory. But, as the traveling agent's instructions noted, recruiters were not to assign X class towns "if the Sales Representative has no facilities for working them inexpensively."[23] Since few rural women had access to private transportation, it did not make economic sense to expect a representative to cover additional territory.

According to population statistics of the representatives listed in *Outlook*, the vast majority of prize-winning representatives came from class one towns. Out of 785 towns listed in the 1910 census search, approximately 20 percent had populations over 10,000, even though the CPC had not traditionally placed much emphasis on recruiting in cities. However, there were also a significant number of prizewinners from class three and four towns. Among representatives from towns under 10,000, the average population was 2,500. CPC recruiters, therefore, did work in large cities even though there was no attempt in the first fifty years of the company's history to differentiate them or to devise a recruiting and sales management plan to organize those workers. Despite the success of representatives who worked large cities, CPC managers tended to treat dense urban markets as over-sized towns. According to the CPC's 1922 district statistics, more than 80 percent of active representatives worked in towns with populations under 2,000, and of those, nearly 20 percent were from towns with populations of fewer than 500.[24]

Not all rural women were necessarily farm women. Although most CPC representatives lived in small towns, the women located in the census search resided in villages near other shops, tradesmen, and independent or professional business people, not out on the back roads. Even among those representatives found in the census search who lived on farms, there is little indication that agriculture or animal husbandry made up the lion's share of their families' income; only four husbands of CPC representatives listed their occupation as "farmer." More likely the non-farming families in these rural towns might have kept some livestock or maintained a garden, or perhaps they rented out their land.

The distinction between farm and non-farm is important to understanding the state of the rural economy in the early twentieth century and the gendered division of labor among families that worked the land. Farm women, whose domestic labor was devalued in the capitalist marketplace in the nineteenth century, developed work relationships with other women and families that emphasized community and reciprocal and long-term bonds of mutual aid instead of market-based competitiveness.[25] Farm communities in the eastern United States, living on the cusp of economic change, found that the growing and increasingly incorporated market threatened farmers' relationship to their land and the market. These communities responded with a form of "rural feminism," in which women's positive view of work helped them resist the new forms of modern consumption in the late nineteenth century.[26] Farm women's work, although segregated from men's by sex, allowed women to work cooperatively and collectively at odds with the emerging capitalist marketplace.[27] These patterns seemed to extend forward into the twentieth century, shaping the experience of rural CPC women, who turned to one another for help accessing new products.

The census survey also shows that CPC women came from very mobile families. More than 90 percent of the women in the census search were either born in a different state from the one in which they resided, or their parents had moved from a different state. Most were also native to the United States; the CPC was not an organization of immigrant or first-generation American women. Coupled with the company's reluctance to enter urban markets, this reluctance to employ immigrants appears to be a bias of both the corporate headquarters and the recruiters themselves. The image of the CPC representative was a preserve for whiteness. If CPC representatives had come from similar, rural backgrounds, it is entirely feasible that their parents, particularly their mothers, would have lived a life in which they developed the types of community bonds and perhaps carried forward a social or rural brand of feminism. Nevertheless, CPC women would have occupied a middle ground between their mothers and grandmothers, who resisted the capitalist market, and the company that promised to support the entry of this generation into that very market through the selling of goods. Like their grandmothers, CPC representatives relied on women's social networks, exploiting their bonds of mutual cooperation, appealing to women's interests in supporting the economic endeavors of a fellow resident. Unlike their grandmothers, CPC women in the 1910s and 1920s colluded with men who were part of a distant company, not a part of their families or communities. Representatives were not resisting the capitalist market; instead, they found a place in it that served their short-term needs without destroying the cooperative neighborhood networks that preceded it. CPC work, in other words, appealed to an older form of proprietary capitalism by employing a language of ownership, loyalty, and independence that would have still been common in rural communities, regardless of one's place of residence in town. While the products may have represented a new trend of commercial markets, the work ethic driving a successful sales career felt distinctly agrarian.

Like CPC women, their customers also lived in villages or town centers. There is very little evidence that many representatives walked or cycled to families who lived miles away in the countryside. Although she probably brought her catalog out to friends and family who might have lived farther away from town, a representative was more likely to knock on the doors of strangers at homes in town. Proximity to the country store, railroad depot, school, and post office afforded women in town faster access to new consumer products, services, and trends, and representatives could benefit from competition in the more populated villages and town centers.

While McConnell and the managers hoped recruiting agents could appoint women to work in the smallest towns, they hoped at the same time to locate women with some measure of social clout and respectability. This, in effect, led them to women who were older, married, and white. Despite the large numbers of women working in the South, no traveling agents and few representatives were women of color. CPC literature, beauty catalogs, product development and marketing strategies, and eventually the advertisements in the national advertising campaigns clearly associated whiteness with business and respectability. Had they been offered, CPC products would have appealed to black women, especially the household products, food additives, fragrances, and soaps. The hair care products were probably less suitable, and African American women such as Madame C. J. Walker and Annie Turnbo Malone were manufacturing and selling customized hair and skin care products around the same time.[28]

The CPC assumed that most black women and recent immigrants were not eligible to work as representatives. In a small section buried in the middle of the 1924 Traveling Agent's manual, the company addressed the question of recruiting black women in an essay titled "A Delicate Question."[29] Here the CPC stated that agents should not appoint "colored" representatives; however, it also recognized that "it is a poor rule that has no exceptions, so that we leave it to the good judgment of a Traveler." The CPC and its agents judged the efficacy of city markets in part by the racial makeup of its residents: in the 1920s, a town of 3,000 might need two workers, if they declined full time work, whereas "a town of 20,000 might have nearly [a large] colored or foreign population, when three or four [representatives] would be sufficient."[30] In both rural towns and urban districts, the CPC did not "approve of the appointment of a colored Representative" but tried to allow for exceptions. In several large cities, it said, "there is sometimes a good colored section in that town where a nice business could be done, if a *reliable* colored Representative could be appointed." As a rule, however, it stated, "Colored are not reliable."[31]

Once appointed, Black representatives were discriminated against by the company. Recruiters marked the contracts for black women as "Colored," were required to secure additional deposits for their sample cases and catalogs, and made clear that black representatives were restricted to sell only in black sections of towns. Unlike white representatives, black representatives were ineligible to purchase goods on credit. "*Cash must accompany orders*" in all instances, the guidebook insisted, eliminating the credit options available to whites. Refusal to extend credit penalized both the few black representatives in the CPC and the black consumers who had to pay for products in advance. Although scattered evidence suggests that black women worked successfully in both urban and rural districts in the pre–World War II era, neither published sales literature nor census analysis positively identifies a single black representative.

Demographics further confirm CPC managers and recruiters' efforts to secure "middle-aged" married women as ideal representatives. According to an analysis of the thirty-nine representatives located in the 1910 census, the average age of the representative was 47.5, although they ranged in age from fourteen to seventy-three years old.[32] Twenty of the thirty-nine representatives had children under age eighteen living at home, and of them, ten had children under age ten. Given the broad range of age and family responsibility, therefore, it's clear that CPC work accommodated a variety of women, but especially those with families who wanted to combine the tasks of child care, housekeeping, and work.

Of particular interest is the way women labeled their occupations for census takers. Although twenty-seven of the thirty-nine women declared "none," thirteen others identified an occupation, of whom ten claimed CPC work: their occupations appeared as "saleswoman, toilet goods," "canvasser," "canvasser, perfume," "agent, dry goods" "saleslady, toiletries," and "solicitor, merchandise." The other three women listed cook, laundress, and pattern maker, and Jane Sproule listed "own income." Once again, the short average tenure rate already limits the number of women from 1905 to 1910 who might still have worked as CPC representatives when the census taker appeared in 1910; like many working-class women who worked part time, others may not have considered sales work an occupation worth mentioning. But chances are that very few who had been listed in CPC literature in 1907 continued to maintain active contracts when the census was taken three years later. That may also account for why women claimed "none" when asked about their occupation.

However, the women who took their CPC work seriously were more likely successful at it. Of the women who claimed it as an occupation, more than half (eight) were among the 15 percent who had appeared in multiple listings, and five out of seven others appeared in *Outlook* between 1906 and 1908; they had maintained their contracts well past the average four months and were part of the elite 15 percent who remained with the company for more than two years. They were among the most highly successful representatives. As such, the women who identified CPC work as their occupation probably viewed it as more than a mere extension of their household duties, but rather as a business and livelihood.

"Inquire for widow ladies. Or ambitious married ladies . . .,"
Instructions for General Agents, **1915**

The profiles of successful representatives indicate that such women came from a variety of family situations and economic strata although class (as both an economic and a cultural factor) is more difficult to determine. The demographic profiles of the women who later became traveling agents, or recruiters, are remarkably similar; all of those women had to work as door-to-door representatives at one point. Most had no dependent children living at home. Pauline Megargel from Moscow, Pennsylvania, for example, whose name appeared just once in 1907, lived by herself, had never married, and had no children. Forty-four-year-old Sarah Rader from Moundsville, West Virginia, lived with her husband (age sixty) and two of her four children, ages twenty-two and twenty-three. Annette Dillon of Coffeyville, Kansas, age thirty-three, lived at home with her father and stepmother and her four siblings, ranging from age eleven to nineteen; her father, George, was a salesman for a drug store. Katherine Anderson, age forty and divorced, lived with sisters Louise and Alice Fisher in Arkansas City, Kansas; her two children apparently lived elsewhere. Forty-one-year-old Addie Bunker, single, rented her home in Silver City, New Mexico. And Jennie Prevey of Millbank, South Dakota, forty-nine and widowed with four of her five children living with her (ages fourteen, seventeen, twenty-five, and twenty-seven in 1910), also rented rooms in her home to three lodgers; we can only speculate about which of Prevey's jobs, as boarding house keeper or "saleswoman, toilet goods," paid more of her expenses. If she lived close to the railroad depot, we can also speculate as to whether a CPC traveling agent stopped at her house in 1908 looking for prospects.

Notable exceptions to the rule of single or widowed women with no children under age eighteen living at home are Jane Sproule, Lottie Napper, and Anna Fiddler. Both Sproule and Napper were widowed and claimed custody of their children. Sproule, from Cavalier, North Dakota (population 652), first appeared in *Outlook* in June 1906, at which time she would have been forty-nine years old. She was listed as a widow in the 1910 census, and in 1906 her two sons would have been nine and fifteen years old. Sproule's name appeared no fewer than eight times in those five years, frequently in the top twenty earnings categories; she was clearly one of CPC's most productive saleswomen. According to a 1926 recruiting booklet, her lifetime commission earnings with CPC totaled approximately $8,800.[33] She may have conducted her business while her children attended school, or she may have relied on the help of her neighbors to watch her children while she went out to deliver products and collect orders. Mrs. Lottie Napper from Pocatello, Idaho (population 9,000), who first appeared in *Outlook* in August 1909, enlisted the labor of her seventeen-year-old daughter, who also listed "solicitor, merchandise" as her occupation, and the two may have worked as a team. Napper, aged thirty-three and widowed by the time of the 1910 census, and her daughter also shared their home with a fifty-seven-year-old lodger, whose room and board fees probably contributed to the family's income.

It is tempting to argue that in order to be a successful, high-earning, long-term sales agent, one could not afford the distraction of very young children. Anna Fiddler of Geddes, South Dakota (population 710), however, challenges that assumption. Aged thirty-three and married for nine years to George, a helper in a brick yard, Fiddler sold CPC products while balancing the needs of her four children, ranging in age from one to eight. Fiddler could very well have been pregnant with or have recently given birth to her youngest son when she gathered orders large enough to get her name in *Outlook* in March, May, June, and August of 1909. Her husband had not been out of work during the twelve months prior to the census taker's arrival, so we can only guess whether it was debt, financial need, or a driven personality that propelled Anna Fiddler with a sample case in hand to knock on her neighbors' doors in 1909.

"Inquire for ladies with sickly (or lazy) husbands . . . "
Instructions for General Agents, 1915

Ironically, although the vast majority of California Perfume Company representatives were married, very few talked about their husbands when they
wrote to the company about their experiences or progress. The "absent husband" is one of the earliest tropes in CPC and Avon literature and one that
continued through its history. Granted, among the families of top representatives, husbands were unlikely to be around at all. But among those
who were married and had families, their reluctance to talk about the men
in their lives supports the view that they regarded the CPC business as their
own. As historian Mary Neth noted, women's access to earnings were negotiated, in part, through men. "Egalitarian" family structures existed in the
sense that men didn't interfere with women's work.[34] Like housework, a
representative's sales work was her individual responsibility in part because it was framed around neighborly visiting and consumption. Just as
a farm husband could exclude his wife from the financial decisions of the
family farm, she could claim ownership over her CPC business. Her earnings entered the family economy at her own discretion, and her husband's
approval or disapproval seemed not to have affected how she carried on her
business relationship with the company.

CPC recruiters consciously sought out married women to work as representatives, although generally speaking, both men and women frequently
resisted the prospect of married women working. Mrs. A. L. Pedrick, a traveling agent in the northwestern division, listed a husband's objection, or fear
of it, as the third most likely protest given by a prospect. Whenever Pedrick
heard, "I want to talk it over with my husband," she wrote, "I keep smiling
and think 'darn' inside." Of course a wife would want to consult her husband;
the $5 deposit was no small affair for most families. Pedrick, though, eager
to get her prospect to sign the contract before she thought of too many other
objections, claimed that she responded with one of three arguments; expe-
diency, responsibility, and independence. "If you were down town and saw
something marked down [to] $5 and you knew that would be the one sale
day . . . would you run home to talk it over?" she asked. Or, appealing to
power and perhaps women's desire to make their own decisions, Pedrick
offered, "Why not start saying, 'I am the Master of my fate, the Captain of my
soul,' or however you like to put it since it really means "I am a Sales Manager
for [CPC] Gold Medal goods.' "[35]

Traveling agents who recruited women as representatives supplied many anecdotes about the resistance they encountered, as well as their success in overcoming it. In all of them, agents implicitly acknowledged a husband's right to object and, ultimately, even to refuse to give his wife permission to sign the contract. Some travelers addressed the suspicious or reluctant husband directly, selling *him* the opportunity for his wife to have a representative position and talking to him as much as she did to the woman herself. The agent's manuals suggested this very tack as well, believing that husbands objected not to their wives working and being outside the home for a few hours a day, but to the type of work: "selling." Travelers addressed this objection by emphasizing business, not sales. In almost every case, agents assumed that husbands would listen to and approve a business proposition—especially one that was "so perfectly suited" for a woman's abilities, hours, and domestic responsibilities. In cases where women seemed reluctant to accept the CPC contract, agents appealed to the authority of the husband. "You scarcely ever find a man who really wants to interfere with his wife's plans," traveling agent Mrs. Mallicoat wrote, "but if you do and the woman appears to be the right person for the work, try to make it convenient to meet the husband and explain the proposition. You can convince him of the value of it much quicker than you can the wife."[36]

In November 1926, the CPC published traveling agent Miss Veral Studebaker's letter, titled "The Adamant Husband," as a CP Chat, a daily memo mailed to all agents. "I had two promising workers today all ready and eager to work when Mr. Husband interrupts. He has the advantage there, as he furnished the $5.00 [deposit] and likes to show his authority. But finally found one whose husband agrees to help. 'May his tribe increase,'" she wrote. The Chats editor, Brian Davis, printed Studebaker's letter, then added his own analysis, one that presented them as a progressive company, a leader in the new trend for women's advancement and economic potential. "Hardheaded" husbands, he wrote, "don't know that woman is advancing, that her place in the world is wherever she wishes to go. And because of this antediluvian idea, you are an antagonist of his." The agent's best strategy to dispel his dark looks and snappy remarks, and to beat his defense, was to appeal to his economic instinct and show weekly reports of nearby, successful representatives as proof of what his wife could earn: "Bullet orders fired from a well aimed gun will penetrate the hardest pate," Davis concluded.[37]

The agent's income-earning proposition was on shaky ground so long as the husband had control over the $5 deposit for the sample case and materials. On the other hand, if a wife had money of her own, the agent encouraged her to accept or reject the contract by her own judgment; CPC managers and agents encouraged women to act independently. The cash for the deposit could have come from husbands or wives, although the company recognized and reinforced married women's subordinate marital status when it came to credit. If a representative had a letter of credit on file signed by three references in her hometown, she could submit an order to the company and take up to three weeks to pay for it. This allowed her to postpone collecting money from her customers until she delivered the products and, ideally, secured a second order, which she would submit along with payment for the first. Agents often sought out these references to secure their signatures, or the company would send them letters after receiving the contract to verify the application. CPC managers suggested that recruiters use the husband's first name on the contract: "Men whose names are given as references," the manual said, "sometimes do not know the maiden name of your Appointee, whereas they will know the husband's name. Of course this does not apply in the case of widows."[38] A husband's connection to the world of credit depended on a social and economic network that favored men, but this did not mean that CPC managers thought husbands had any control over their wives' businesses.

Husbands seem to have played a minor role in how representatives viewed their work, however, and once the contract was signed, a company manager no longer seemed compelled to seek their approval or participation in the business. Once a woman was on file at a CPC regional sales office, the company dealt solely with her and no manual, publication, or piece of official correspondence ever mentioned her husband again. For the vast majority of representatives, the small scale and low total income would have done little to alter or threaten traditional gender roles in the family. Historically, husbands sometimes tried to control a woman's business by virtue of their legal control of property, and occasionally husbands ruined a successful business.[39] Husbands, however, would have little incentive to interfere with a CPC business. They may have regarded door-to-door work of lesser consequence than a larger or more established independent concern, making it less threatening to their household authority.[40] Direct sales involved risking less capital—representatives did not invest in inventory or equipment, but only required seasonal catalogs, order forms, and samples of face powders and perfumes. The CPC pitched door-to-door work as something women could "fit in" with their domestic duties. Unlike dressmakers or shop owners, but perhaps like boarding house keepers, CPC representatives accommodated their sales work to housework. Occasionally the work supplemented women's domestic duties, as representatives could purchase household products for their own use at wholesale prices.

A CPC business confirmed rather than challenged women's gendered roles as housekeepers and managers of the family economy. Therefore, it is best understood as an element of a family economy in which married women held a subordinate and supporting role, especially in a rural economy where women helped one another. McConnell defined the CPC as fitting neatly into women's domestic role, designed neither to interfere with her primary duties (caring for her home and family) nor subordinate them.

"How 'Tis Done": Business Secrets of the Most (and Least) Successful CPC Representatives

Although women's family and social situations affected their business, there was no standard profile or way to predict who would succeed or fail at the work. Personality mattered and McConnell thrived on training the fresh and optimistic, those who had not yet discovered the difficulties bound up in transforming social relationships into business. Most women, however, had no work experience with direct sales. Indeed, McConnell preferred women who had not worked in the line before because he did not want to have to "correct" the "bad habits" they might have learned from other firms. "You need have had no special training or experience," he wrote in a recruiting booklet. "We tell you just how to go about it. It is easy to succeed with the instructions we give you."[41] His training and motivation techniques were geared toward getting new representatives out to quick starts before inertia, inherent in the unsupervised nature of the work, set in to their routines.

New representatives received some instructions from the traveling agent at the time of the appointment, but most of the information was in the sales manual. Also, repeated tips on selling appeared in the monthly newsletters and in the weekly correspondence that managers sent during the first four weeks of the contract. When a new recruit signed her contract, she also signed an intent slip that outlined her work plan. Ideally, a recruiter would have convinced a woman to start canvassing immediately, but of course many women put the inevitable task off for a few days, some claiming that they needed time to get their household affairs in order before they started leaving their homes for a few hours each day. Catalogs, a sample case filled with a variety of CPC's most popular products, a sales manual, order book, and *Outlook* accompanied her contract, so each new representative had the tools to start immediately. Sometimes a traveling agent, when she succeeded in recruiting a new representative, would have already gathered a few orders from women nearby whom she had unsuccessfully attempted to recruit; in lieu of a contract, the agent passed the new orders on to her new representative as proof of the products' popularity. They were also a kind of signing bonus because the recruit, not the traveling agent, kept the commissions when she delivered the products. Sometimes the traveling agent would accompany the new representative on her first few sales calls to show her how it was done, but the representative did not leave to begin her sales calls until she had committed to start canvassing and to sending in a wholesale order of at least thirty dollars.

Traveling agents helped new representatives determine where they might start calling by making a list of friends, family, and neighbors. Early in the company's history, sales literature emphasized that representatives should call upon "the best families" first. "Select ten or a dozen of the most influential families in your territory," the 1899 manual suggested. "Call upon these most influential people, introduce yourself in an easy, pleasing manner . . . state that you have a line of goods you would like to show them; open your sample case . . . "[42] Their endorsement then served as a calling card and proof of the company's reputation. Ironically, the class-based language was soon dropped, as if McConnell knew that the women who worked for him were not comfortable with it. He hedged his bets, urging women not to be intimidated and to approach both rich and poor households: "Remember there is no family who is too rich or who lives in too much style for you to call on with our goods. . . . One customer's money is as good as another's."[43]

CPC literature constantly encouraged representatives to do a "thorough" canvass, to "call on every house in their territory," and to "work up a good order" before submitting it to the company. The company provided "leave catalogs," small paper versions, for representatives to give to customers; but as a rule, it was their job to go over the color plate catalog with customers inside the home. If the representative did not want to lug along a full sample case each time, the company suggested that she carry just one or two "leader" items. *Outlook* editors generally highlighted a seasonal product that they urged representatives to push and frequently backed it up with a contest, offering a special prize to the representative who sold the most or who sold over a particular limit. CPC also provided representatives with a customer logbook to note a customer's past purchases. Representatives could then try to judge when a customer might be running low on a particular item and suggest it during a sales call, or make recommendations for products that a customer had not yet tried. Once the representative had collected a good wholesale order (ideally this would be more than $30 so she could receive a full wholesale discount, free shipping, and free samples), she submitted it to the company, delivered the items when they arrived, and took a new order.

Canvassing was real work, McConnell said. Representatives needed to plan for it and dedicate themselves to it. "Allow nothing to come between yourself and your duty," he wrote. "If you are to start out in the morning at nine o'clock, be just as prompt and just as particular as though you were coming to our office to report for work. . . . And canvass just as conscientiously as though you were working right in our office." He believed that the only time women should give up for the day was when they were truly tired and exhausted, "mentally or physically." It was better to go home and rest, he said, than to risk "showing up the goods" in an uninteresting manner and becoming a "bore to your customers."[44] McConnell warned though, in familiar Progressive-era style exhortations, against mistaking tiredness for laziness. Given that most representatives would canvass their territory on foot, *Outlook* regularly carried articles on walking.[45] "What better way to keep the system in trim, the blood circulating properly and repairing the worn parts of the body than a brisk walk in the bracing atmosphere of January. And is there any more interesting way than a call on friends and acquaintances for business and for profit. . . . Utilize it, not only for health but for that little private savings account."[46]

Despite training and motivational rhetoric that encouraged women to work full time developing their businesses, managers knew that women would not actually do that. McConnell wanted women who were available to handle the trade four to six hours a day, and although he hoped women would canvass full-time and urged them to do so, he did not intend the CPC to displace their domestic duties: "Arrange your home affairs so as to give as much of your time as you possibly can to this work," he wrote. He dedicated a 1923 recruiting pamphlet, "Converting Spare Hours into Dollars" to "those who can *make* spare time possible by efficiency in their daily routine of duties."[47] Some women reported their hours and routine when they submitted their weekly report cards, or when they wrote letters of appreciation. Mrs. George Allen of Colorado, for example, worked her CPC business around her two children, ages three and five: "I can give from two to five hours every day, as my report shows," she said. "I find that Saturday is not always a profitable day to intrude on my patrons."[48]

Those who succeeded tended consistently to spend more time working their business. Although some worked it as if it were a full-time job, others devoted the same hours week after week to their work. "My hours are from eight until eleven-thirty in the morning, and from one until five in the afternoon, rain or shine," wrote Mrs. Albert King of Newburyport, Massachusetts. For more than twenty years, Mrs. Albert King earned the highest honors within the CPC organization. Year after year, she made sales that were more than three times the annual totals of her nearest rivals. In July 1905, the earliest her name appears in the extant literature, she submitted the highest wholesale order in the entire organization: $300.80 retail, which earned her $120.32 for the month. In July 1906, she submitted the second highest order, $320.70 retail ($128 in commissions), for which she won an extra $10 in gold. She clearly worked as part of a team, for the CPC often listed *Mr.* Albert King

It is a little over a year since I took out a contract with you and would like to say I never worked for a better firm and have never sold anything that hasn't been satisfactory. The fates have

been against me this year in many ways. My mother has been in the hospital for over a month and the order I am enclosing is very small. I am also sending a small photo of myself, and I do hope New York State will win the Prize, and only wish I was able to help more.
Contract No. E155, N. Y.   MISS MABEL STEIH.

Figure 2.2. Miss Marie Steih, New York, had proudly worked as a representative for a year. She sent her photograph along with an apology for sending a small order. *CPC Outlook*, March 1917. (Courtesy of Hagley Museum and Library.)

as the monthly prizewinner. Mr. King was not her husband but her son. In fact, three of the King children, her sixteen-year-old daughter, fifteen-year-old son, and another son (age unclear) assisted their mother, and together they developed a thriving family retail business. "The people were so pleased with the goods," she wrote, "and we had such good success, that after we had been to the people several times, we arranged our work systematically."[49]

The Kings divided Taunton into sections and planned to call at every house once every five weeks. Their plan resulted in a twenty-year selling dynasty in CPC. In July 1914, son Nathan won a company contest by selling 478 packages of CPC Baby and Elite Powder; he earned $15 worth of crystal cut glass. (His closest competitor, Miss Olive E. Decker of New York, sold 326 packages and won $10 worth.)[50] Mrs. King, too, tried for every contest. In August, she sold 100 packages of Shampoo Cream and Liquid (tied for second place) and earned $10 in cut glass. By 1921, Mrs. King had submitted a total of $34,117.25 in wholesale orders to the CPC ($54,587.60 retail). At a 40 percent commission, she had kept $20,470.35 for herself—or approximately $1,950 per year, not counting contests and prizes; by 1926, her lifetime submissions totaled $47,152.49 in wholesale, and commissions of $28,291.94.[51]

Eugene Snow also made notable progress in Newburyport, Massachusetts. He started work with the company in July 1909, "giving his spare time to the local work" and frequently turning in orders that put him in the top twenty producers. In 1914, he signed on as a traveling agent and recruited in the New England area for approximately ten years, when he returned to local sales. His name appeared in CPC/Avon representative tributes as late as 1948. Eugene Snow and the King family clearly considered CPC work their careers and their business.

Other women, perhaps as many as 10 to 20 percent of the entire sales force, had no intention of trying to build a sales base. These women eventually appeared on the "situation" reports for traveling agents, which the company provided to agents when they entered towns to reappoint a representative. In most cases, the company chose to replace representatives when women had failed to respond to company correspondence, or did not submit orders that they promised. Mrs. Emma Ellis of Arbuckle, California, for example, appointed in August 1925, never wrote to the company to explain her lack of activity and as a result CPC sent a recruiter to appoint a new worker there in December. Similarly, Mrs. Will Hughs, appointed in June 1925, wrote to the company in August that she had been ill, but promised to start right out. "To date, we have had no report of service, nor have we had any business from her," the report stated.[52]

Some women did not wait for an agent to show up in town and wrote directly to CPC to cancel their contracts. Mrs. L. E. Durkee of Albany, Oregon, appointed in April 1925, sent in only three orders through June, amounting to a total of $31 wholesale: "She wrote us in September that she would not continue the work." Similarly, Mrs. Roy Glenn of Sisson, California, claimed that she had too much other work. She had worked for a year, submitting wholesale orders totaling $65: "She recently wrote us that she has so much work to do at home that she hasn't the time."[53] Miss Mary Weirich of Dunsmuir, California, claimed similar woes. She submitted wholesale orders totaling $65 between June and November 1925, but she wrote to say, "the work was too hard on her and that she was giving it up."[54] All of these women acknowledged that they had an obligation to fulfill their contracts with CPC, but that they did not have the time or energy to do the work "properly." They had considered their business to be part of their work; however, not all women felt it their duty to take on the extra load.

Some women clearly used their CPC contracts to serve only their own family needs, occasionally purchasing products at wholesale without having canvassed their neighborhoods. Mrs. Robert Sorenson, appointed in August, sent in an order for $9.00, another in September for $4.35. "This is of course insufficient business for the district," traveling agent Lela Eastman's manager wrote. Mrs. H. B. Cole also sent in tiny orders: $6.73 in July, $2.02 in August, and $4.32 in September. "This business is not sufficient to warrant our holding the district open for her any longer."[55] In Kent, Washington, managers suggested that a new representative be appointed to replace Mrs. G. B. Creed. She sent in several small orders between June 23 and November totaling $13.16: "Mrs. Creed evidently [sic] orders only for [herself and a] few friends. Kent has a population of 3,000 and should be producing [good business.] Appoint a live wire here who will give her full time to the CPC work."[56]

In between the Kings and women like Mrs. Creed lay the vast majority of "live wires" whom the CPC relied on to distribute products and increase corporate profits. McConnell used the Kings, Mr. Snow, and the hundreds of other women who succeeded with CPC work as examples of successful full-time workers. At the same time he recognized that most women stayed with the company for only a few months and produced less than $100 in business before "retiring." Throughout the 1910s and '20s, turnover rates among the representative staff were very high, often approaching 90 to 100 percent every year. Spectacular as those numbers sound, an average "good" year can help illustrate the CPC recruiter's task and the scope of problems CPC confronted on an annual basis.

Tenure rates for the representative staff (i.e., the length of time they actively worked their CPC contracts before canceling or being terminated) varied from year to year. According to the 1927 recruiting report, the New York Office appointed 10,816 women as representatives in 1927, of whom (according to the 1928 statistics) only 14 percent (1,542) were still working at the end of 1928. According to tenure and sales reports of the New York office, which organized more than 12,000 representatives, of the total number of representatives on file at the end of 1928, nearly 60 percent were "new," meaning they had been appointed that year. The remaining 40 percent had been appointed in previous years. In other words, McConnell relied on a solid core of experienced representatives to balance the larger percentage of short-term representatives. These experienced representatives received enough benefits from their association with the California Perfume Company to continue on a longer-term basis.

Tenure directly correlated to average order size an important indicator for CPC analysts. In all its literature, the CPC encouraged representatives to submit orders of $30 or more: as an incentive, these representatives earned free shipping, in addition to $10 commission. However, as the reports make clear, barely one-third of representatives reached this threshold. The others, consequently, had to pay their own shipping costs. Individually, most representatives were not very productive in sales. According to a sales report analysis for the same group in 1928, the vast majority of women earned far less than $250 (wholesale) a year. Despite the company's encouragement to pull together wholesale orders of $100 or more a month ($1,200 a year), 21 percent of women produced less than $10 in wholesale orders a year, barely enough to cover the CPC's recruiting costs.[57] The top 25 percent of representatives who had worked for more than a year produced nearly 75 percent of CPC business.

Sales and Consumption in Rural Women's Social Networks

Those women who commented on their other paid jobs noted that they preferred the CPC because it required fewer hours and often resulted in higher pay and other non-cash benefits. "I like my new job very much," Miss Lillian Menard of Massachusetts wrote. "It is better than the shop any time."[58] Mrs. Ed Sanford of Wisconsin claimed that she found the work undemanding: "Am very glad that I took up this work because it is the easiest of all I have to do."[59]

Although Mrs. Sanford's declaration does not specify what her other work included, she was presumably alluding to her non-wage labor (her house-work and family care responsibilities) and not necessarily to other paid work. Sales work remained one of the few options rural women had for earning money and was not a substitute for industrial homework or piecework, which were not as available in the rural villages where most CPC representa-tives worked. Rural women may have also found that sales work fitted more neatly into their lives. Few opportunities for wage work existed for married women in rural America, and commissioned sales work could fill the need for occasional, seasonal earnings.[60]

The vast number of women who did contract with the CPC lived within a social and cultural system that did not supply opportunities to work with companies that paid wages. Although practically every small town fea-tured independent and entrepreneurial women in business, as dressmakers, shopkeepers, or laundresses, for example, nearly all "women's trades" in the early twentieth century were in the midst of decline. Ready-to-wear clothing, for example, was out-selling items made by skilled needle workers, and the numbers of servants steadily declined throughout the early twentieth cen-tury. Furthermore, women's individual businesses were often subject to dis-criminatory credit auditors and policies that served to limit the scope of their endeavors.

Sales work, on the other hand, was familiar, both because women had ex-perience with it as consumers, and because, as the century wore on, women had more opportunities to engage in it as a money-making venture. There appeared to have been numerous opportunities for women to contract with other direct selling concerns. Many representatives wrote about their ability to establish a better reputation for themselves and CPC products in con-trast to other direct sales concerns. Some, like Mrs. J. R. Allen in Kentucky, turned down other companies that offered her better commissions on their products: "I have so many companies that try to offer me an agency for their line . . .," she wrote for *Outlook*, the representative magazine, "[but] I am so proud to represent your line that I could not consider their propositions at all."[61] In fact, fourteen of seventy testimonials written by CPC's most suc-cessful representatives and published in the 1922 recruiting booklet, "Does

It Pay?" referred to competition from other direct sales concerns, which suggests that the number of recruiters who regularly canvassed small towns in search of agents was high. Several others even mentioned a personal history of selling; as such, a CPC contract fit a pattern for some women, who were already familiar with the type of work it required.

Even if a new representative did not have experience working for another direct sales concern, she was familiar with how the business operated, for many products were available through non-retail venues. Although most women purchased their supplies through retail stores, mail order, and direct canvassing, many women also formed purchasing "clubs," submitting bulk orders for products at reduced prices. For example, the Larkin Soap Company competed directly with the CPC for market coverage and indirectly for representatives. For example, as noted by historian Lu Ann Jones, itinerant merchants from the W. T. Rawleigh Company, which sold vitamins and supplements, "represented the so-called incorporation of America and a new and intensified phase in the creation of a national market for brand-name consumer goods." But more importantly, she argues, "gender, race, and local customs shaped the way southerners encountered the market."[62] Employing men as salesmen, Rawleigh proudly boasted modern training principles much like the CPC's, following the company's rules of scientific salesmanship. Women welcomed the salesmen as a break from their household routines and an opportunity to make "autonomous" purchases. The wide array of buying opportunities in rural America rested on the wheels of peddlers. Most of these representatives, like those of J. R. Watkins who sold soap door to door, moved through town in regular schedules, but others sought to create a foothold by infiltrating women's neighborhood networks via buying clubs that formed by small groups of families to increase their purchasing power. Some direct sales companies in this period sought them out and actively promoted them.

One arena of stiff competition that faced the CPC was in the selling of soaps, which made up more than half of CPC's product line. Such staple products were available through any number of retail venues with price and product size figured prominently in consumers' purchasing decisions. Larkin Soap dominated this market, and its soap buyers clubs were fairly widespread. A Larkin customer combined her order with those of her neighbors; the more soap they ordered together, the less expensive was each individual product. Frequently, prospective representatives referred to Larkin directly as a reason they did not think the CPC would be a viable business in their towns. the company responded in two ways. The first was to assure their products' superiority, in quality and quantity, and even considering the higher price, the CPC product was an economical alternative. The second response was to try to recruit the woman who organized the club; she was, after all, already expressing a "business-like" mind by talking friends and neighbors into joining a purchasing cooperative and gathering orders, and therefore exhibiting the behavior of an ideal representative.

CPC editors happily printed letters from representatives who had ousted Larkin from their neighborhood purchasing circles, as well as any other "inferior" competitor. "Dear Sirs": wrote Mrs. S. Ream of Stonington, Illinois. "I herein send you my third weekly report, and also my first order for $97.05. I have solicited the town pretty thoroughly. I find fourteen Larkin Clubs, three Bullock and Ward agents, and four others of as many companies. Under the circumstances I think I have made a good order." Similarly, Dennis J. Adams of Gouverneur, New York, "found Spragueville had many Larkin Soap Clubs, yet I took orders to the amount of $14.00 Friday." Fanny Baarman of Zeeland, Michigan, reported: "I have no difficulty in selling your goods. There are a number of Soap Clubs and agents for other companies, but the people are more pleased with the articles we carry and promise me an order for more." Finally, expressing the zeal of the true believer in direct sales opportunities, Mrs. Mary A. Wesley of Terre Haute, Indiana, submitted her first order and claimed, "I feel the ice is broken, and now, with an effort, I can swim to the shore of victory over my enemy, the Larkins!"[63]

Women's unpaid labor as club organizers and/or savvy shoppers continued well into the twentieth century. CPC managers recognized the value and need for women's social and economic networks and turned this into a "business opportunity." CPC literature frequently portrayed the soap clubs as potential, yet ineffective, competition. It thus affirmed women's role as active consumers. Their efforts to save money, as opposed to producing it, had become fully integrated with their role as housekeepers.[64] Indeed, the CPC contract and bonus offers appeared as a step up from either soap clubs or other canvassing concerns. Although the company did not condone it, many representatives may have sold CPC products to friends and family at reduced retail prices, thereby giving women an opportunity to include other women as co-beneficiaries of their "exclusive" sales rights and to make a profit on sales to women whom they could treat more formally as customers. However, there was no way for CPC managers to know how much women collected at the point of sale, for representatives submitted orders and payments based on wholesale prices. Although various state laws prohibited representatives from selling above published retail prices, a practice presented to consumers in language that showed the company had their interests at heart, there was nothing to prevent representatives from selling below them. Women's consumer activities, their productive and reproductive labor within the home, and their entrepreneurial behavior, therefore, overlapped.

Gender and Business

Business means many things. It is an activity, a transaction. It is also an organization, and it is an ideology. Networks based on gender not only shaped but were also reshaped by every aspect of CPC culture. From the business relationships between executives and representatives and consumers, to the standards of conduct, and even in the definition of work and business, gender expectations profoundly affected the way CPC sales managers and representatives practiced and experienced business as a cultural institution. Gendered perceptions of women's wage-earning potential—for example, their desire for money and their ability to handle finances and a trade—shaped the way both CPC men and women regarded, defined, and promoted business. And it functioned in the way representatives viewed themselves and their business in relationship to their families and communities, mediating the transactions between women representatives and their customers, who were also their friends and neighbors.

The CPC business, as an organization and as an activity, was fluid. At the corporate level, it so resembled a contemporary "firm," vertically integrated and managed by departments and modern accounting methods, that it is nearly impossible to consider CPC as anything less than a progressive twentieth-century business. At the other end of the spectrum, the individual women who served as the CPC's distribution channels and as its sole means of advertising and service, worked so infrequently and generated such small individual sales that is it difficult to see them as anything other than half-hearted part-time workers. They occasionally acted as entrepreneurs but they were not fully business "owners." Indeed, except for a select few, their CPC responsibilities were not the highest priority of these women. Nevertheless, representatives participated in business at the CPC's organizational level in the corporation and in the personal, domestic arena through their transactions with women over catalogs and coffee in kitchens and front parlors.

CPC business should not be judged by standards set by either organized labor or by exponents of the "self-made man," both of which mask the historical experience and objectives of women in business. Women's patterns of entrepreneurship and labor follow uniquely gendered paths. That CPC work was not "full-time"—that women could not earn raises, claim seniority, bargain for higher commissions, or claim benefits to guard against sickness—were not perceived as problems to either the company's managers or its representatives, in part because they defined and accepted the work as "business," not as "labor." The rhetoric of "owning" a CPC "business," which camouflaged the actual economic activities in which women engaged, shifted the responsibility of success or failure squarely onto the shoulders of the individual representative. The company believed this and promoted it in nearly every piece of communication; the successful representative proudly judged and claimed her own achievements by this ideology, and even the unsuccessful representative seemed to blame no one but herself if she did not profit from the system. That she did not work it or make a living at it did not contradict the fact that a CPC contract was a potential business opportunity. Although there are no clear lines separating the business of representatives from the business at corporate headquarters, the two existed in a mutually reinforcing relationship, which was dominated by the men at the top.

Representatives were so far removed from the firm that traditional worker-control mechanisms proved both impractical and ineffective. However, McConnell profited by avoiding the costs that most businesses incurred in the supervision of workers. Representatives did not take up physical space at CPC; they did not work machines as employees at a factory, or sit at desks as most white-collar women did. McConnell could afford to "hire" inefficient workers because, in doing so, he did not risk his own resources; women did not take up space at his business, regardless of whether or not they worked efficiently. Instead he passed those costs on to representatives, who also had to invest very little in order to conduct their businesses. "You get the same profit that the owner of a store receives from the things he sells. And you don't have to pay out a cent for rent, light, heat, clerk hire and other expenses," McConnell had explained to his representatives. Ironically, the CPC paid significantly less for these expenses, too.

The CPC, in this formulation, existed as a representative's "support network." Every communication, from the traveling agent's recruiting pitch and initial instructions to the sales manuals and publications, told women that they were in control, that they had the power to succeed. Indeed, so long as women produced orders, McConnell did support and reward their efforts, and he terminated the contracts of only those representatives who had ceased to communicate with the company. Theoretically, the CPC representative could have conducted her business by whatever means she saw fit, but most women followed the company's instructions. Although they did not all succeed either in performing to service standards or in generating sales, most women accepted the premise of the company's ideals and attempted to re-create the CPC business personality described in its sales literature.

The physical and long-term isolation of individual women lent them a degree of control over their work and the ability to invent variations of the business personality that the CPC suggested in its literature. Door-to-door representatives worked in unregulated environments, which had both advantages and disadvantages. It gave them some power over the pace of their workday. Unlike sales clerks, they did not negotiate, bargain with, or face supervisors, co-workers—or even consumers, for that matter—on a daily basis. They had the right to work five hours a week or forty-five hours a week and to choose their own customers. For most representatives, the weather had more influence over when and how they worked than a CPC manager or publication.

However, the arrangement did not guarantee results for either McConnell or his representatives. Representatives' independence or isolation, depending on one's perspective, could work against them. Their connection to the company existed primarily through company literature, which served as the women's only access to the lives of fellow representatives, and which privileged the successful. A woman in a small town in Texas, for example, may never have known how thousands of other women like her could not, or did not know how to, pull together a $30 order. What would have happened had the thousands of women who quit CPC each year known how common their experiences of failure and low sales levels were? Could they have forced the company to change some of its policies and won benefits similar to those that were becoming available to salaried salesmen in wholesale and distribution firms? Would they have created a work-based consciousness of their position as representatives and demanded more profits or a different compensation system? Many businessmen began direct sales companies to avoid the potential for worker solidarity. Indeed, business analysts throughout the twentieth century have pointed out that one of the advantages to direct selling the corporations was workers' inability and disinclination to organize.

On the other hand, keeping women in the dark about shared business problems was not entirely beneficial to the CPC, either. Although representatives' isolation ultimately propped up the paternalistic relationship, keeping women in a subordinate position to male managers and maintaining the pretense that managers existed only to help them, it also prevented women from sharing ideas and supporting one another. Women who became discouraged very early on and quit trying to secure orders soon after signing their contracts, or who never ventured out their front doors in the first place, cost the company in recruiting and replacement expenses. It also resulted in long-term sales losses. Sales analysis within the company showed that women who repeatedly worked their territories gathered larger orders, in part because of their own increased confidence in their ability to sell, and also because of the consumers' assurance of representatives' reliability. In a market flooded with traveling salesmen, purchasing clubs, and mail-order catalogs, consumers became more reluctant to purchase from fly-by-night concerns. Representatives' inability to exchange information, formally or informally, therefore, negatively affected the CPC's bottom line, and the unregulated, unsupervised nature of direct selling often worked against the company's costs and profits interests. Ultimately the company's need for active representatives led managers to downplay the language of domesticity, emphasizing instead language promoting independent business and control. The company's success hinged on convincing women to try, on selling women a business.

3

Agents and Agency

The Work and Business Culture of California Perfume Company Traveling Agents, 1890s–1930s

My sole object is to help some other ambitious, struggling woman to join the California Perfume Company's great army of workers; for there is more to be realized in this work than in anything open to women—a broad assertion, but I speak whereof I know.

Mrs. C. A. Wood, "Travel Talks," c. 1920

The success or failure of the California Perfume Company hinged on the entrepreneurial efforts of the traveling agents. They recruited and trained an army of representatives across the country and were the only direct personal connection between the company and its female workforce. No other means existed under the CPC's business model to forge the links in the chain that formed a profitable direct sales team. Traveling agents were remarkably independent for business women and their success was a reflection of their reputations, fortitude, and savvy.

The CPC employed women as traveling agents from the early 1890s, when Mrs. P. F. E. Albee first set out with the new perfume sample case, to the early 1940s, when the company began settling them in city-sales-office management positions. Every year throughout the first third of the twentieth century, approximately 150 traveling agents searched the countryside year round, riding trains, living out of suitcases in hotels and boarding houses, and stopping in every tiny town to appoint new representatives to sell products door-to-door in their hometowns. Depending on her schedule, the average traveling agent could sign up four or five new representatives a week, and in this way, CPC recruited thousands of women to sell door-to-door every year. The agents sold CPC's second most important product: the business opportunity. The nature of their work meant traveling alone for eight to twelve months of the year, which gave these women a unique position in the company organization.[1]

The most successful California Perfume Company traveling agents treated their recruiting careers not only as a means to earn an income but as if it were their calling. Before formal public relations departments codified the vernacular of corporate goodwill, CPC traveling agents proselytized the company's good works, drawing women into its fold one by one.[2] In their recruiting pitches, traveling agents sometimes aimed to "save" women and help them to pick up the pieces of personal disaster or simply to give them the opportunity for a better life. Preaching a gospel of positive thinking and self-help, and bestowing "income earning opportunities" on women throughout the land, travelers as a group developed a respectable business personality based on charisma and independence.[3] On a much less poetic level, they also performed a very basic business function; they identified and trained the women who sold CPC products and in this they strongly influenced the business character and culture of the company. As a distinctive brand of middle managers, traveling agents provided a vital and integral link between representatives and the CPC management structure.

Personally and professionally, traveling agents comprise a historically important and unusual group of businesswomen. Using information teased out of the monthly newsletters, business correspondence, and travelers' personal records, this chapter creates a profile of agents' careers, their lives on the road, and their business culture. It shows how traveling agents defined themselves in the business world and what being "in business" meant to them. Analyzing traveling agents as a group also illustrates many aspects of CPC's business organization, strategy, and culture, including the values and patterns of decision making within the corporate hierarchy, the role of the individual in the organization, and the nature of the business relationships that individuals cultivated with each other and with management.

All traveling agents began their CPC careers as successful door-to-door sales representatives. Before they could recruit for CPC, they had to prove themselves as "business women" by being good representatives. McConnell required each woman to accumulate a minimum of $250 in wholesale orders from personal selling, thus ensuring that each one knew the CPC line of goods. Some women achieved this requirement in a matter of months; others worked for several years before going out on the road. McConnell intended to use this rule to keep from committing to an unproven prospect, for many women who eagerly began selling with high enthusiasm soon hit a lull and stopped producing. A woman also had to convince herself of the value of being a CPC agent before she tried to prove it to someone else. A traveling agent who did not first work as a sales representative lost one of her best recruiting tools: the ability to speak about her own experience. Travelers often displayed their own sales records and recounted their challenges and rewards to help persuade prospects to sign contracts.

Traveling agents worked on the road, moving from town to town to recruit and train new sales agents. Most covered areas that were somewhat close to their home state; others took advantage of the opportunity to travel and requested far away regions of the country. The very nature of the job limited the number of women who could take on this kind of work. The CPC needed both a specific demographic and a personality type. The reputation of the company, McConnell frequently said, was built on the respectability and "business sense" of his traveling agents. The same argument about the poor reputation of traveling salesmen that drove McConnell to design a community-based representative sales force also applied to the traveling agent staff, but of course with the important caveat that the traveling agent did indeed work on the road and therefore she could not build "community" trust, nor could she hook in to her neighborhood networks. Instead, she had to cultivate a respectable business personality, and the uniqueness of her very appearance on the road probably helped make a serious impression.

The transformation of American business as it spread across the land was propelled by better communications, ready capital, and civic improvements in small towns and cities across the CPC's territories. The automobile, abundant railroads, and later buses crisscrossed the Midwest and West. Political and social upheaval, the Progressive Era, competition from national retailers, even war did not seem to impede the CPC's core business. The system the company built was resilient and relied expressly on the traveling agent, who with suitcase and trunk covered as many as twenty to twenty-five towns in three to four weeks.

Sales division managers in corporate headquarters approved the applications of new travelers. However, a distinctive culture among agents developed because the CPC relied almost wholly on existing agents in the field, not company management officials, to recommend, recruit, and train new travelers. After all, CPC managers in Manhattan and Kansas City rarely, if ever, met any of the women in person, even after they had traveled for the company for years. The criteria for hiring an agent were almost entirely

MISS MYRTLE HOLT.

Miss Holt has traveled as General Agent for our Company almost continually for the last seven years. She has traveled over Michigan, Wisconsin, Indiana, Illinois, and, during the year of 1905, spent almost her entire time in Colorado. We have no doubt very many of our workers will be glad to meet her again.

Figure. 3.1. Miss Myrtle Holt worked as a CPC traveling agent for seven years, recruiting representatives in Michigan, Wisconsin, Indiana, and Illinois. "She spent most of 1905 in Colorado." *CPC Outlook*, May 1906. (Courtesy of Hagley Museum and Library.)

subjective and depended on the judgment of other women in the field. According to the traveling agents' 1915 manual, the agent who recruited a new representative took note of whether she felt the recruit would be qualified as a traveler someday. She especially considered the woman's family obligations and character before recommending that she be admitted to the ranks of agency: "whether he or she is so situated at home that trips of two or three months at a time away from home will be possible; that there are no family ties which would prevent the party" from being a traveling agent.[4] Although early in its history, the CPC had employed men as traveling agents, such as Mr. Eugene Snow from Newburyport, Massachusetts, CPC policy by the 1920s specifically stated that the company would only hire women: "We do not employ men as traveling [agents] under any circumstances. Appointing men [as local representatives] with this object in view is not good policy."[5]

Effectively then, women judged one another and advised the company on a prospect's appropriateness for the work.

The 1915 manual suggested that agents take note of a new recruit's appearance: "One of the main qualifications of a successful [Traveling] Agent is cleanliness and good taste. . . . It is one of the most important indexes to character."[6] The manual also very straightforwardly advised the traveling agent to "provide yourself with a neat traveling suit of serviceable material and quiet color, made simply but stylishly, in which you will feel well-dressed wherever you may chance to be on your journey."[7] McConnell warned his traveling staff that many people would "judge them by their appearance," and while "their opinion is not worth much," he said, "the person who is tastefully attired

Figure. 3.2. "Mr. A. Eugene Snow joined the CPC organization in July 1909, giving his spare time to the local work and doing an exceptionally good business in one of the cities of Eastern Massachusetts. With his careful conscientious method of instruction, the Sales Manager appointed by Mr. Snow is bound to make good and there is no doubt that during his travels through New England this year that many live wires will enroll under the CPC banner." *CPC Outlook,* March 1915. (Courtesy of Hagley Museum and Library.)

receives a consideration from strangers that is not extended to a shabbily or carelessly dressed person, or one much given to fads, and your attire will add to or detract from the dignity you would assume for your work."[8] Traveling agent Emma Buster supported this advice later in a CPC Chat: "I always try to be very clean and neat as the people judge the CPC by the travelers they employ."[9] In 1926, a recruit had been turned down for a traveling agency because of her poor appearance. When an experienced traveler assigned to drill her for the traveling position met her, she reported, "If her clothing had been made from pieces of cloth taken from a rag bag, she could not have looked worse, and, secondly, that she used 'dope' or drugs."[10] Sloppiness in personal habits translated into inattention to business practice and reflected a class position from which CPC tried to dissociate itself.

Travelers learned to fit their public image to conventional standards of business codes for women: quiet, serviceable, stylish, and confident. Although CPC repeatedly emphasized a woman's skills, abilities, and knowledge, most company literature favored other characteristics: good judgment, determination, maturity, cheerfulness, tact, pride, intuition, loyalty, confidence, perseverance, energy, persuasiveness, dignity, and honesty. At least, that is what CPC managers believed their best agents possessed; without onsite supervision and with little feedback other than an agent's recruiting record and an occasional letter from a new representative complimenting (or complaining about) an agent's conduct, the company could not enforce these criteria.

Tracking Agents

CPC managers had to take into account a traveling agent's needs, how far she could travel and for how long before returning home, her ability to work in both small towns and small cities, and whether she occasionally required additional training before being routed to new areas. At the same time, managers needed to spread out their traveling force in order to ensure complete coverage of the country. Keeping these women moving and informed was in itself a remarkable feat of organization and communication. Despite the differences among work tasks and styles between home office managers and traveling agents, ultimately the constant two-way communication between them created a strong and fairly uniform corporate culture, marked by a mutual understanding of individual and company goals.

The Manhattan sales office handled agents east of the Mississippi River, divided into the Eastern and Southern divisions, and the Kansas City office handled agents west of the Mississippi, divided into the Central and Western divisions. The general sales manager oversaw the entire routing operation; under him were Eastern (Manhattan) and Western (Kansas City) sales managers and their division (or regional) managers (all male); then each state had a field manager (often female). The routing rooms looked like a military command center or a political campaign headquarters. Detailed maps of each state lined the walls, marked by various colored tacks that denoted whether a town was being worked by an active representative, or a "failed" representative (a woman on contract but who had not submitted enough orders), or if it was an open territory, where a representative had resigned and no one had yet filled her place.

Field managers in the central offices tried to send a traveling agent over each route at least once a year. Travelers received their routes, consisting of approximately twenty towns along local train and trolley lines, every three or four weeks at a time. Field managers in New York or Kansas City chose first a railroad line, then identified towns either that needed a new representative or where the company required the agent to follow up on a current representative. (The 1924 handbook asked travelers to forward bus schedules so field managers could update routes and include more towns "on the interior" or off the train and trolley lines.) They provided a situation report for each town that included information on the former representative and her business history, and on the town itself, including population and the types of industry there. Travelers kept field managers up to date on conditions in various towns; they often sent updated information in reports or included notes on their recruiting slips, which were filed in field offices and included in routing information for the next traveler. The rapid growth of towns in the Midwest and West in the early twentieth century meant that travelers' judgments about new or growing towns became key in charting market coverage.

The advance planning and organization work required to create a schedule and keep an agent supplied, given that all information passed through the mail, is impressive. Before a traveler started a new route, field managers wrote to inactive representatives warning them that their sales privileges were about to be revoked. The letters, called "DSOW" (for "District Supervisor On Way"), were first sent after a representative had not sent in an order for ninety days. They were also sent to representatives who had repeatedly sent in small orders, which managers deemed probably only for personal use.

A representative usually received two warning notices in which the company requested that she either write to explain her situation and outline a work plan, or ideally that she submit an order. If she responded positively, assuring the company of her plans to work, then the field manager sent the traveling agent a letter at three different addresses along her route requesting that she cancel the town. It meant that travelers' schedules could be amended just days or hours before they worked a town. Files on active and inactive representatives were cross-referenced to the billing office, routing office, and the traveling agent who had recruited her and was therefore eligible to receive bonuses and commissions on her orders. Travelers were under no obligation to visit representatives who had not responded unless it was to try to collect money.

Travelers received supplies of recruiting materials and sales "outfits" numbering ten kits at a time, at a rate of about every two weeks for agents on a twenty-per-month quota. The CPC provided agents with a "traveling trunk," the one piece of luggage for which the company reimbursed expenses (to cover storage or portage fees, for example). It carried new representative contract packets, sales manuals, product literature, sample cases, and company magazines. Given the size of the trunk, the CPC required that agents carry only ten sets at a time. Generally it was the field manager's job to keep track of a traveler's supplies, but sometimes agents ran out, either because they had failed to mail in their new contracts in a timely manner or because they recruited faster than expected. In her diary, traveling agent Louise Fogartie wrote about being on a recruiting streak in which she distributed outfits faster than the company could replace them. Fogartie had to wait two days for fresh materials and unfortunately lost valuable recruiting time.

Field managers also kept track of each traveler's daily activities, records of which travelers ideally submitted along with the contracts they negotiated that day. In addition to receiving routes and recruiting materials on a regular basis, agents also received daily correspondence from headquarters. Five or six times a week, one of a variety of men at headquarters wrote a somewhat informal memo, a Chat, which was then mailed to every active traveler in the field. Chats contained a wide range of information on new products, updates on monthly and quarterly sales, personal recruiting stories, and even jokes. Managers also used the Chats for motivation. Once a month, the Chats carried a report on the top ten travelers' performance, listing the number of appointments they made, the number of quality bonuses they received, and occasionally the total sales by the women each had recruited. Chats were intended for internal use and not for the eyes of regular representatives. Checking for them at the post office was the traveler's first order of business in a new town because mail often carried important messages, but mostly, the letters kept travelers in daily contact with the company. For the system to work, field managers in New York or Kansas City needed to know where every active agent would be weeks ahead of time and required an impressive level of coordination, prediction, and planning.

Independence on the road came with a mix of personal, professional, and financial costs and benefits. Travelers generally followed the schedules provided by their field managers and paid for their housing and board from their salaries and not from an expense account. If they were to slow down or spend too many days working a town, they lost money. On the flip side, unsuccessful travelers sometimes moved on from a town too quickly, and field managers at headquarters warned that this gave the CPC a bad reputation in the community; recruiters who could not locate a woman to be a representative in her hometown, they said, called into question the quality of the products and the company, thus putting pressure on the traveler. But sheer distance from the home office also afforded women independence. Travelers exercised some control over their own schedules. No one was ever waiting in a town for them to arrive, nor did they make advance reservations or have to keep appointments.

Training for the Position

The 1915 "Manual of Instruction," over 250 pages long and written by both CPC managers and traveling agents, detailed company recruiting policies and procedures and dispensed practical advice. Recruiting instructions were intended only as guidelines, for in reality there was no one formula, no standard procedure that agents could have used in every recruiting situation or in every town. More than a step-by-step procedure book for recruiting representatives, the manual resembled an assembly of essays, letters, and anecdotes that offered advice for traveling agents on how to cope with living on the road. CPC managers frequently asked experienced travelers to write about their methods, the ways they handled difficult cases, their strategies for efficiently organizing traveling trunks, and their methods for guarding against the unpleasant people whom they met on their travels. Managers edited agents' contributions

Our General Agents.

MRS. MARIE METCALFE.

A traveler for the California Perfume Company
for nearly eleven years. While a resident of the
State of Maine, yet in the capacity of General
Agent for "C. P." goods, Mrs. Metcalfe has
traveled through a score of States appointing a
large number of successful Depot Managers, and
making hosts of friends in every locality she has
visited.

Figure 3.3. Mrs. Marie Metcalfe of Maine began traveling for CPC in 1895.
CPC Outlook, August 1906. (Courtesy of Hagley Museum and Library.)

and published them either anonymously or directly, first as a Chat and
then as part of the manual. Consequently, most of the manual's guidelines
and advice were generated not by sales managers at the home office but
by the women who actually lived their jobs on the road, thus adding credibility to the recommendations it made.

More important than the guidebook, however, was a new agent's training
in the field with an experienced agent. Ideally, this week-long training
would both introduce the practical nature of CPC's business strategy and
provide firsthand examples of how a seasoned businesswoman handled
herself with prospects and in public. Trainees would observe the basics of
recruiting: asking for prospects' names, interviewing techniques, dealing
with objections, filling out contracts, collecting the deposit, and more.
A skilled traveler would also put on display her business character, showing
through a variety of interviews how to handle various personality types

she encountered in the field. The quality of that experience certainly varied among individuals.

Like most travelers, Louise Fogartie had no formal business experience before she began working for the CPC in 1928. In 1930, following her mother's long illness and death, Fogartie requested a traveling position. Thirty years old and single, Fogartie saw an opportunity to travel and get away from Asheville, North Carolina, the town she had lived in all her life. The CPC accepted her application and assigned Mrs. Mary Turlington, an agent working in the southern division, to train Louise in Washington, DC. Turlington had worked more than ten years as a traveler, and CPC home-office managers praised her thorough approach to agency work. "We hardly need add that her kindly disposition and earnest character have left an invaluable store of goodwill and friendship along the routes she has covered," read

Mrs. Margaret B. Leatherbury.

The above is no doubt a familiar face to many of our Southern Depot Managers.

Mrs. Leatherbury, after doing a successful business as Depot Manager, started as one of our Southern travelers four years ago, during which time she has been in parts of nearly all of the Southern States, appointing and instructing a large number of successful Representatives for "C. P." goods.

She now starts on her 1906 Fall trip, so do not be surprised if she should drop in to see you.

Figure 3.4. Mrs. Margaret Leatherbury had worked as a CPC representative before she began as a traveling agent in 1902. The company emphasized her good judgment in choosing successful representatives. *CPC Outlook*, September 1906. (Courtesy of Hagley Museum and Library.)

a short biography of Turlington in CPC *Outlook,* seven years before Mary met Louise. "It is just that feature of her work and her personality that helps to build up CPC business as well as lasting appreciation and loyalty on the part of those she has won for CPC Service."[11] Fogartie enjoyed her time with Mrs. Turlington, who, in addition to teaching her the business, entertained her and showed her the sights in Washington. Louise confided to her diary that she wanted to emulate her, personally and professionally.

After Fogartie had shadowed Mrs. Turlington on recruiting trips in Washington, DC, for several days, she prepared to go out by herself. Nervous, she wrote, "I surely hope I can make an appointment. It will be my first, and I am anxious to get started in this work." Fogartie succeeded; she "landed" her first recruit that day and claimed Mrs. Johnson of Congress Heights as "my first victim." "Of course I have more confidence in myself now that I know I can do it," she wrote.[12] She signed up another woman in Brightwood on Monday, and three more women that week. "I've been working so hard— have made five appointments so far, and am real proud of the fact."[13] Three days later, Fogartie set out on her first solo route through northern Maryland.

Lela Eastman's training experience was not so inspiring. Eastman first signed a CPC contract in 1924 to be a door-to-door representative in Hood River, Oregon. She was already selling Real Silk hosiery (another direct selling concern that operated well into the postwar period), but transferred her business to another local woman when the CPC traveling agent arrived in town and recruited her. Eastman took on CPC work, she said, in part because of the opportunity to travel if she were successful, a prospect Real Silk had not offered. Unlike Fogartie, Eastman had several years of experience in business situations. She had worked for many years as an assistant in Hood River's dental office where she vulcanized false teeth. The dentist was also Hood River's mayor, and Eastman was in regular contact with local business leaders and town officials, experience that she later claimed was the bedrock of her sales and managerial career.

In April 1925, just eight months after she began selling CPC products and despite suffering serious health problems, Eastman began her new career as a traveling agent. "I went on the road when they said they wanted me. If I would have had to crawl, I would have gone," Eastman later claimed.[14] She trained in San Francisco with traveling agent Mrs. F. M. Findley, who, Eastman believed, did not prepare her well for her new job. "I didn't like her," Eastman later said. "She smoked until I just couldn't take it . . . and she wasn't thorough, but she trained me anyway." On her third day, working solo for the first time, Eastman had convinced a woman to join the CPC, only to learn later that she did not have the money for the deposit on the catalog and sample case. Although CPC had many suggestions about what to do in such a situation, Findley had not prepared Eastman to meet this basic objection. So Eastman moved on and finally signed up the third woman she interviewed. She returned to the hotel very late at night, finding both Mrs. Findley and the hotel clerk very worried. After hearing Eastman's tale, Findley asked what she would have done if she had not gotten anyone, to which Eastman replied, "I wouldn't have come back."[15] Surely Eastman meant to imply that she would have still been out looking for her recruit and not that she would have quit the company, for she was very determined to work as a traveler, if only she could be out on her own.

Perhaps Eastman and Findley simply did not like one another or perhaps Findley was not a very good trainer. She was, however, a very successful traveler, averaging twenty-five appointments per month, most of whom produced substantial orders.[16] Findley's selection, training, and motivation techniques had surely played an important role in her successful searches for representatives. Her methods, which she may not have shared with Eastman, also included a fair bit of sport and wiliness. In describing how she "baited" prospects, she outlined her plan in a CPC Chat for other traveling agents: "When I find the prospect I want, I want her mighty bad. It never enters my head that I may not get her," she wrote. After explaining the CPC opportunity, Findley would ask her prospect if she wanted the sales district. "If she says no, then I ask why. If her excuse is a least bit weak, I tear it all down and step on it. . . . I do not make my talk a hard-boiled proposition. I just make a few funny remarks to make her laugh, but those remarks have fish hooks baited with CPC that she never suspects at all."[17] All those motivational stories in the manual about fishing had succeeded in entering into Findley's vernacular.

However, CPC work meant more to Findley than the opportunity to outwit prospects, for she also believed in giving women a business opportunity and even referred to her recruiting position as a "calling." North-Western Division Manager Henry Bachler described Findley's "unbounded confidence" as the basis of all successful business transactions. In February 1925, just two months before she met Eastman, Findley had published another letter in a CPC Chat extolling the virtues of training new representatives. A woman had the potential to turn her life around with CPC, Findley believed, if she were properly trained: "This seems to me to be the main thing we are placed on the road and paid for," she wrote. "It seems to me the Supervisor who does not do her best is not only cheating herself, but the Representative and the Company. I believe I have always understood we are not out to 'sell' anything, but for something vastly more important."[18]

These four women represent a cross section of CPC travelers. Like the representative staff from which they came, most used the title "Mrs." Only Louise Fogartie, thirty years old and single, did not have immediate family responsibilities to balance. Mrs. Mary Turlington, however, had a young son and actually left in the midst of her training because she had received a message that he had "swallowed poison." Turlington rushed home; he was fine, but it is not entirely clear who had been caring for him while she was away working. Mrs. Lela Eastman had divorced her husband and for a while left their son with his father's family in Texas before bringing him up to stay with her parents in San Francisco while she went to work in Hood River, Oregon. Mrs. F. M. Findley, for whom the least information exists, was widowed; she claimed that she had begun her career out of economic necessity. It would be interesting to know how other women in Turlington's and Eastman's communities viewed them: were they respected for working in their careers? Were they blamed for "abandoning" their children? All that is known is that the four women ended up under the umbrella of the CPC organization.

Earning Potential

Between 1915 and 1925 (the only years for which figures are available), traveling agents earned an impressive starting salary (for women) of $100 per month, plus bonuses and some expenses.[19] To Lela Eastman, who earned only $12.50 cents a month as a dental assistant, it meant a substantial increase in her monthly income. A traveling agency paid women extraordinarily well, almost equal to what men made in similar positions.[20] Home-office managers assigned individual traveling agents monthly recruiting "quotas" (usually around twenty appointments per month), but they were not docked salary for falling short. They earned a $1 bonus for every representative appointed, plus a $3 "Quality Bonus" for every new recruit who submitted an initial net order totaling $30 or more. The CPC also offered benefits, such as savings clubs and profit sharing plans, and sponsored contests and awards to keep women working toward their goals.

Compared to the regular representative's earnings, the traveling agent's monthly salary alone was a significant raise. Representatives earned a 40 percent commission on personal sales, and a top-producing representative who sent in a $100 order each month—a very high level—would have earned just $40 in commission (plus non-monetary prizes). However, unlike representatives, traveling agents earned a substantial amount of their income from commissions and bonuses. Therefore, the CPC argued, the size of a paycheck became their individual responsibility. "Remember, the size of the check always depends on YOU and you alone," the guidebook stated. "The kind of work you do, that is the number of people you appoint, the kind of people you appoint, and the amount of money it costs to appoint them is really what determines the size of your salary."[21] Individual travelers already steeped in the philosophy that success depended on hard work and believing that the CPC was completely fair also adopted the rhetoric.

A traveling agent's salary seems less generous when expense reimbursement policies are taken into account. The CPC paid for agents' transportation, including their maps, trunk repairs, and transfers as well as advertising, telegrams, and other correspondence expenses, but they did not reimburse for the costs of lodging and meals, laundry charges, or excess baggage charges unless the company was responsible.[22] The CPC mailed expense checks in advance, forwarding $20 or $30 at a time to ensure that agents had enough money, but only on Thanksgiving and Christmas did the company offer to pay for "a full dinner with all the trimmings" for travelers who chose to work through the holidays.[23] Although agents usually stayed in small towns in the rural countryside where lodging and meals were cheaper than in large cities, these expenses probably cost about 30 percent to 40 percent of their guaranteed monthly salary. Louise Fogartie, for example, tried to keep her room and board expenses to a dollar a day, or $30 a month.

Requiring agents to cover the cost of their lodgings and meals served as a control mechanism by forcing inefficient travelers to incur part of the costs of their trade. "The chief advantage of this plan," the official bulletin noted, "is the reward it yields the economical traveler. If you save a dollar, you save it for yourself: when you search out a moderate priced boarding house, the difference is yours. It means just that much more salary—for you."[24] The system also kept agents moving, for there was no incentive for them to stay in a town for an extra day to rest. Similarly, agents who fell ill on the road found themselves in a difficult position, for they paid their expenses with no hope of earning them back in bonuses. Although there is no direct evidence to suggest it, travelers could have padded their accounts to recover some personal expenses. The CPC did not require receipts for every expenditure, and it is not unreasonable to think that some travelers added incidental charges (such as street car fare within city limits, another expense the company did not pay) onto the cost of other allowed expenses.

By 1926, Lela Eastman had established herself as one of the top ten recruiters in the Western Division in just her second year on the road. Her experience, while perhaps atypical, illustrates the earning potential of a CPC traveling agency. In 1925, in addition to her $100 monthly salary, Eastman had averaged twenty-one appointments per month in ten months, earning her an extra $210 per year in appointment bonuses. Thirty percent of her recruits had submitted initial orders of more than $30, from which she earned an additional $190 in Quality Bonus awards that year. In January 1926, the CPC raised her salary to $115 per month and Eastman's Division Sales Manager, Henry Bachler, encouraged her to improve her work by increasing the average yearly business obtained by her appointments. In February, Eastman was already ahead of her average, and along with final words of encouragement, Bachler advanced her an expense check for $20 so she would not run short of funds. If she maintained the same rate in 1926, Eastman could look forward to earning more than $1,550 for ten months' work, more than 30 percent of which came from bonuses.[25] In Eastman's case, the salary and bonus structure gave her a solid income, but just how much money Eastman had to spend on food and lodging expenses is unknown. However, neither Eastman nor any other traveler ever went on record as objecting to the CPC's reimbursement policy.

While Eastman's success may have been extraordinary, her ability to appoint strong representatives was not due to access to a better class of towns. Rather, given that 30 percent of her new recruits submitted high initial orders, a standard fewer than 10 percent of representatives companywide achieved, her accomplishment probably rested on her initial training and personal motivational style. Eastman usually worked in California, Oregon, and Washington, following the current Routes 5 and 101 from Mexico to Canada. The vast majority of her towns were class four and X class—all with fewer than 500 inhabitants. In August 1927, Eastman was routed east into Idaho, Montana, Wyoming, and North Dakota. There were slim pickings in those states, but Bachler believed Eastman could find women who could produce good business in these sparsely populated states. "Circle, Montana has a population of 300, or approximately 75 families," he wrote in one situation report. The representative there, Mrs. G. M. Gilbert, had not done any business since she was appointed on July 9, but Bachler believed that Eastman's efforts to get "a good worker who will call on every family in this town" could produce at least $35 of business each month. In nearby Sidney, Montana, population 700 (or 140 families, according to the situation report), Mrs. A. M. Setter, working since June, had ordered only $8.06 in CPC goods and a special demonstration set worth $6. The company had not received payment for either, and Bachler asked Eastman to collect the money and appoint a new representative. A full-time worker, Bachler thought, would produce $60 to $75 in business each month in Sidney.[26]

According to Eastman's November 1927 "Bonus Report," her new Wyoming recruits were able to meet higher sales targets. Throughout small towns in Wyoming, Montana, and Nevada, Eastman's newly appointed representatives submitted bonus-winning orders. Mrs. Hetty Williams, beginning October 11 in Guernsey, Wyoming, sent in an order for $42.17. Mrs. Viola Broyles of Wheatland, Wyoming, appointed the very next day, sent in an order for $29.60. Residents of Cheyenne gave Mrs. W. Miller $32.52 in orders, and Miss Sara Williams hustled $57.75 worth of business in Rock Springs, Wyoming. Mrs. M. Arruiti in McDermitt, Nevada, sent in an order for $62.62 just twelve days after she was appointed.[27] All told, Eastman's fall recruiting drive earned her an extra $27 in quality bonuses and $90 in appointment bonuses from September to November in addition to a raised monthly salary of $130. Eastman's appointment rate climbed even higher toward the end of the year, earning her the $40 cash prize in the contest among all traveling agents in the Western Division for highest number of quality appointments during the second half of 1927.[28] Later, in May 1928, her salary was increased to $140 a month.[29]

Eastman was unique in the CPC traveling force for yet another reason, which may have contributed to her high monthly appointment rate. In early October 1927, Eastman left her temporary headquarters in Cheyenne, Wyoming, and headed to Nevada, bypassing Utah altogether because it was managed by Southeastern Division travelers. The chief reason for moving Eastman south, Bachler explained, was to move her into Pacific Coast territory as quickly as possible: "I realize you are traveling with your Ford and it won't be long before some of the roads will be rather difficult to cover."[30] Indeed, Eastman was driving an automobile. "I don't think anyone else had a car," Eastman said in a 1972 interview. "But I had a little old Ford coupe, and I had kewpie dolls [painted] on the side of it."[31] Henry Bachler did not approve of the car; he was annoyed, not that she had purchased it for herself, but that she had done it without his permission.[32]

She needed to buy it, Eastman explained. She had been in Walla Walla, Washington, one Saturday in October. She got to town about noon, signed up her representative, dropped the contract in the mail, and went back to the train depot. "It was one of those hicky hicky towns" in eastern Washington, Eastman explained. The next train wasn't leaving until Monday, and the town was filled with loggers. Eastman could not find a room for the night and ended up sleeping in a screened porch. "And that's when I bought my car." Eastman told Bachler, "I'm not sitting around waiting for trains to come two or three days later. I said when I get through I want to get out of here."[33] Bachler objected: "Who told you, you could buy a car?" he asked, but he also agreed to pay Eastman the equivalent of bus expenses for the use of her car.[34] Thirty years later, when Eastman had established herself as the top grossing manager in the West Coast division, Bachler admitted that Eastman should have told him to mind his own business.

"My adventure alone": Life on the Road

When Louise Fogartie set out on Tuesday, February 11, 1930, for Gaithersburg, Maryland, to begin her new career, she called it "my adventure alone," a phrase that captured her excitement and nervousness. Writers of CPC newsletters, training manuals, and business correspondence usually downplayed the solitary nature of agency work, emphasizing concepts like "independence" instead. CPC writers held up "experience" as the greatest teacher in the traveling trades, making it seem both romantic and brave for women to learn the agency position, and they promised that the company was always there to offer a "kind word" and "helping hand."

CPC literature frequently cited boredom and loneliness as two of travelers' greatest hazards. The small towns that women frequented did not afford many distractions, so agents advised each other in company newsletters to take part in community activities. CPC traveling agent Emma Buster wrote that she always tried "to enter into whatever entertainment the little town [could] afford. I go to Sunday school, church, hospitals, etc, which helps me keep homesickness away. This leaves a rather good impression of me with the people in that town."[35] Similarly, Lela Eastman said she had traveled with photographs of her family, which she put out wherever she stayed.

Attending community functions not only promoted the traveler's image in very small towns she visited, but it also served personal needs of feeling "at home" and "secure." Louise Fogartie's main form of entertainment came in the form of church services and Sunday school. Practicing her religion across many denominations, Louise attended whatever service was local— Catholic, Methodist, Baptist, Episcopalian, Wesleyan—and if there were more than one church available, she was frequently willing to put in double time. "Went to church twice today," she wrote in Charleston, West Virginia.[36] In the tiny town of Griffin, Georgia, a town she liked "real well," she "played Golf, went to the movies once and to church three times."[37] In Walkersville, West Virginia, where she spent a "*long*, lonesome Sunday," she was surprised to find no services available on Sunday, despite there being two churches. "It isn't any wonder that I saw the boys, large and small, playing marbles this morning," she wrote.[38]

Fogartie often relied on local acquaintances to accompany her to community events. The people she met at boarding houses, where she frequently stayed, often became the center of her social life. On February 22, 1930, one of the girls staying in the same boarding house in Martinsburg invited Fogartie to join her at the movies, and then to the "Basket Ball" game: "Was my first game to watch and I was very much interested in the game." She attended another in Walkersville, West Virginia, in March: "Went to a Basket Ball game tonight and enjoyed it, getting *real* interested in B Ball now."[39] Two days later, though, her new boarding-house companions were not as social. "For instance," Fogartie explained, "the folks heard me say I would like to go the B. Ball last night, and none of them invited me to go along with them— had to ask the 15 year old girl if I could go along with her."[40] By December, while traveling in Georgia, Fogartie frequently went through Atlanta, where she discovered "indoor golf," the theater, and movies. Still relying on local acquaintances to accompany her, she confessed that "I like the 'young man' who has been giving me free tickets to the show just lots—believe me he is real good looking."[41] Fogartie consistently sought the companionship of women while traveling alone; convention restricted her ability, but not her desire, to meet men.

Remarkably, home-office managers did not appear overly concerned about their travelers' personal safety, nor did they seem worried about their reputation as women on the road. Neither Louise Fogartie nor Lela Eastman ever referred to being treated as unusual while on the road. Both were very resourceful and did not balk at having to contend with finding transportation on rail lines, taking buses, or even catching a ride with the occasional postman. Under the cloak of the CPC, they knew they had a right to participate in the economic sphere while on the trains or checking into boarding houses and hotels, gathering mail at post offices along their routes, tracking representatives, interviewing and following up with new recruits, training new agents, and cashing in their monthly paychecks and bonuses. Fogartie and Eastman also negotiated with a steady stream of men in public. They frequently asked postmasters, hotelkeepers, trainmen, and shop owners for recommendations, and they ran credit checks with the individuals whom recruits listed as references on their applications. Agents' dealings with these men, however, took place in the context of business, which made contact both justifiable and confined.

The agent's manual encouraged travelers to stay at boarding houses instead of hotels, not just because they were cheaper, but for safety and integrity—advice that came from other women, not just male managers. Many agents concurred, but set aside the image of impropriety, writing instead that they found it cleaner and more "home like" to stay at boarding houses. "When we are discouraged and are just longing for a word of sympathy and a hearty 'cheer up' from someone, our thoughts naturally drift to home and the folks . . ." one anonymous traveler wrote.[42] Lela Eastman noted, "The nearest approach to home conditions and companionship after a hard day's work on the road is to be found in the good, cheerful, respectable boarding-house, where everybody tries to be pleasant to the stranger and show a sincere interest in you and your business, and where there is in evidence none of that formal and abrupt atmosphere which seems to characterize the hotel."[43]

In addition to companionship, a boarding house environment served a traveler's business purpose, for it proved an excellent environment in which to find recruits. Boarding-house keepers frequently recommended women in the town they thought might be suited for CPC work, and occasionally travelers found a new recruit among the keeper's family or the other guests. "One of our most successful travelers," the guidebook stated, "always makes it a point to stop at a boarding-house. . . . And do you know she has time and again found people right in the house who were looking for just such an opportunity as a CPC Sales District offer."[44] Louise Fogartie followed this advice and signed up at least three boarding-house keepers and another boarder during her travels in West Virginia, Georgia, and Kentucky in 1930. In Rockmart, Georgia, (population 3,500) the "little lady here in the Hotel" took the agency from Fogartie. Mixing business and pleasure, Louise stayed there for the entire weekend. "The folks running this hotel (Marble Hill Hotel) are very nice," she noted. "I'm very glad indeed that I came here, as they are so nice to me."[45] Her behavior also affirmed the integrity of the CPC opportunity. Contrary to popular perceptions of itinerant salesmen peddling substandard products or fraudulent money-making schemes in small towns, Fogartie's willingness to stay with the woman she had most recently appointed likely built trust for CPC's business and a reputation for fair and honest dealings.

Despite a schedule that required travelers to recruit in new towns every day, many women found temporary housing in larger towns and worked smaller ones nearby over the course of two or more days. When Louise Fogartie's schedule included towns spaced some distance apart, it was unusual enough that it warranted her comment: "Spent the night in a different town every nite [sic] last week. Don't think this has ever happened before."[46] In order to create some sense of stability, Fogartie frequently set up base in a central location and worked nearby assignments by bus or other local transportation. For example, after taking a room in Terra Alta, West Virginia, high up in the mountains and coalfields, she worked the small town of Aurora, catching a ride there with the mailman. "Thot [sic] I'd never stand it until we could get there, as the roads were so rough. However it was to my advantage to go with him, as he didn't charge me anything."[47] The next day she "had an easy time getting someone and got another free ride as far as Oakland, Md., and then got the Bus from there." Staying four days in Terra Alta allowed Fogartie to leave her baggage in one place and obtain cheaper transportation.

Just as the manual had suggested, Louise Fogartie used boarding houses more frequently than hotels. Still, hotels figured prominently in her diary. She stayed at a hotel no fewer than fourteen times her first year. On February 24, barely one month into her work, in Franklin, West Virginia, she wrote: "It is my first time to stop at a hotel, have been in private homes since I've been traveling, seems to be a nice little hotel."[48] However, she had to choose her lodgings carefully. Three months later in Mullens, West Virginia, Fogartie chose a boarding house only after inquiring for hotels: "I feel very fortunate in getting a room with her as the hotels here could not be recommended."[49] The only time Fogartie alluded to her unique position as a woman traveling agent was in connection with her choices of lodging. In Elkins, West Virginia, she noted that she had moved out of one hotel because she felt uncomfortable there. "Have changed Hotels—didn't like the first one (Elkins Hotel) as I was the only woman there, and have heard that it used to be considered not so good. Staying now at the Tygart Hotel, and have a nice room."[50] Unwilling to risk associating herself with a hotel's seedy reputation, Fogartie drew attention to one of the only precautions she felt she had to take as a lone woman on the road.

Despite what CPC writers warned, not all hotels were impersonal or anonymous. Fogartie made many friends at these establishments, which suggests that CPC managers may have been somewhat overprotective in their advice. "I stayed at the [Pinnacle] Hotel here," she wrote. "The folks were simply lovely to me, so of course I enjoyed my little stay in Cumberland Gap very much."[51] At Mrs. Dickey's hotel in Murphy, North Carolina, Louise was impressed by the proprietor's fanaticism with pets and curios; the roof was occupied by a monkey and a parrot, and the lobby adorned with large owls and stuffed birds. Louise made friends with another girl boarding there who invited her to Sunday school and church: "We went to the Baptist."[52]

The CPC Sisterhood of Travelers

Maintaining gendered respectability sometimes cost CPC agents considerably in terms of their professional development. Since it was important for them to work independently, they could not risk associating with "promiscuous" or mixed-sex audiences that could damage their reputations. As a result, traveling agents remained physically isolated from both their company and each other and professionally disengaged from the sizable ranks of traveling salesmen. Male sales agents, too, faced an increasingly hostile clientele in the early twentieth century. Men responded to this changing and threatening environment by forming professional associations and organizations, such as the Order of United Commercial Travelers and International Federation of Commercial Travelers of the United States, designed to protect their public image and commercial interests.[53] But CPC women lacked access to commercial travelers' special meeting places in hotels and the easy camaraderie of salesmen in railroad smoker cars that excluded women. Nor were women eligible to join the "brotherhoods" male travelers formed, such as the Gideons and the UTC. Members of the Commercial Travelers' brotherhoods garnered support, lobbied for job rights and securities, and built a stronger allegiance to their trade and to each other than to their employers.[54]

CPC agents' allegiance had always been to their company, as individuals linked to the corporate organization, or more precisely, in the respectable company vernacular, to their "House." As a result, CPC agents sought out the company of other women whom they met as part of their travels. Some agents who worked the same territory year after year built networks of friends who ran boarding houses where they stayed on a regular basis. But this hardly helped them create a shared business culture that improved their understanding of the trade, developed their professional image, or taught them alternative means of selling. Agents also had no means to collectively negotiate compensation or privileges from the company.

Instead, CPC career women learned how to conduct themselves in a professional manner through stories they shared with each other, most of which were mediated by their managers. Every month from 1905 to the late 1920s, *Outlook* printed, along with information on products and sales updates, a column called "Our General Agents" that featured one or two traveling agents in the field. The column usually included a photo and brief biography of the traveler and a message to her recruits. These profiles highlighted a variety of personal and business characteristics that the CPC encouraged other agents and representatives to emulate. Whereas instruction manuals tended to focus on work habits, tasks, and procedures, the "Our General Agents" column offered a more personal look at agents' lives and women's styles of professional deportment. Here, in images and words, gender, personality, and work were more intimately and conspicuously entwined.

The biographies and letters that appeared in the "Our General Agents" column and the recruiting and bonus reports published frequently in the "Daily Chats" were the only spaces where agents could get to know their fellow workers and corporate managers. Therefore, to the extent that the CPC developed a common business culture among agents and representatives during its first fifty years, it existed solely on the printed page in monthly newsletters, daily correspondence, and published sales records. This left the company's fortunes almost solely in the hands of the traveling agent and her skills at recruiting and encouraging representatives.

The travelers who were most involved with CPC business, who appeared most frequently in Chats and saw their selling and recruiting stories featured in *Outlook*, came from the ranks of the most successful. The CPC preached loudest to its choir, to those women like Fogartie and Eastman whose lives and personalities were most suited to life on the road, who enjoyed travel, and who worked best when they worked independently. Many women, whose stories cannot be told because their careers were not stellar (and consequently not documented by CPC) or who left no other record of their

It has always been the policy of the Company to employ as Travelers those who have been successful in the local canvass. Hence when Mrs. Mary Ella Moore, after doing a most satisfactory business in a city of New Jersey, from 1909 to 1913, was placed on the road, we knew that she could present the C P C proposition properly and demonstrate its value from the standpoint of her personal experience. When sending her photograph a short time ago, she wrote: "It has been my privilege and pleasure to be connected with the C P Company as Sales Manager and General Agent for nearly six years and I believe they are pleased with my work. I assure you that I attribute my success wholly to the high grade of their goods and the loyalty of the C P Company. I am confident their quality of goods has no equal and I hope to remain with the Company until old age compels me to retire."

Figure 3.5. Mrs. Mary Ella Moore began her career with the CPC in 1909. She intended to make it her life's work. *CPC Outlook*, February 1915. (Courtesy of Hagley Museum and Library.)

performance, probably resigned from the CPC for a variety of reasons, including family, health, money, loneliness, or just plain boredom. It is difficult to discern just how CPC travelers conducted their business on a day-to-day basis, how much they bought into the prescriptive literature generated by the company, and whether or not they used the motivational literature to manage or alter their business practices. But those who did engage earned substantial benefits in the form of travel opportunity and especially in cash.

Personal Profiles of Traveling Agents

The CPC did not save biographical information on its traveling agents, and census searches are practically impossible given that the company

Figure 3.6. Miss Elizabeth Butts of North Carolina had worked for just six months when she was featured in the "Our General Agents" column. She marked her entry to the ranks of professional businesswomen with a portrait of herself hard at work writing correspondence while wearing a feather boa, hat, and leather gloves. *Outlook*, May 1916. (Courtesy of Hagley Museum and Library.)

rarely identified an agent's hometown. However, personal biographies and testimonials published in company literature from 1905 to 1936 offer two subjective profiles of CPC women. The majority of CPC travelers had been married; most who used the title Mrs., however, were widowed by the time they started traveling. Other travelers used the title Miss, but judging by those women who included their pictures for publication, "Miss" most frequently denoted a much older woman. CPC traveling agents tended to be either unmarried women (young and old) or widowed women. The traveling agent's job required that she leave her home for several months at a time. Not surprisingly, most travelers who gave clues about their family responsibilities suggested that their careers had commenced shortly after home commitments became less time consuming—either their children had grown and were living on their own, or other family members were available to look after them. Of the forty-six agents featured in the 1920 "Travel Talks" recruiting brochure, for example, thirty-nine (85 percent) identified themselves as Mrs., four (8 percent) as Miss; three others did not give a title. This trend aligns with women's titles in other CPC publications. Marital status did not relate directly to age, however. On average, most of the traveling agents who appeared in the photographs seem to be middle-aged to elderly. Some women, such as Mrs. E. Earle Clyde, looked to be in their thirties or forties, while women such as Miss Flora A. Prout were more likely past their sixties.[55] Very few agents mentioned their age, but Mrs. M.A.S. of Missouri wrote that she had begun working for the CPC in 1908 when she was fifty-eight years old. In 1920, at seventy years of age, she may have been the CPC's oldest traveling agent on the road.

Women worked as CPC traveling agents for longer periods than either women in the workforce in general or those who worked as CPC sales representatives. Thirty-nine (of forty six) travelers featured in "Travel Talks" either mentioned the date they started traveling or the number of years they had worked as an agent; on average, they had logged six or more years of experience. "Many of them have been traveling for years," the introduction stated, "the highest kind of a testimonial as to their opinion of the California Perfume Company, and its relations with them, financially and otherwise."[56] Mrs. H.E.G. of Michigan, who started traveling in 1899, had the longest tenure, at twenty-one years; the shortest belonged to Miss L.S. of Ontario, who had written for "Travel Talks" after just two weeks on the road.[57] Many women also noted that they took hiatuses, as long as a year or two, because of illness or family responsibilities.

While traveling seemed possible mainly for women without young children, such as unmarried women, or those without elderly parents needing care, agents were not free from family obligations. According to the biographies and testimonials published in the "Our General Agents" column of the *Outlook* and brochures like "Travel Talks," travelers who were either married or widowed reported that sudden, difficult situations drove them to find full-time work. Husbands died, leaving widowed mothers in desperate circumstances, frequently in debt and without sufficient income. At the same time, most travelers named their families as their top priority for working.

Mrs. C. A. Wood, a CPC traveling agent who worked for the company from approximately 1908 to 1924, wrote in her testimonial about how she used the CPC to save her family when "tragedy struck." When her husband died, Wood was suddenly left without income. "Ten years ago," she wrote in a letter published in *Outlook*, "when I became the bread winner of my little family (my daughter in her teens and myself), I scarcely knew what to do or which way to turn."[58] She had taught school for a few years during her "young-lady-hood," presumably before she was married, so her "mind naturally turned

HATTIE M. R. GOSS

Mrs. Goss hails from Michigan and is, we believe, the SENIOR GENERAL AGENT of our Organization.

She may not want us to tell that it was back in June 1899 when she first began working as a General Agent, but she has made such a creditable record, it would be a shame to omit this important detail.

For a while, Mrs. Goss was compelled to stay at home, because of her mother's poor health, but with this exception her record is an unbroken string of successes won and difficulties overcome.

What a story Mrs. Goss could tell if she could start at the beginning and relate her experiences of these twenty-two years! Think of the thousands of friends she has made and of the hundreds of towns and cities she has visited! Certainly if she could supply these notes, one would have the material at hand for a book that would be replete with human interest.

Figure 3.7. Mrs. Hattie Goss from Michigan began working for CPC in 1899. In her twenty-second year with the company she was traveling in the Pacific Northwest. CPC hailed her as "noble" and "tireless." *CPC Outlook*, September 1921. (Courtesy of Hagley Museum and Library.)

to school work." "Out of necessity" she first accepted a matronship of an academy, but the salary was "inadequate to meet our actual expenses," she wrote, so she sought another way to finance her daughter's education at a music conservatory and a year abroad. Eventually she started selling CPC products, and in 1908 accepted a position as an agent. After seven years of traveling, Wood proudly reported, she had earned enough money to send her daughter to school; she "holds a diploma from each of two conservatories of music in our own beloved land."[59]

Like Wood, many traveling agents had worked other jobs but found the salary and commitment of a CPC agency more appealing and lucrative. Indeed, many women's testimonials referred to the limited financial opportunities available to older women. R.F.O. of Texas wrote, "Being a widow with no encumbrance I do not care to maintain a home and live alone, neither would I enjoy being with relatives or friends."[60] Miss E.S.T. of Missouri wrote that "after teaching more than ten years the inevitable happened. Health too poor to continue [to] teach, must go south [sic] . . . but I had no money, never had traveled further from home than two hundred miles, had not advanced mentally, rather the other thing. Was induced to take a traveling agency. In less than two years have regained my health, accumulated some property, traveled from the lakes to the gulf, crossed the continent several times, developed mental alertness I never thought possible for humble littles."[61] Miss E.S.T. had started her letter by declaring "that nothing but an urgent duty will induce me to give [traveling] up." Similarly, Mrs. J.H.L. of Indiana began working in 1914 and soon after found herself and her family in grim circumstances: "A little while after I took up traveling work my father failed in health which made him fail in his business; he borrowed money on our home, and he passed away about four years ago, leaving us in debt for over $1,200." By working on the road, she could claim to have almost paid for her home. In addition, she invested over $1,000 and "bought me a horse and buggy; helped give my little niece a trip to Miami, Florida, and several other things. I would not take anything for my experience in traveling for I know it is very profitable, both physically and also financially."[62]

Many travelers emphasized their narrow wage-earning choices prior to finding CPC. "I was formerly a school teacher," Mrs. M.N.W. of Illinois wrote, "but (even with salaries raised) I can save more money as General [Traveling] Agent."[63] Mrs. M.A.D. of Kentucky took up traveling in August 1909: "Twelve years ago, through financial loss[,] I found it necessary to earn, at which time I took the General Agency for the California Perfume Co.," she wrote. "Today can truly say it has been a blessing to me, financially and otherwise."[64] Mrs. M.A.D. outlined many other benefits she received, including the means to provide for and put a loved one through college, and "to put away a substantial amount that any woman would be proud of."[65] She advised women to take the "opportunity" to travel, for "it will put you in an

Our General Agents

Six years ago to-day I became identified with the California Perfume Company.

For over two years I was their local representative, after which I was appointed as one of their General Agents. In this capacity I am still acting.

During the entire period that I have been in their employ, there has never been a moment that I have regretted having joined the sales force of this great organization, for while at times the work has been very arduous and trying, yet I realized that I was being benefited not only financially but also physically and intellectually.

Our business relations have always been of the most pleasant nature and I can say in all truthfulness that I have never yet been in the employ of a more appreciative or considerate people. In every instance they have lived up to the strictest letter of their contract.

In the above, I feel that I echo the sentiments of all persons who have been honored with a position with this Company.

During my incumbency as General Agent, I have covered four states and have met numbers of their old Representatives. With few exceptions, they all have nothing but words of commendation and praise for the California Perfume Co.

I have never had the pleasure of meeting but one member of the firm, Mr. Scheele, whom I met last May, in Atlanta, at the General Agents' Convention.

I hope, however, that in the not far distant future I may be enabled to visit New York City and shake hands with Mr. McConnell and his other Co-workers.   Very sincerely,

MRS. S. M. E. BROWN.

Figure 3.8. Mrs. S. M. E. Brown worked for two years as a CPC representatives before becoming a traveling agent. Her letter emphasized the financial benefits of the work, as well as the pleasant business relationship. She hoped to shake hands with Mr. McConnell some day. *CPC Outlook*, June 1916. (Courtesy of Hagley Museum and Library.)

independent position, [and] I thank you a thousand times that the CPC came to me, because it is such a fine opportunity for a woman, and would advise all who have to earn or who want to do so, to take the General Agency for the California Co."[66]

Mrs. M.A.D.'s statement repeated a familiar theme among traveling agents: despite their confidence in their abilities as businesswomen, they had not gone looking for such work. Indeed, many talked of a CPC agency as if it were a gift bestowed on them. Similarly, differentiating between women who "have" to earn and those who "want" to implicitly acknowledged the profiles of women most appropriate for CPC work—either women in desperate circumstances and or women free from immediate family responsibility. As such, traveling agents who were outside of the domestic realm or who were escaping their entrance into it, became the company's most vigorous defenders. Most traveling agents supported women's work, a sentiment echoed in CPC recruiting and motivational literature, for they recognized that families needed support beyond women's capacity for love and nurture. They explicitly required money. In this way, most travelers did not directly challenge social conventions about women's place in the home. They were, however, quick to support the general need for financial options for both those women who did not have family responsibilities and those forced, under straitened economic circumstances, to take drastic measures to save their families.

In reality, many traveling agents did have pressing family obligations, including financial commitments and grown children, grandchildren, sick parents, and others who relied on them for support. But unlike the tone of contemporary, prescriptive literature that characterized responsible women's

Figure 3.9. Mrs. Ella Bacon Bond of District C51, Connecticut, "has been with us 25 years and now celebrates her silver anniversary with an expression of her thoughts as poetry.... 'Now I'm testing the end of my business career/ So I'm sending my co-workers lines of cheer./ And to young beginners I wish to say/ You'll never regret that you started that day/ To work for the well known CPC.'" *CPC Outlook*, September 1922. (Courtesy of Hagley Museum and Library.)

roles as domestic caretakers, no CPC account of travelers suggested that these women had abandoned their families while they were on the road. Indeed, family obligations could also indicate a woman's experience and a mature sense of responsibility: "We need someone who has sufficiently matured so that good judgment can be exercised," McConnell wrote.[67] An agent's relationship with her family remained essential to the measure of respectability in her business reputation. At the same time her freedom from immediate responsibilities functioned as her calling card into the rank of travelers. Ultimately, though, CPC writers focused on a traveler's contributions to business and professionalism; women's proficiency and skill, as well as their goals, methods, and contributions predominated. Not once did the CPC offer a tribute or congratulations to a dedicated and successful traveler who left to get married. Husbands were, and remained throughout the company's history, absent from women's lives and success. Tellingly, in a workforce dominated by widows, remarriage was never hailed as a desirable goal. Nor, for that matter, did the CPC offer them a management position in the regional offices of Morton Grove, Davenport, or New York City. But for decades, the CPC's business relied almost completely on this group of dedicated women who recruited thousands of representatives across the byways of the country. The traveling agents represented a unique group of business women. They were, without a doubt, responsible for establishing a national market for the CPC.

4

"The Dawn of a New Era"

Introducing Avon Products and a Depression-Proof Business Strategy

While trying to recruit a representative in LaGrange, Georgia, in November 1930, a year after the stock market crashed in New York City, traveling agent Louise Fogartie received a letter from her brother and learned that the banks had closed in her hometown of Asheville, North Carolina. She lost everything. "Went to Thanksgiving services this morning, and tried very hard to be thankful, but it was hard when I would think about my little savings gone," she wrote in her diary.[1] Considering the plight of so many working Americans, Fogartie was relatively fortunate. Five years of savings had disappeared, but she still had her job, which guaranteed her a monthly salary of $100. By May 1931, Fogartie actually received a raise, a $10 increase on her monthly salary, and an extra bonus for training a new traveling agent: "Gotta raise in salary old Diary, and am I glad? *You bet!*"[2] As the country fell further into the Depression, the California Perfume Company prospered. Hundreds of thousands of people turned to direct sales and found a quick, if temporary, solution to earn some money.

Fogartie's success in recruiting new representatives varied, but the CPC never reduced quotas. Some regions offered her no hope of finding a worker. She could not locate an agent in Lexington, Georgia, for example: "It's another one of those 'hard boiled' towns, where everyone tries to discourage me." she wrote.[3] But she managed to appoint a representative each day on her way to Union Point, thirty miles away: "I appointed the second lady I talked with this morning, and believe she will do good as this is a busy little mill town, and the mill is running full time."[4]

During the winter and spring of 1931, Fogartie continued her trek through the South, working Alabama, Georgia, Florida, and Kentucky. Her recruiting quota remained at five appointments per week, or twenty women per month. The $10 increase in her salary, however, probably only offset the losses she suffered during weeks when she could only make two or three appointments. The CPC awarded her a $1 signing bonus for each new recruit. Since Fogartie usually met her monthly quota, she did not lose her base salary. However, given that fewer women, especially in those depressed towns, were able to collect "good-sized" wholesale orders, she frequently missed out on the $3 quality bonus awards that CPC gave to a recruiter when her representative's first order totaled $30 or more.[5] Therefore, most traveling agents like Fogartie could maintain their salaries, which allowed them to continue pitching a positive business message. Even so, women's success in selling products door-to-door varied by how hard-hit their towns were by the economy, and overall, representatives' sales barely improved.

Although representatives did not earn as much money during the Depression as they had in the 1920s, the California Perfume Company survived and profited in the 1930s. It did so because its managers had refined their recruiting, training, and motivating techniques and had developed new sales and management schemes. The direct sales business proposition continued to meet the needs of both short- and long-term representatives who had built consumer bases in rural areas and who recognized and responded to the CPC's merchandising tradition. In contrast to businesses that simply did not have enough work to offer, CPC and many other companies in the direct selling industry remained unabashedly labor-intensive and glutted during the Depression.

In 1930, more than 25,000 women throughout the nation looked to the CPC to supplement their income. They generated more than $2.5 million in annual sales. Three years later, following a concerted effort by the company to increase the size of the sales force, the representative corps had increased to 30,000, and sales climbed commensurately. As one California Perfume Company report stated in 1931, "When most firms were glad to make two thirds of the profits they enjoyed the year before, our sales were *greater* than the previous year."[6] The trend continued, and the CPC posted sales increases of 10 to 15 percent every single year between 1930 and 1938. "Seemingly depressions have little ill effect on [our] business, for which we are indeed thankful. People can hardly believe us when we say we are doing more business this year than last, and that last year was a good year," president David H. McConnell wrote in 1933. When the stock market had crashed in 1929, he calmly explained, the forty-year-old California Perfume Company had already survived three depressions. The CPC's unique distribution methods, its hand-picked traveling and sales force, the high quality of the line of products, and the "general morale of the whole CPC family—these reasons explain why we go ahead when other concerns cease to grow or fail completely."[7]

Indeed, throughout the 1930s, the California Perfume Company continually added to the number of its new representatives, introduced new products, increased production, and opened new markets to expand its consumer base. This chapter explores the company's business strategy during the these years of economic hardship. It argues that the CPC's unique market niche in rural America, its devotion to selling a business opportunity to women, and its strong commitment to maintaining its door-to-door sales and service strategy made this prosperity possible. It first focuses on the company's business structure and key new strategies it employed to meet the economic crisis, including recruiting methods, accelerated sales, product and market development, and national advertising, which for all intents and purposes had not existed before 1936. Significantly, some of the company's most important strategies, including the introduction of the "Avon" brand cosmetics and skin care line in 1929, the targeting of urban markets in 1935, and the development of a national advertising campaign in 1936, had been conceived and developed much earlier in the company's history. The Depression, therefore, did not stimulate institutional innovation but instead reinforced the CPC's traditional approach to managing its workforce.

Key to this strategy was the motivational literature the company used to teach its scattered female workforce how to manage their direct selling businesses. An essential component of the California Perfume Company's management strategy since its founding, this literature used an evangelical style to shape women's selling and business behavior. During the Depression, the literature took on a new emphasis and made women's consumption and business efforts an implicit part of a national and patriotic struggle to combat the economic crisis. In doing so, it bestowed political meaning on women's economic activity, blending an individual self-help, "Horatia Alger" celebration with an ironic anti-corporate defense of proprietary capitalism. Company literature assured women that a career in direct selling would give them the power to create and control their own wealth. Company leaders promised to democratize business and to support equality, opportunity, and fairness while defending the role of an ethical business in an economically depressed society.[8] The CPC's motivational literature appealed to resilient American ideals of work, ownership, and the self-made individual. The literature, produced by both CPC male managers and female representatives' personal stories, served to build a relationship between the company and its female sales agents that reflected a peculiar combination of paternalism, compassion, self-help, and economic self-interest—a mindset that characterized the CPC's, and indeed the entire direct selling industry's, management style throughout the Depression.

In the postwar era, business analysts created several explanations for how Avon had survived the Depression.[9] At first glance, the direct sales formula alone seemed to account for its success. People needed money and direct sales contracts offered them a way to earn some quick cash. Indeed, the entire direct selling industry, which overall employed more than a quarter million men and women nationwide each year during the 1930s, seemed surprisingly "Depression proof." Even the CPC, in the midst of the crisis, thought of itself as such: "We are convinced that the right company, with the right products, with the right selling representatives, can develop a depression-proof business," wrote W. J. Alley, CPC's secretary and treasurer in 1933.[10] Direct sales had that reputation. Like the CPC, Fuller Brush (founded in 1911) posted sales increases throughout the 1930s. Starting with a $5 million total for 1930, Fuller increased sales $1 million each year until 1938. Sears spun off Encyclopaedia Britannica in 1933, turning it into a direct selling company offering just one product; it, too, prospered throughout the Depression. Stanley Home Products, founded in 1929 by former stereopticon salesman and Fuller Brush Company executive Frank Stanley Beveridge, also became a very successful direct selling company during these years.[11] Yet many other direct selling companies went out of business in the 1930s. According to one report presented to the National Association of Direct Selling companies, more than one-third of the 6,000 companies in business before the Depression folded, and for many of the same reasons as other businesses: improper management, insufficient finances, and manufacturing products that had lost their markets.[12]

The simplicity of direct sales appealed to both recruits and entrepreneurs, but only the most efficient and well-managed companies made direct selling look easy. On the surface it appeared merely to involve distributing samples, catalogs, and order books, and offering a straight 30 or 40 percent commission to sales agents, who received payment only for the products they actually sold. Representatives who did not sell products did not get paid and therefore cost the company very little in terms of salaries, office space, and labor costs. Similarly, recruiting seemed just a matter of finding people who had lost their jobs or who needed a source of quick cash, for direct selling did not require special skills or previous sales experience. Many traditional retailers and manufacturers fell into the trap of thinking that direct sales could be an inexpensive way to distribute products and cut manpower. Yet direct sales distribution did not neatly translate into a lifeline for traditional businesses.

Managing a direct sales company defied the bureaucratic-efficiency logic of modern firms, and few had the CPC's experience to draw on. Traditional producers and retailers, operating under a mistaken impression that direct sales provided a low-overhead, low-maintenance distribution option, found that maintaining a direct sales force required unusually high expenses, especially in shipping and recruiting. Moreover, it only worked for certain types of products. Companies had to create items small enough that individual representatives could deliver them, like cosmetics, brushes, cookware, and vacuums, for example, rather than heavy appliances like refrigerators or products difficult to install. Direct sales also required higher distribution costs, for companies shipped to representatives only the products they ordered, no matter how small the request, unlike large retail marketers who received products in bulk. Keeping records for thousands of representatives scattered throughout the country rather than for a few hundred marketers, plus funding new equipment, samples, and warehousing all became new overhead expenses borne by the manufacturer.

Furthermore, individual agents earned higher commissions (generally 30 to 40 percent of the products' selling prices) than the wholesale-retail margins available to retail stores. Crucially, most direct sales representatives received their products on credit. Generally, representatives took orders from customers, received the products from the company, collected payments on delivery, and then paid the wholesale invoice. Many companies did demand that representatives submit payment at the time of the order; however, most consumers could be tempted to give larger orders when they were told that they did not have to pay for them until they were delivered several weeks later. Not surprisingly, companies that extended credit to thousands of representatives lost money, as representatives could not reliably collect from customers during the Depression. To make up for losses, some companies invested in credit and collection departments, which further drove up costs.[13]

Traditional firms that switched to or added a direct sales force also found that recruiting expenses drained away profits. Unlike the CPC, which employed a traveling force to recruit women on a face-to-face basis, some companies cut corners by recruiting through newspaper advertisements or direct mail inquiries. Under this system, prospective contractors received information and samples through the mail but never met a company official. Such companies found it difficult, if not impossible, to check recruits for suitability or references. Even several experienced direct sales firms tried this method. In 1958, sociologist Raymond Ries studied a direct sales company, which he called "Tiebolt" (a fictitious name to protect the confidentiality of his subjects), that sold lawn products, including shrubs, small trees, seeds, bulbs, and landscaping designs via an independent door-to-door marketing force. In the 1930s, Tiebolt mailed out more than 40,000 information packets and sales kits a year to men who had responded to letters and advertisements that pitched the business and sales opportunity. Usually, only 6,000 (or 15 percent) of those who received the information actually submitted an order; of them, 96 percent would submit fewer than three orders before quitting.[14] The system was entirely inefficient, and Tiebolt, like many companies struggling during the Depression, found that it made more sense to maintain branch offices with salaried managers who recruited, trained, and managed sales on the local level. Local branch managers alleviated credit issues by providing training and encouragement to representatives and teaching them how to collect payments from customers, thus benefiting both the representative and the company.[15] Direct selling, therefore, was not necessarily a viable solution for companies to either help withstand or make money during the Depression. Management and recruiting techniques, necessary for maintaining a direct sales representative staff, could not easily be incorporated into an inexperienced firm's existing structure.

The CPC's success paralleled the increased sales of beauty products market-wide during the 1930s. During the first third of the twentieth century, the beauty industry as a whole experienced spectacular increases in the types of products manufactured and in overall sales.[16] But the CPC's success during the Depression cannot be explained by pointing to the growing trend in color cosmetics, such as tinted lipsticks, rouge, and eye liners, during that era. The company's strongest sales continued to stem from its toiletries, household products, and skin care lines, not from sales of cosmetics. Women did not look to the CPC for variety or for indulging in the latest trend product. Indeed, the company sold more basic toiletries, such as toothpaste, shampoo, and soap, than it did cosmetics.

In the 1920s, the California Perfume Company had carried an extensive line of toiletries and skin care products but only a very limited line of "color" cosmetics, including tinted face powders and rouges. It introduced its first lipstick in 1917 as part of the "Daphne" fragrance line and sold it in shades "light" and "dark." Despite the growing popularity of these products, it did not expand its color cosmetics line, or even its popular lipstick line, until after World War II.[17] The CPC's product designers did watch beauty industry trends closely, however. Skin care products like soaps, astringents, moisturizers, massage creams, bleaching creams, and night creams, which formed the foundation of the beauty trade, became popular among American urban and rural women alike early in the century. In the 1920s, many companies had organized skin care products into "systems," which celebrities and "scientific" and beauty experts endorsed.[18] In 1928, the CPC followed suit and launched its own celebrity-endorsed skin care system under the name Gertrude Recordon, the skin care expert who formulated the products, but it failed after just one year.[19]

A second family-line of cosmetics promised better results: Avon. The very first product to carry the "Avon" name was not makeup but a powdered general cleanser, called "Avon Maid" featuring a cartoon image of a young woman with a handkerchief tied around her head who wielded a dust rag. In 1929, the CPC launched "Avon"—the cosmetics brand—with a notice to representatives on special letterhead portentously claiming "The Dawn of a New Era."

McConnell took the Avon name, corporate folklore says, because the hills around Stratford-upon-Avon in England reminded him of the landscape in Suffern, New York. To strengthen the connection, the first logo was a large, rounded "A" filled with the image of Anne Hathaway's house. The first "Avon" brand color cosmetics product, a face powder and lipstick compact in a blue and silver package design, appeared in catalogs just in time for Christmas.[20] By 1934, the CPC had repositioned most of its line of cleansers, toners, massage creams, and moisturizers under the new Avon family line.

The California Perfume Company seemed poised to succeed if only because it had developed the right product at the right time. In this context, its profitability during the 1930s is not surprising, for while not completely Depression-proof, both color cosmetics and skin care categories remained strong sellers industry-wide. "Women who went without new clothes," historian Kathy Peiss noted, "could still afford to indulge in a new lipstick." Avon's offerings, available in an expanded color line with coordinating rouges, including shades named Light, Medium, Dark, and Vivid, sold for just 52 cents.[21]

The CPC representatives also sold to a population underserved by modern retail establishments. More than 80 percent of the Avon sales force lived in towns of fewer than 2,500, more than two-thirds of which lay west of the

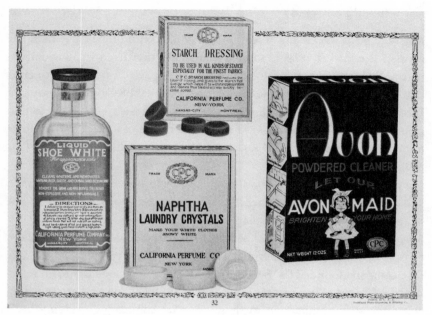

Figure 4.1. "Avon Maid." Color Plate Catalog, 1924. The first two Avon brand products appeared in the 1924 catalog, the "Avon Maid" powdered cleanser, and a boxed gift set of Avon rouge and lipstick. CPC soon dropped Avon Maid in favor of building the brand name color cosmetics that would soon define their company. (Courtesy of Hagley Museum and Library.)

Figure 4.2. Avon brand compact and lipstick, 1924. (Courtesy of Hagley Museum and Library.)

Mississippi River. While women in these small communities may have had access to general stores and catalog merchants, they lived well beyond the reach of department stores and retail chains popular in northeastern cities that set beauty trends. Despite the increasing availability of color cosmetics, rural women remained much more reluctant than their city sisters to purchase and use color cosmetics.[22] Farm women's use of lipstick and perfume increased throughout the 1930s, but other products like eye makeup and rouge held little appeal.

Even within city markets, though, cosmetics were a volatile trade, and many companies experienced only short bursts of success. Several firms, such as Tangee and Armand, did not survive the 1930s. Max Factor, Maybelline, and Revlon (founded in 1908, 1914, and 1932, respectively) prospered through and after the Depression. The venerable Ponds skin care company founded in 1846 also survived.[23] Avon came late to an established color cosmetics market in the 1930s. Its color line appeared remarkably limited in comparison to those of other companies, carrying fewer product categories—lipstick, rouge, tinted face powders, cake mascara, and nail enamel—and a conservative color palette. Soaps, toothpaste, shampoo, and shaving creams, and home-use items, such as baking products, flavoring extracts, and household cleaners, not its lipsticks, skin care products, and perfumes, carried CPC sales throughout the Depression.

Although the CPC's overall business strategy did not change significantly during the 1930s, the face and character of its top managers did. The firm's patriarch, David McConnell Sr., seventy-two years of age in 1930, had taken a backseat in corporate decision making and allowed his twenty-eight-year-old son, David McConnell Jr., to lead the company. The heir apparent began working for his father in 1923 after graduating from Princeton and served short stints in every major department until he was named executive vice president and general manager in 1927. From an early age, he was groomed to take control of the business.[24] McConnell Jr. was part of a new generation of corporate managers eager to implement modern scientific business-management techniques.

At the same time that McConnell's son joined the CPC ranks, a young manager in the Kansas City sales office, John Ewald, made his name known throughout the CPC organization. Ewald had joined the company as a billing clerk in 1917 when he was sixteen years old. By 1925, he had become general manager of the Kansas City branch office, and four years later, he was transferred to New York City to become general sales manager of the entire national organization. Other young executives, such as Henry Bachler, Mark

Figure 4.3. David H. McConnell Jr. worked with his father's company after graduating from Princeton University. He assumed leadership in 1937 and oversaw the creation of the Avon brand, the development of national advertising, and the expansion into city markets. He died suddenly in 1944. (Courtesy of Hagley Museum and Library.)

Taylor, Philip Brockman, Alphonse Williams, and Wayne Hicklin, had also started their careers with the CPC in the late 1920s and early 1930s, moving through various departments and branch offices where they learned about the full nature of "the business" and gained a larger perspective on the company as a whole. They started their careers young (the average age of the CPC executive staff in 1935 was twenty-nine years) and stayed with the company for most of their working lives.[25] The innovative nature and quality of the recruitment and sales management programs they developed reflected their broad range of experience and knowledge of the inter-related nature of company departments. Men like McConnell Jr. and Ewald, and many others who worked under their leadership, accepted and remade a corporate culture at the CPC that both respected their corporate heritage and built on the economic, political, and social challenges they faced in the 1930s.

Although few CPC executives had any formal training in business management techniques or philosophy, they all exhibited an enthusiastic embrace of popular business rhetoric espoused in contemporary journals and magazines, such as *Fortune*, *Sales Management*, *Success*, and *Specialty Salesman*, turning away from the paternalistic tone invoked by McConnell Sr. throughout his leadership. CPC managers used this information to explain and justify various policy changes. Editorials and short articles from these magazines, frequently reprinted in *CPC Outlook* and "Chats," also gave women in rural towns, who would never set foot inside formal CPC office space and who had probably never worked in an office or business setting, a window on emerging business culture.

Developing City Markets and a National Advertising Campaign

In 1926, David McConnell Jr. asked top managers to think seriously about how to improve sales in cities; it was time to introduce products to towns with populations of more than 5,000. Recruiting in large cities had always posed problems for CPC traveling agents, and McConnell Jr. and his managers identified three characteristics of city and urban districts that made creating a market difficult: the relatively impersonal relationships between city residents, the difficulty in defining territories for representatives to work, and competition with other employers for women's part-time labor. Representatives in cities seemed reluctant, apparently, to develop a regular trade among their neighbors. Perhaps the size of districts overwhelmed them, or perhaps they found CPC instructions to "canvass every home" unmanageable. Moreover, since CPC could not draw more distinct territories in city neighborhoods than in rural regions, representatives and business in cities floundered.

Until the 1930s, CPC managers had not thought through the unique problems and challenges of city markets, nor did they have a sense of differentiation among types or sizes of cities. Sales manuals essentially recommended that cities be treated as oversized small towns and did little to adapt their approach to recruiting and training representatives or merchandising products. "There are two ways of working Sales Districts of five thousand up to a million population," the 1924 guidebook stated: direct inquiry or by advertising in daily papers.[26] The CPC recommended that traveling agents find a local person to describe various sections of the city so that they could divide into districts that would each comprise some "good population," a phrase carrying both class and race implications. The CPC had often reflected a bias against African Americans as both clients and representatives, and there was an overt dismissal of immigrants as viable canvassers. The assumption gleaned from the company's literature was not one of purposely neglecting large cities but of underlying racial and ethnic biases common to white-owned and operated businesses. This likely played into the company's reluctance to open urban markets to its products. As C. J. Walker and other entrepreneurs proved, there was a demand by women of color for beauty products, especially hair care products, and lipsticks suited to their needs. As the CPC branched tentatively into urban areas, success varied by agent and city; most urban representatives quit sooner than their rural counterparts, and many complained that they did not like to approach houses where they did not know the occupants, for they received cooler receptions.

In 1935, McConnell Jr. organized three initial test markets in Houston and San Antonio, Texas, and Wichita, Kansas, "because they were very much like country towns." As one executive recalled, "In Texas the problem wasn't getting in [the door], it was getting [back] out[;] they wanted you to have cake and coffee."[27] The CPC soon authorized eleven city sales offices in Texas, Kansas, Nebraska, Oklahoma, and Minnesota in 1936; twenty-three more opened in 1937, all in states west of the Mississippi River.[28] CPC executives believed that the character of midwestern and western towns made them more conducive to the direct selling approach; as a result, Wayne Hicklin and Russel Rooks, executives at the Kansas City branch office (which handled all sales west of the Mississippi), promoted the city sales offices faster than did the managers in New York. Although the new city sales offices would eventually come to dominate the Avon sales system, in the 1930s the sporadic sales they generated barely covered their high start-up costs. During the Depression, therefore, city markets had almost no impact on the corporation's overall profit or income.[29]

In the context of the entire direct selling industry, as in the cosmetics industry, the CPC lagged behind the times precisely because it had waited so long to develop urban markets. The vast majority of direct sales companies, including Fuller Brush, Stanley Home Products, and Real Silk Hosiery, sold almost exclusively in urban areas. Fuller Brush, for example, was founded in Hartford, Connecticut, a city market. Fuller hired permanent managers to recruit, train, and monitor their local sales representatives.[30] CPC managers were reluctant to market in cities in part because of competition from department stores and other retail outlets since Avon-brand products and services would not stand out. Potential customers, increasingly aware of brand-name goods, did not recognize the Avon name and, just as important, did not know where to find the products. These problems did not seem as noticeable in rural districts because the relationship between the sales agent and the customer trumped the product itself. In smaller rural markets, representatives used their local reputations and intimate knowledge of social networks as their calling card, whereas representatives in relatively impersonal and transitory city markets needed to rely on consumers' recognition of the product. Meeting these problems in urban areas, therefore, required a reorganization of representative recruitment and training strategies, as well as a new conception of selling territories and markets. National advertising became a key component in this merchandising strategy.

Avon (as the entire company was officially known after 1937) made its most serious efforts to work through these issues during World War II. However, the company's first attempt to create a brand-name awareness came with a newly designed continuous national advertising campaign in the mid-1930s. CPC/Avon's first mass-circulation advertisement, designed by the Monroe Dreher advertising firm, appeared in *Good Housekeeping* in November 1936. It featured a two-page stylized drawing of Avon cosmetics and a text insert explaining where consumers could purchase them. The next year, Dreher composed story-line advertisements with copy that both highlighted the services of the Avon representative and positioned their offerings as glamour products. Each advertisement ended by inviting magazine readers to welcome Avon callers.

Radio advertising also helped to create brand-name awareness and boost sales. Lela Eastman, one of CPC's most successful traveling agents in the Pacific Northwest and the first city sales office manager in Pasadena, California, believed that the company's name change made an enormous difference. She quickly realized the advertising advantages of the Avon name. Eastman had just opened the Pasadena sales office and took it upon herself to spread the word about the "new" company. "I was told that they changed the name from California Perfume Company to Avon," Eastman recalled, "because [during the Depression] when the girls would go to the doors saying they represented the California Perfume Company the people would say, my dear, we can't afford food. We can't afford perfumes. So . . . you'd say Avon and people didn't know what you were talking about."[31]

How I discovered the AVON way to *Loveliness!*

Visiting Janet is always a pleasure. She's a charming hostess—and has such perfect taste. Her home, her wardrobe and everything about her is always correct and smart. A recent week-end at her house was lucky for me ...

I started to "freshen up"... and made a marvelous discovery! I found a collection of amazingly exquisite cosmetics... fragrant bath salts... heavenly soap... delightful creams and face powder. I tried every one. They were so lovely I just *had* to ask Janet about them ...

When I came downstairs she was talking to a friend. "This is Miss Martin," said Janet. "She brings me Avon cosmetics. They are salon quality—the finest I've ever seen—and I select them right here at home." "Wonderful," I agreed, "but aren't they expensive?" "Not at all," Janet replied, "they're *easy on your budget*."...

As soon as I got home, I looked up the Avon Representative who lives in my neighborhood. She came right over with her cosmetics and selection charts. With her help, I quickly found an ideal combination of face powder, lipstick and rouge ... and picked out many other lovely things. They are all simply *perfect*.

P. S. By the way, here's something I forgot to tell you. A few days later, Ted (friend husband) said, "What's going on here? You actually look younger every day!" His words gave me a thrill. I didn't tell Ted my new beauty secret—but believe me, I'm using nothing but Avon cosmetics from now on!

Avon COSMETICS equal the most expensive sold anywhere—yet our prices are amazingly reasonable. Avon's 52 years of experience ... the Good Housekeeping seal of approval ... and our money-back guarantee ... insure your *complete satisfaction*. Begin today to follow the Avon Way to loveliness!

Exceptional values in exquisite cosmetics: Avon velvet-textured Face Powder, in 2

weights and 8 flattering shades—78¢ a box. Avon Perfumes in 12 enchanting fragrances —52¢ to $1.04 a flaconette. Avon Bleach Cream, to lighten complexion for Fall fashions—52¢. Avon Lipstick, in 4 becoming tones—52¢. Avon Rouge in 4 shades to harmonize with the Lipstick—52¢. Avon Astringent—78¢. Avon Tissue Cream—78¢. Avon de luxe Manicure Set, complete—$1.67.

If you are not receiving regular Avon service, mail a postcard to Avon Products, 30 Rockefeller Plaza, New York City. Our Representative in your community will call—without obligation on your part.

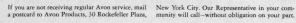

A Personalized Service that Comes to Your Home

Figure 4.4. "How I discovered the Avon way to loveliness." Avon began advertising in *Good Housekeeping* in 1936. Storyboard advertisements like this one featured Avon products and developed expectations of an Avon Lady's sales call.

Radio advertising seemed like a logical next step to Eastman. In an oral interview conducted by Avon in 1972, Eastman took credit for developing the first radio ad. "I decided that if I could put the word Avon in their mind, it would happen just like that and it happened almost in the twinkling of an eye," she said. "People in the home were listening to the radio and the man came on and with a nice voice telling about Avon, telling about their credentials, and that a lovely lady would call at their home to show them the merchandise. And then he would tell them that she would have a little gift for them. And it went over big. Many girls would tell me that they would knock on the door and say that they were the Avon representative and the people would say come in, I just heard your ad over the radio."[32]

When McConnell Jr. announced the first national advertising campaign, several executives were skeptical of its usefulness. "National advertising was hard to sell," Wayne Hicklin recalled, "but Mr. McConnell Jr. and Mr. Ewald insisted it would be good. Many of us in the branches thought that was the most peculiar thing; how would that help us? It didn't help right then, but the cumulative effect over four or five years was very evident."[33] Executives disagreed about the efficacy of mass advertising and the use of local radio spots, and few in Avon initially saw it as something the company needed to pull it through the Depression. Most preferred a more conservative approach, such as establishing higher recruiting goals, a tried and true method for increasing the size of the representative staff, the amount of orders, and cash the company received. Despite the success of other companies' investments in city branch offices and national advertising, most Avon executives believed that a new approach would not serve the vast majority of Avon representatives who continued to work in rural districts.

Increasing the number of agents' appointments changed only the scale of Avon's business but did not symbolize a fundamental shift in company strategy. Higher recruiting goals resulted in a larger representative staff. Eventually the base number of contracts on file leveled out at about 25,000 from 1933 to 1937. Sales grew from just under $2.8 million in 1929 to $3.6 million in 1936 and by 1939 nearly doubled to $6.5 million. The turnover rate during the Depression era rose dramatically—recruiters had to appoint between 25,000 and 30,000 new women every year just to maintain an average of 25,000 active representatives. The CPC's ability to compensate for high turnover and low individual sales saved the company during the 1930s when annual turnover rates skyrocketed to well over 200 percent.[34] Although Avon had to step up the pace of recruitment, managing a temporary, part-time, and low-earning sales force did not present any fundamental challenges to its existing system.

Continued sales increases in the mid- and late 1930s, in light of the stable number of representatives, resulted from two merchandising strategies. John Ewald, then CPC's general manager, instituted various plans to encourage women to make more sales. Traditionally, the CPC had required representatives to submit an order, preferably of $30 or more, every month. Ewald thought that representatives took too much time canvassing their territory and believed that he could increase the number of orders by making the selling cycle three weeks instead of four. This maneuver would increase the number of orders from a steady worker to eighteen per year rather than twelve. The new mind-game managers played with representatives essentially became a speed-up.

McConnell Sr., who in the early 1930s still held considerable power within the company, was not initially convinced of the value of the three-week campaign. "It wasn't easy to sell the home office," Hicklin said. He and his executives in Manhattan "thought Kansas City was a lot of little young upstarts. [But] eventually the home office was sold and overnight that was put into effect."[35] The CPC adopted Ewald's scheme with very little fanfare in August 1932. It informed recruiters of the new plan just days before they told representatives: "I am sure you will be mighty enthusiastic over the new twenty day sales campaign," Kansas City manager O. F. Blattler told his traveling agents. "We are expecting, because of this, that it will stimulate quicker interest in the minds of our Sales Representatives resulting in a greater volume of business for the period indicated."[36] In the representatives' newsletter, *Avon Outlook*, John Ewald introduced the new twenty-day campaign format along with a special offer to sell Avon Ariel and Vernafleur face powders, regularly 75 cents each, at two for a dollar.[37] The three-week selling campaign combined with the new "two for a dollar sale" showed instant results; the number and size of representatives' orders rose dramatically. "We had just as big orders in three weeks as we had in a month," Hicklin said.[38] The success of the shorter sales campaign taught CPC executives that representatives willingly followed instructions or "suggestions," which managers could use to control how a representative conducted her "business."

Not all of Ewald's plans proved successful, however. One failure in particular may have had a greater impact on the way the entire CPC management team approached the 1930s than any other. In 1932, Ewald had convinced McConnell Sr. to test out a new system for paying the door-to-door sales representatives a fixed monthly salary of $15 per month for agreeing to work full time. McConnell Sr. reluctantly agreed. Within just three months, the plan proved a fiasco. Representatives did not increase the number of hours they spent on their business, and the size of their orders actually decreased. According to Wayne Hicklin, then the western division sales manager, guaranteeing salary under absentee management could not work. "When you've got people out there the best thing to do is give 'em an incentive where if they work they make money," he said. Under such circumstances the independent contractor relationship proved more sensible than a traditional one with fixed salaries: "We have to sell them on what they should do. . . . We're challenged, we have all these people, we've got to keep selling and getting them to do things they don't think they can do."[39] McConnell, Ewald, and many others learned that fixed salaries proved to be an incentive for unsupervised representatives *not* to work, and they never tried it again. Avon managers opted not to follow the trend of increasing corporate control of its sales staff. Placing workers on salary and promising them benefits proved ineffective in such flexible work environments.

The failed salary plan also exposed how management strategies worked within business structures that reflected assumptions about gender. Fuller Brush had also tried a similar initiative, and although the records are not clear, Avon may have hired Fuller Brush managers to try converting its system.[40] However, most Fuller Brush men worked full-time, unlike part-time Avon Ladies.[41] Avon's managers accepted the realization that its representatives treated their sales business as providing a supplementary, rather than a primary, source of income. Ultimately, the collapse of Ewald's salary plan showed management that radical changes to a proven system seemed unjustifiable in the midst of an economic crisis. Selling representatives on their jobs, however, as Hicklin suggested, resulted in a unique and effective method for increasing sales: motivation.

Motivational Literature: A Strategy for Emotional Control

Following Ewald's unsuccessful fixed salary experiment, CPC/Avon managers recommitted themselves to energizing representatives with emotional techniques that exaggerated each representative's commitment to the company and suggested that she had a moral obligation to serve it.[42] Motivational literature became key to CPC strategy, for it served instructional purposes, conveyed a sense of business ownership and responsibility, and encouraged women to set goals for themselves—a logical consequence of being unable to assign them specific tasks or enforce strict objectives. The technique placed responsibility for the success of the business directly in the hands of representatives; but without a formal, bureaucratic connection between women and the company, the CPC took an enormous risk, as the company had no system for enforcing a representative's activity. Not only did the representative work without supervision, but the company also set remarkably low sales quotas for her to maintain an active contract status. For example, the CPC sent letters of inquiry after a representative had not submitted an order for three months and did not threaten to replace her until about six months had gone by, in part because the company did not have enough recruiters available to reassign territories. Indeed, unlike commercial salesmen who maintained client lists and reported to supervisors, the company could not monitor a representative's day-to-day performance without on-site staff.

Motivational literature served to train representatives for their jobs by encouraging them to be diligent about their work habits. The representative's job required a degree of self-confidence that even a socially active woman in the midst of a strong economy found daunting. It necessitated that she knock on the doors of strangers and ask for a sale, facing rejection in two of every five households she approached. Most women simply gave up, as the low annual sales figures suggest. Without on-site supervision to help women through the first few difficult days, CPC lost many representatives due to lack of interest in the work or low morale from rejection.[43] These circumstances, not unique to the direct sales industry, drove the company's use of motivational literature from its inception as a business strategy. Managers believed that each woman needed to feel a part of the larger organization and to be aware of and believe that her success depended on her own aptitude, ingenuity, and willingness to work.

CPC's optimism seemed strangely out of place in the context of both national economic disaster and its own corporate history of high turnover and low individual sales. The inefficiency of the CPC system went hand in hand with the emotional, inefficient technique of distributing motivational literature and success stories to create direct selling's most visible, consistent, impossible to measure, and ultimately effective means of "irrational management." Motivational literature during the Depression emphasized that a woman should work virtuously and act responsibly for herself, her career, her family, her community, and the company itself. Editors relied on women to write the stories and allegories that supported the self-help theme, and ultimately representatives themselves came to define and defend the Oz-like promise of CPC business opportunities. Not only did the CPC message hold cultural appeal, for in the world of direct selling the success ethic was more than a rhetorical trope; it was also a central organizing feature of the company's business strategy.

American businesses rarely applied positive thinking, goal setting, and evangelical spirit—characteristics of modern management, progressive ideology, and religious philosophy—so directly to rural women. CPC liter-ature directly appealed to women as wives and mothers as well as women living in rural, agrarian states who had a long tradition of combining outside work with household management. Women, the CPC said, had to take re-sponsibility for the economic security of both their neighborhoods and the nation by entering business. "The enterprise and will to work, reflected in the splendid sales of thousands of our Representatives, gives me faith that prosperity is not far away," McConnell wrote. "Women—the ones you meet on your sales trips—still do 80% of the spending. . . . It is your responsibility to give them the opportunity to secure your merchandise. . . . When people get into the buying habit again, the wheels of industry will turn at full speed and there will be work for all."[44] To the women of a nation that still believed in the moral strength of the individual's entrepreneurial power and social responsibility, Avon's message resonated with particular urgency during the Depression.

McConnell and his managers believed that every woman, paid in direct proportion to her productivity, had the potential to earn and prosper, regard-less of experience or social background. Emphasizing the independent na-ture of agency work, Avon writers always described a woman's association with the company as a result of a well-thought out, independent, and pro-gressive choice, and they made the representative's success or failure a direct corollary of her time and effort. According to McConnell, positive thinking generated the individual's economic success. In *Outlook* and all company cor-respondence, he reminded his representatives that despite the Depression, rewards were limitless for those who wanted to work. "Pessimists are whim-pering over the unemployment situation," McConnell wrote in a 1931 edito-rial; "people are out of work, they say, and cannot find jobs." This confused him, for on his desk next to the reports on national unemployment were sev-eral sales reports for orders of more than $100 each: "Instead of being turned from doors," one representative wrote, "I am called back."[45]

Outlook editors employed a variety of rhetorical strategies for making their motivational messages more powerful. Most significantly, they encouraged women to write their personal stories and strategies for success. Assigning authorship to ideas about success and ownership, and employing rhetoric that linked representatives' responsibility to their communities belied the fact that negotiations between individual representatives and Avon took place between two very unequal parties. In order to foster representatives' trust, managers continually assured them of the corporation's paternalistic goodwill, a technique that allowed representatives to speak both for themselves and the company in the literature.

Representatives' voices had always played a conspicuous role in Avon's publications. The CPC used women's stories to teach lessons about the free-enterprise system and to emphasize the potential of the individual to succeed despite any limitations, establishing a business vernacular that supported a political and economic vision of social democracy. Avon featured personal stories from representatives in its earliest newsletters and manuals as a way to prove to women that no obstacle could justify why they stopped selling or serve as an excuse for why they were not earning money and improving their character. Many women claimed to have benefited physically, psychologically, and financially from Avon's positive outlook: "From a physical viewpoint I can say my work has been of more benefit to me than all the money I have ever spent," Mrs. Charles McNutt wrote from Oklahoma. "I sincerely believe that most ills are caused by a mental state of mind. I find that my work creates a diversion of thought, that in no way can be associated with the ordinary ills of today."[46]

Stories from other women who suffered from sickness, the death of a spouse, bankruptcy, or debt and who had learned to turn hardships into incentives pervaded Avon literature. "[Avon] has helped me financially, but most of all it kept me from doing a lot of worrying," wrote Mrs. Fred Them of Indiana. "For instance, three years ago I lost one of my babies and could not stand to be at home." She went to work for the CPC: "It did not take me long to get started and I have had such wonderful results." Another representative, Mrs. Cora Coffin of Massachusetts, wrote that she had started Avon work when she was "on the verge of a nervous breakdown." "I began to regain my health from the start. . . . My three children were young . . . and my husband being an ordinary working man, he was unable to meet all the expenses. So I always dressed the children from my earnings," she wrote.[47] According to these women, their fresh sense of power and possibility came from their new business acumen. "These women have *learned their own value*. . . . They plan to get what they want," General Manager John Ewald wrote in his 1931 editorial, "Success Is Not An Accident."[48]

Overall, the direct selling industry seemed to have thrived on morality tales, particularly those written by representatives who had overcome hardships. "Before I took up this work . . . I was a widow alone, no one to depend on and living in fear all the time," wrote Hattie McGoovan of Oklahoma. "Since I have been with the Company I have paid off $1,500 of debts left me by the ex-husband five years before, have a comfortable place to live, am living well and enjoying life to the fullest extent, for to be really happy one must be serving our fellow beings and building and making progress, which I am doing every day with the aid of the California Perfume Company."

Avon had featured exotic stories from representatives in its earliest newsletters. In the 1920s, the CPC had featured a woman in Alaska who used sled dogs and Eskimo guides to deliver her soaps to customers in the frozen tundra. In the January 1931 *Outlook*, under the heading "You Can't Keep a Good Representative Down," representative Miss Susie Robinson received praise for selling Avon merchandise from her own hospital bed following an operation. She had taken more than $15 in orders from nurses, doctors, janitors, and even other patients and used the money to pay her hospital bill. "There are not many people who would think of turning their ills to such good account," the *Outlook* editor commented.[49]

Thousands of women like McGoovan and Robinson shared their experiences and, in each instance, Avon singled out their business opportunity as the catalyst for their accomplishments. These success stories "are taken from our records as an inspiration to you, to have the things these women have—new clothes, nice homes, paid up doctors' bills, comforts for aged ones, [and] education for the younger generation," the *Outlook* editor wrote. "When you join the ranks of the [Avon] organization, your future success is in your hands. . . . How you capitalize on it depends on your own efforts."[50] Positive thinking and hard work became the simple and obvious solutions to any problem, including the Depression. As John Ewald wrote, "Those who use Hard Luck as an alibi for lack of effort, and prefer to bemoan their hard lot rather than cure it, are the victims of their own lack of foresight."[51]

In its most insidious form, Avon literature even suggested that business could become a substitute for social networks. "Sometimes a Representative will start out with the traditions of an older age. She will decide to make a few social calls. She will take her sales portfolio along, hoping to pick up a little business as she goes," began one editorial entitled "Our Work Is the Test of Our Value." "But if she is the forward-looking, up-to-date type, she soon drops this attitude for that of the new age. She goes out to WORK—like her progressive sisters everywhere. She finds her social life as she goes. For in her portfolio she carries the key to every woman's confidence and friendliness— the desire to appear at one's best before the world."[52]

At Avon and the CPC before it, the beauty culture went beyond personal application of red rouges and vivid lipstick; it was colored green with economic incentives for those selected as "ambassadors of beauty" in their neighborhoods. Ironically, the chorus of women's voices that reaffirmed the CPC and Avon's business strategy, and its moral and emotional support of independent business owners, provided the ammunition the CPC/Avon needed when government regulation threatened the direct sales business contract. Singing the praises of the CPC and Avon—its business characterized by fairness, unlimited potential, and quality—Avon women enthusiastically supported the continuation of a business contract that afforded them no security or benefits beyond their commissions.[53]

Avon and the New Deal

Throughout the early part of President Franklin D. Roosevelt's first term, progressive federal legislation, commonly referred to as the "New Deal," resulted in a vast shifting of the economic and social landscape. While the majority of the new laws addressed unemployment and the banking crisis, one piece of legislation that affected industry, including direct sales firms, was the National Labor Relations Act of 1935. Also known as the Wagner Act, the bill gave labor the right to organize and set workplace standards.

Throughout the Depression, hundreds of thousands of people turned to direct selling to supplement their incomes and there were nearly 3,000 companies, some that operated locally and some nationwide, that sold products door-to-door. The companies and their representatives worked in the midst of a growing national conversation about work and labor, workers' rights and corporate responsibility. Given direct sales' long history of motivational rhetoric connecting independent effort and opportunity, most representatives did not expect to be covered by new federal legislation like the National Labor Relations Act that mandated businesses to restrict workers' hours, guarantee minimum hourly wages, or pay income taxes.[54] Not all companies operated like Avon did. Fuller Brush, Wearever Cookware, Encyclopedia Britannica, and many others used more structured workforces. Some companies used managers who drove salesmen into neighborhoods, directed them to canvass houses in assigned territories, and picked them up hours later. Other companies required extensive travel and, since the turn of the century, salesmen's organizations had formed as trade groups to lobby for their interests. In 1899, two traveling salesmen in Wisconsin formed the most famous of them, the Gideons, to help protect their spiritual integrity while on the road. Initially attracting salesmen, the group distributed free Bibles to members and left them in hotel rooms to support Christian morality in a lifestyle that potentially invited moral danger. The strongest trade organizations, however, organized direct sales corporate interests. The CPC had joined other direct sellers to form the National Association of Direct Selling Companies (NADSC) in 1910, an umbrella trade organization that lobbied on behalf of its member companies. Originally known as the Agents Credit Association, it offered financial support and services for companies. As the Wagner Act was being written, direct sales companies feared that if laws regulating worker rights were applied to them it would have devastating consequences. Although Avon had always supported Roosevelt's efforts, most federal programs required little from Avon other than lip service. It was easy for Avon to boost the 1933–34 National Recovery Act as it required little more than placing Blue Eagle stickers on recruiting literature packets and catalogs, but the threat of regulation by the Social Security Administration and the Wagner Act presented an impracticable situation to the entire direct sales industry.

The NADSC successfully appealed to the Federal Trade Commission in 1936 to officially classify direct sales representatives as "independent contractors."[55] The unsupervised nature of representative work, the NADSC argued, made it impossible for companies like Avon to monitor employees' hours and the quality of their work, factors that did not affect how the company had previously regulated or rewarded representatives, who only had to meet minimum order quotas. Ultimately, the FTC's independent-contractor ruling exempted direct selling companies from paying representatives' Social Security taxes and from adhering to minimum wage requirements. However, it also carried legal restrictions on what direct selling companies could and could not do regarding their representatives. Thereafter companies could neither "hire" nor "fire" representatives, nor could they restrict representatives' activities either by establishing protected territories or by enforcing product pricing. Other laws prevented representatives from charging more than published prices, but representatives could reduce prices. Moreover, direct sales employers could not require representatives to submit documentation of their business activities beyond the paperwork required for processing orders. But, as with many New Deal initiatives, the federal government could not establish the mechanisms needed to enforce its new law, and Avon did not feel the full impact of the 1936 legislation until several decades later when the federal government established regulatory committees to monitor the direct selling industry.[56]

Meanwhile, by 1936, Avon managers could rely heavily on their company's fifty-year-history in managing its sizable sales force. McConnell was a leader in the industry, and his company represented the model of how to build a successful direct selling organization. Avon clearly filled a need for customers and distributors alike. Given his perfected motivational techniques, even a lackadaisical sales representative could profit the company so long as overhead was kept low enough, whereas the costs of transforming the independent sales force into a mass of "employees" would have been overwhelming. Therefore, while the contractor rulings of 1936 would eventually become significant for Avon, they made little impact on its organization and management style at the time. Avon remained devoted to treating its distributors as independent business owners, and it was as likely to use the phrase "Now you are in business for yourself" in 1940 as it did in 1920.[57]

In the early years of the Depression, Avon had touted direct selling as a vehicle for developing women's agency to alleviate a national crisis. As the decade wore on, its need to emphasize women's role in business as a necessary and valuable component in helping the country to survive became more subdued. By 1936 the firm had dropped all references to the economic crisis. Avon's business strategy rhetoric ignored the Depression and instead placed a heavy emphasis on sales techniques, service skill development, product information, and how-to beauty advice. Structural changes within the organization coincided with this shift in emphasis. A new group of managers had firmly taken control. When Avon's patriarchal head and founder, David McConnell Sr., died in 1937, his son fully took the helm. Avon knew that it had survived the long-running crisis and began in 1938 a plan to open new city markets.

The economic crisis certainly increased the degree and intensity of Avon's message to representatives, providing fodder for the "conquer and overcome" theme in the motivational literature; the myth of the "self-made [wo]man"

Figure 4.5. Sales representative business manual (1936).(Courtesy of Hagley Museum and Library.) .

became more exaggerated and embellished as a result. Yet organizationally, the most important changes enacted at Avon between 1929 and 1938 had been planned before the economic crisis took its full toll. Development of the color cosmetics line, late in the broader context of the beauty industry, began at Avon only in 1928. The reorganization of city markets, a priority in the late 1920s, remained untested before 1935 and had little or no effect on Avon's bottom line until World War II. Even the first national advertising campaign could not explain Avon's success during the Depression.[58] Ultimately, Avon's

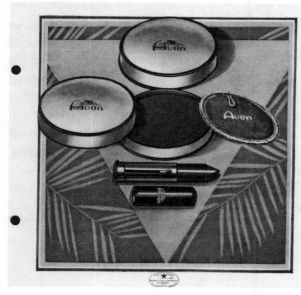

AVON DRESSING TABLE ROUGE

Avon Dressing Table Rouge gives a charming, natural effect, indescribably youthful. It will cling for hours, is absolutely pure, and will not clog the pores.

Generous in size, fragrantly perfumed, and attractively boxed with wool puff. Four popular shades to enhance the beauty of every type of complexion: vivid (orange), light, medium and dark. Desirable to have more than one shade for day and evening use.

Per Box, 47 cents

AVON LIP STICK

Avon Lip Stick is made of the purest ingredients and is guaranteed absolutely harmless. It is easily applied and is reasonably indelible but will come off when desired. Even the conservative woman today considers it good taste to have her lips tinted. But their color must harmonize with her complexion. So Avon Lip Stick has been created in four shades — vivid, light, medium and dark—to suit any type. It is delicately scented.

Each, 52 cents

Shades of rouge and lip stick available are shown on color chart elsewhere in this book.

Figure 4.6. Avon brand rouge and lipstick, Color Plate Catalog, 1939. (Courtesy of Hagley Museum and Library.)

AVON SINGLE ROUGE COMPACT
(Purse Size)

Avon Compact Rouge imparts a youthful warmth and brilliance of color which blends perfectly with the skin, and which stays fresh and glowing for hours. The Rouge cake is generous in quantity allowing full and easy applications. It is absolutely pure and harmless and will not clog the pores.

The thin blue and silver metal compact case has been especially designed for carrying in the purse, and comes complete with mirror and luxurious puff. Illustration shows actual size. The rouge is obtainable in four beautiful shades, as shown on color chart.

Price complete, 52c

Figure 4.7. Avon rouge, advertising borrowed art deco influences, Color Plate Catalog, 1939. (Courtesy of Hagley Museum and Library.)

sales growth stemmed from face-to-face transactions in parlors and kitchens between individual women in rural America. That said, a few spontaneous decisions in the early 1930s had long-term consequences, such as General Manager John Ewald's decision in 1932 to reduce the period of the selling campaign and offering product specials such as the two-for-a-dollar sale on face powder. However, the major changes of the 1930s were planned earlier and reflected David McConnell Jr.'s leadership. Ultimately, Avon's success in the 1930s was underwritten by its ideological and managerial commitment to and mastery of direct sales and its unique market niche in rural America, despite this regional sector being hard hit by the economic depression. The company opened new market areas, found new strategies for motivating their representatives, dodged the repercussions of the Wagner Act, and thrived under new management.

5

The Men and Women of Avon

City Sales and the Gender Division of Management

In August 1935, as Lela Eastman cruised through the Southwest in her Ford decorated with hand-painted kewpie dolls, she received a letter from her division manager, Wayne Hicklin, asking her to become Avon's first city sales office manager on the West Coast. After twelve years on the road, she gladly accepted the opportunity. Eastman's new job would be to recruit and provide regular encouragement, sales advice, and product information to her representatives, all of whom would be working within the city of Pasadena. In return, Avon offered Eastman control of an office as well as a commission and bonus plan geared directly to her staff's annual production. In many ways the job closely resembled the work she performed as a traveling agent, but it involved markedly different tasks and increased responsibilities.

Eastman settled in Pasadena in 1935 with only vague instructions from Avon headquarters. City sales office management positions offered travelers like Eastman a more stable lifestyle and more influence within Avon's managerial ranks. Like all the female city managers that Avon appointed, Eastman assumed sole responsibility for setting up her office, continuing the independent style of decision making required of all traveling agents. Hicklin and his superiors trusted Eastman's initiative and gave her, and many other traveling agents like her, space and time to get their businesses started. She negotiated leases for office space and ordered furniture, supplies, and telephone service: "Just as soon as your organization is developed a little more there," Hicklin wrote to Eastman, "we have several ideas and plans which we will be glad to work with you on in the effort to get a larger volume of business."[1]

The new organization allowed Avon women to create a whole new middle-management layer of the Avon corporate pyramid. Eastman learned to become a manager, in the modern bureaucratic sense, through her own experience. Together, the traveling agents that Avon pulled off the roads in the years just before World War II created a new and separate career ladder within the corporation. They did not join or replace male managers, for their job categories had not existed before within the company, and men continued to control the company's operations at the executive level. But from their positions, the women of Avon carved out a place and a voice in management that rested on more than mere feminine sensibility; success required a sophisticated sense of personnel, salesmanship, training, and economic judgment. By the end of the war, they had established themselves as mid-level corporate managers, then an unusual position for working women.

The new system of city and field management changed the company's hierarchical structure and organization. For the first time, women had access to an exclusive managerial career track where they occupied meaningful and influential supervisory positions. Ensconced in city sales offices far removed from corporate headquarters and dealing almost exclusively with female sales representatives, these women had to excel at working with and managing other women. Their entry into middle management prompted discussion among the men of Avon of a wide range of issues about Avon's corporate philosophy, including ideas about women's initiative, responsibility, business leadership, and success. At headquarters, men articulated paternalistic interpretations of women's ability to manage and their style of leadership. Distance mattered, though, for the physical separation ultimately allowed the women of Avon significant independence and control over their jobs. The new managerial relationship was at the root of Avon's extraordinary rise within the cosmetics and direct selling industries: 26,000 Avon representatives produced $8 million in sales in 1940; by 1953, more than 125,000 representatives produced $47 million. Women middle managers were essentially responsible for the growth of the company.

The Branch Management System

Avon had planned to establish city sales offices in the late 1930s as part of a larger scheme developed by David McConnell Jr., then general manager and executive vice president, to increase the size and profitability of Avon's urban market. The opening of city markets coordinated with the strategies of building the Avon brand skin care and cosmetics line and creating a national market via a continuous national advertising campaign. By 1939, Avon Products, Incorporated, was poised for a new era. The timing for these major changes was fortuitous; they were under way long enough before the United States entered the war that Avon's managers felt compelled to continue them even when they had to turn their attention to wartime production. It also meant that, at the war's end, Avon had established a solid platform of city sales offices from which it could expand into fast-growing suburban areas.

David McConnell Jr. and Russel Rooks, the two men most responsible for envisioning and initiating the branch management system in the 1930s, saw the city sales office as a corrective for recruiting problems and a way to facilitate the management of sales in urban areas. Representatives had received inadequate training; very little encouragement, except what could be mailed; and little incentive to continue selling beyond their initial commitment to submit a $30 order. Unlike rural representatives, urban women did not approach selling as part and parcel of their neighborly rounds. They quit sooner than their rural counterparts; and some felt daunted by impossibly large districts, which could sometimes mean assignments of 10,000 households. They more often had to approach homes where they did not know the residents and experienced more competition from stores that sold toiletries and household products. Few had the experience of selling cosmetics and beauty products that had come to dominate the Avon line.

McConnell Jr. and his executives imagined that a city sales office, staffed by a full-time permanent manager, would address these issues and ultimately help improve sales performance. The traveling agent's responsibility had been too limited. She controlled only partial information on active representatives and exercised little long-term impact on any individual representative's performance. For her, involvement in sales management was restricted to the hour or so that she spent with her recruit explaining how to use the sales manual and catalog. Traveling agents revisited a representative only when her performance was so low that the company threatened to take away her sales privileges, and even then, most representatives received termination notices through the mail. McConnell Jr. had envisioned that onsite managers would make themselves available to provide representatives with standardized training and ongoing sales support and motivation. He also proposed to tie city managers' compensation directly to their representatives' sales performance. In this regard the new city manager's corporate and personal influence increased exponentially.

When Avon executives developed the city sales office plan, they did not do so with a preconceived managerial strategy. Nor did Avon follow the strategies of other direct sales companies, although many others, including Fuller Brush, Stanley Home Products, Wearever Cookware, and Real Silk Hosiery, were then well established in urban markets. None of those companies, however, had continued to send agents out in the field simply to recruit, as Avon still did. Their systems were not compatible with the expectations of Avon, either at the corporate or door-to-door level, as the men of Avon learned in one attempt to transfer management ideas.

In the early 1930s, McConnell had hired two men from the Fuller Brush Company, which operated under the branch office system, to help organize the shift to urban markets. Fuller's motivational methods didn't fit with Avon's culture. "Kansas City brought in two Fuller Brush men, high-priced guys," Wayne Hicklin, then the western division sales manager of the Kansas City office, recalled. "They hired men and fired them up, [but] it was a miserable flop," he said. Other companies, which used male managers, relied in part on the affordability of automobiles and availability of good roads to draw large territories for salesmen, who could in turn cover longer distances and still return home on a nightly basis. The Fuller Brush concept was to drive their salesmen into a city and assign them significant sections to canvass and then retrieve them when the day was finished. The motivational techniques that these companies wanted Avon to adopt relied too much on assumptions about men's desire for competition and dominance. Fuller Brush based their approach on the idea of competition between representatives rather than encouragement. Avon's city managers would not hold up the success of a representative as a means of berating others for under-performing. Ultimately, the Fuller men failed, Hicklin believed, because their system was not compatible with Avon's management style and, he added, because "men shouldn't sell our product."[2]

Avon's traditional sexual division of labor both within the representative sales force and the traveling agent staff led its top managers to acknowledge consciously that "as men" they needed to organize, manage, and motivate the women in their company in ways that were different from the strategies used by other companies. Avon had developed merchandising and sales techniques over many years expressly for women's experience; the Fuller Brush system could not simply be imposed onto them. Instead, executives relied on the talent and ingenuity of former traveling agents, like Lela Eastman and Louise Fogartie, who freely shared their ideas with each other and with division managers, enabling them to take charge and develop new plans. Female city managers' experience at the grassroots level in setting up offices, recruiting, teaching sales techniques, motivating, and organizing representatives in their districts formed the basis of Avon's corporate style for the new branch office sales development.

Defining Women's Corporate Responsibilities

Methods for recruiting women to sell Avon products door-to-door in the targeted city markets copied the procedures traveling agents had used in rural markets. Initially, new Avon city managers found most recruits through door-to-door inquiries, but some started a new strategy of relying on advertisements in the "help wanted" sections of local newspapers, something that the corporate executives had deemed unnecessary or counterproductive in rural regions. Early on, Avon's executives had wrongly assumed that the direct sales methods representatives used in rural markets would work equally well in city markets and suburban neighborhoods. However, in cities, managers could not guarantee a new recruit an exclusive selling district without first mapping neighborhoods. Beginning in 1942, executives advised managers to acquire city maps from local census offices and to create territories differentiating by wealth and by the concentration of residences or apartment buildings and businesses. Ideally, each territory would include elements of "both classes." Their assumption was quite likely that wealthy neighborhoods meant "white neighborhoods" and by referring to "classes," they were making distinctions about not just income but ethnicity as well. By 1942, city managers were to have broken these neighborhoods into 400-household territories and begun filling them with representatives.

Avon also asked managers to separate white neighborhoods from black. Throughout its history, Avon leadership had envisioned it as a racially white company, but its recruiting advertisements in newspapers and on radio succeeded in attracting black women to the company. By the beginning of World War II, offices in both Washington, DC, and Philadelphia reported "a sizable amount" of black representatives on file. Initially, Avon chose to maintain segregated city sales offices, as southern division manager Paul Madden had suggested at the 1942 managerial conference. "The negro situation in various cities in the Southern Division is increasing," he noted. He suggested that Avon develop "separate training programs and special meetings" for black representatives at the opening of each sales campaign. Other division managers suggested that city managers and assistants not appoint black representatives while recruiting in the field (cold calling); "however, if they come in answer to an advertisement—it is O.K."[3] There are no further details in the Avon records about this suggested segregated approach or about the continuation of existing stringent policies for African American representatives and customers regarding credit and collecting payments on orders before delivery.

Mapping and managing neighborhood data were essential activities for urban managers. "The exclusive territory plan is a fundamental part of a city manager's responsibility and it is up to her to establish a well-developed, exclusive territorial plan to gain any degree of success in her work," the first city sales manual stated.[4] Managers drew grids on their maps, numbered each territory, and used a colored-tack system to indicate status: red tacks marked vacant territories, green tacks marked active ones. Avon left the division and drawing of territories entirely up to the city manager's discretion, but it set the overall goals by which she would be measured: "How many representatives you regularly place in the territories in your city measures your success. How active each person is determines your results. The length of time they continue and the amount of net sales they build contributes each year to your progress."[5]

The territory map, therefore, indicated the shape, extent, and character of the Avon market as well as the success of the manager as an "employer." Avon characterized the cultivation of these elements as the personal responsibility of each city manager: "The dressing tables and bathroom shelves of the women living in those homes represent your market and opportunity for distribution. . . . But it is impossible for them to buy Avon until you have an active Representative in each territory to serve them."[6] By defining the challenge this way, Avon identified a central problem. The manager's task was not a marketing issue of getting women to buy Avon but rather providing the representatives who would perform in the space where it was sold, which was a merchandising issue. The Avon marketplace was not a typical retail outlet. A consumer did not come to an Avon store, nor could she purchase Avon brand products off the shelf. Avon could not sell a product until a representative entered a customer's home. The main problem in city markets, therefore, was not persuading women to buy Avon's products but convincing women to sell them, and so a scripted and structured recruiting pitch was developed.

Every new recruit heard the same "Avon story" that described the advantages of being a representative. In 1940, Avon distributed a step-by-step guide to show managers how to present "The Avon Opportunity" book to a new recruit—here referred to as "Mrs. Sampson."[7] After determining whether the woman a manager had selected was appropriate for a representative position, the manager was to present the book, saying: "From my own observations, Mrs. Sampson, and the information you have given me you appear to have the necessary qualifications for the position we have open." In reality, Avon estimated that only 5 percent of all potential territories were covered; any woman willing to do the work was, by default, mostly qualified. "You have been kind enough to tell me about yourself so now I want to tell you about the House of Avon," the manager was to continue. "The Story of Avon is a story of primary interest to women. It is a simple story of the daily lives and happiness of thousands of women who have been successful and happy with Avon. It is a unique story, one that no other Company can tell. And the reason is, because Avon is a woman's organization."[8] Words used repeatedly in the Avon recruiting pitch—women, dollars, income, need, earnings, happy, independence, security, and prosperity—all spoke to a culture of Depression-era financial fantasy and wartime preparedness.

Avon met the need for women's employment during the Depression head-on.[9] It focused on the conditions of independence and control its representatives achieved in direct sales. The headline on a page in the 1940 recruiting book that read "Thousands of Women Enjoy Avon's Earning Opportunity" featured a beautiful young woman handling nearly $30 in cash (the minimum-sized wholesale order to qualify for the 30 percent discount). Avon suggested to the sales manager that she reassure her potential recruit how easy and respectable an Avon position was.

Permanent opportunity to earn the year round. . . . An income with security plus independence. It's a real blessing for you to feel secure and know that you have a gainful opportunity as long as you give it your time and attention. Avon women know the true value of security, because many have been gainfully employed throughout a lifetime. When you can have a feeling of security and with it have independence, Mrs. Sampson, so that you can use your own originality and initiative, you have a combination that's hard to beat. Avon women are free to live, work and play their own way, which lets them step right out of the crowd. . . . You have a business that is your very own. Our Avon women by their deeds have proven their business management ability. . . . Over 35,000 women find their answer to financial security with Avon. Fine American women who are banded together in one vast organization proving that financial security is within reach of every woman who is sincere, has confidence in herself and the time and desire to earn. Avon Representatives are proud of their organization because it is the most unique family of business women in all the world.[10]

When a city manager recruited a new representative, she presented the assigned territory plan as if the city had always been organized that way. Technically, guaranteeing an exclusive territory was illegal according to the 1937 independent contractor laws that Avon had helped write via the National Association of Direct Sales Companies (NADSC).[11] Avon's lawyers, speaking at the 1942 management conference, outlined the legal status of representatives and helped develop language that managers could use when guiding city representatives' activities. "We cannot assign a certain territory to a Representative as that will show control," they stated. "However we can tell a Representative that she will *benefit* if she works in a certain district."[12] All Avon literature and recruiting scripts, therefore, referred to working only in certain territory as a "suggestion" rather than a right. In other words, Avon's recruiters claimed to have created "exclusive territories" but never plainly said that a representative "must" work the one assigned to her, nor that she was prohibited from selling in other areas. However, at the same time Avon promised to "keep other representatives away" from one's assigned territory. Mark Taylor, the branch manager of the Los Angeles division, said he simply would not fill the orders of representatives who infringed on another representative's territory. "This is a way of getting around 'firing' representatives," he said.[13] Russel Rooks concurred, adding, "We can emphasize the fact that it is for the good of the Representative that she work a certain territory, thus avoiding showing control over Representatives by assigning territories."[14] This semantic play made Avon's activities only barely legal, and indeed the company would eventually have to drop that language, too. But in the 1940s the federal government was not closely monitoring this aspect of the direct selling industry.

Not surprisingly, when a new branch manager showed up in the city and introduced active urban representatives to the new policy of restricted territories they resisted these changes. These representatives had joined Avon before sales offices existed, and according to their contracts they already had rights to an "exclusive" territory that included practically half of a city. In the 1930s, Avon had sought to recruit only three or four representatives for a city with a population of 20,000.[15] These representatives, whom Avon labeled "old" representatives, rightfully sensed encroachment. Under the new plan, the company restricted representatives' work to clearly marked districts or neighborhoods. City managers told "old" representatives, even those who had previously sold to friends and family throughout the city, that they could not serve customers outside the new boundaries. Four-hundred household territories seemed ridiculously small to women who had been guaranteed 5,000 residents, even though it was unrealistic, if not impossible, for those working alone to cover that much ground every three weeks.

Ideally, "old" representatives would be able to continue to work the neighborhood in which they lived; managers assigned new representatives, assuming they had access to transportation to canvass nearby neighborhoods. Regardless of whether a representative was "old" or "new," statistics proved that women who wanted to work a particular neighborhood probably had to wait just a few months to have it assigned to her, since turnover in cities was higher than unorganized rural districts. Theoretically, converting representatives already working in city territories to the new, restricted territory system presented only short-term problems for Avon managers.

Avon's city managers assured all representatives that the territories plan was more efficient, suggesting that Avon had created it for the individual's— not the company's—benefit. According to its recruiting literature, Avon claimed to have already done the work of establishing "an exclusive number of homes" within a representative's easy reach. Territories "concentrated a representative's earning power," helping her to focus on developing a local market, reducing the temptation to skip all over the city, and eliminating the confusion, duplication, and discouragement that came with interference from other representatives. Avon also argued that a territory helped more representatives move more efficiently. By walking less, they could see more customers each working hour. Pamphlets distributed to newly appointed representatives, such as "Getting the Most Value Out of Your Territory" (1942) and "Avon Wants You to Succeed" (1946), repeatedly emphasized the advantages of staying within the territorial bounds set by the company.[16] The plan, Avon said, bred neighborhood familiarity and therefore ensured repeat service: "The Representative is a housewife serving customers in her own neighborhood, adding pleasure in developing friends who are exclusively her own customers in that neighborhood."[17]

While the territory plan may indeed have been more efficient for representatives, it was primarily advantageous to Avon. Territories marked the boundaries of individual markets for future representatives. The plan set limits, but at the same time served to focus each representative's selling activities, requiring her to approach customers with whom she might not otherwise have made contact. Territories also restricted the more intimate and social selling style representatives might have used with women whom they already knew. In effect, managers hoped that territories would mold women into company sales representatives whom Avon could control by confining their access to their immediate neighborhood.

The territory system perpetuated an assumption, common in Avon/ CPC literature since the company's founding and in direct sales companies of all kinds in the postwar era, that every sales representative—as an independent business operative—wanted to claim a district where she would not encounter competition. Executives in the 1930s and 1940s continued to abide by this maxim, even though experience had shown that on average, women only served ten to thirty customers and only a very few were willing to knock on the doors of complete strangers. Avon could have benefited by eliminating territories altogether, but both the men and women of Avon, including representatives who sought to "protect" their territory from other representatives, insisted on clear boundaries even though they intended to sell to less than 10 percent of households in them. The program, however, helped cement the perception that Avon, not the individual, controlled the representative's business.

The quality of the ongoing sales training and motivation program determined a manager's success, both in the eyes of the company and in the balance of the city manager's paycheck. Managers received guaranteed salaries, just as traveling agents had, but they also received ongoing commissions. In contrast with the system used for travelers, a city manager's commission and bonuses were based on her entire unit's sales during each three-week campaign. Traveling agents, on the other hand, had received commissions and bonuses based only on a recruit's first wholesale order, regardless of how long that representative stayed with the company; under the new branch management plan, Avon rewarded city managers for every order in every campaign. In 1945, according to an annual analysis, the average city manager earned $3,164 per year; the best-paid manager (probably Lela Eastman) earned $9,560 ($796/month), while the lowest-paid manager earned $1,771 ($147/ month).[18] High orders directly correlated with a representative's tenure; the longer a representative stayed with the company, the higher the wholesale orders she submitted. Therefore, it was the manager's job and in her personal financial interest to keep representatives active for as long as possible. She would use her new office as a meeting place where representatives could gather to learn more about their business and receive incentives for their work.

The Monday morning sales meeting became the linchpin of a successful city sales office. While the origin of the idea is uncertain, Avon executives most likely borrowed it from other direct sales companies. In the late 1930s, however, Avon had no plans for how the meetings would be run. Avon's executives supported the meeting in principle but left its agenda up to individual female managers. This allowed the mid-level women managers the independence to set the agenda and discover the most effective means of organizing and running the meetings. One purpose, implicit in the planning of city offices, was to build a sense of camaraderie and teamwork among the representative staff, most of whom had never met another Avon representative before. Once again, old representatives resisted the changes. Lela Eastman reported that she had only "seven reluctant representatives" at her first meeting in Los Angeles.[19] Gladys Lathom, the new city manager in Washington, DC, had been an assistant in Eastman's Pasadena office and wrote to her in October 1939 for advice. Lathom lamented her difficulty in establishing a supervisory relationship with representatives who had worked the city before she came. Representatives complained, she said, both about the training and the new geographic restrictions on their business, for many had customers living outside of their new boundaries. Lathom described the litany of representatives' excuses for not attending meetings: "I don't have to come to the meetings, I'm not a child, not going to school, have to do my washing Monday a.m., more important things to do, and a million other excuses," they told her. Still, she wrote to Eastman, a "good percent" of her seventy-three representatives showed up at her last meeting, and "they are beginning to cooperate now."[20]

Eventually word spread about the sales meetings' usefulness: "One Rep told me she had been with Avon twelve years and didn't know half the things I have told her," Lathom said. Although most of the meeting materials parroted the information available in sales manuals, catalogs, newsletters, and product pamphlets—including, for example how to canvass, how to present products, how to ask for an order, and how to submit orders to the company—old and new representatives said they benefited from the reminders managers presented in their meetings.

Meetings also became an attractive new social space for representatives. Managers usually leased office space in a downtown center. The presence of women in commercial buildings forced Avon's managers to think about representatives' respectability as business women. Lela Eastman remained cautious about where women could travel in the city. She moved her office several times, starting first in the Bank of America building in 1935, then moving into meeting space in a hospital, then to the Beaux Arts building near the Los Angeles bus depot, each time seeking out a better neighborhood that all representatives could get to easily and safely. Eastman left the bus depot, she said, because "it was a bad neighborhood and I didn't like to ask the girls to come there." Women's presence in a business environment challenged the views of other clients in and around the Avon city offices, for managers like Eastman brought a new business culture to traditional office spaces. Eastman's enthusiasm and the energy her representatives created even got them evicted. She had to leave the Beaux Arts building, she recalled, because her meetings were too raucous: "They put us out because we had so many women coming . . . to meetings. And they'd stand around in the halls and talk and . . . there was screaming and laughing . . . so they made us move out."[21] Other times the sheer spectacle of women in the beauty business attracted onlookers. Eastman held meetings on Monday mornings and Thursday evenings. Thursday was dedicated to training for new representatives, but all representatives came on Monday to learn about the new campaigns and see demonstrations. Eastman invited a beauty parlor owner to teach her representatives about makeup application. "I never told anybody, not a soul," she said, "but I would take the ugliest woman in the room, the straggliest looking woman in the room and fix her up so she was really very pretty. And I—oh, the men, when they used to come up here. . . . They were well known. And even other companies would get their people to sneak in."[22]

Although the sales meetings may have been distracting or amusing to the men in the gray flannel suits who peered in, the degree of enthusiasm a manager could build among her representatives was an important part of sales management and the key to her ongoing success. Avon managers sought to motivate their representatives through reward and recognition. The supportive atmosphere of an Avon sales meeting stood in sharp contrast to the competitiveness of other direct sales companies. Companies that contracted almost exclusively with men, such as Fuller Brush, "Tiebolt," Encyclopedia Britannica, and Wearever, sponsored competitions for nearly every type of sales activity and, in most cases, only the man who won received a prize.[23] To help build solidarity and a sense of "mission" among her staff, Eastman decided to run contests differently. She and many other managers offered prizes, usually items from the Avon line, for activities as simple as attending the meeting or for bringing a friend, and as difficult as securing the highest numbers of new customers, or for submitting wholesale orders over $30 and $50. "I think your idea of giving a prize to the one who has the greatest amount of sales is a splendid idea," Wayne Hicklin wrote to Eastman.[24] But female managers quickly realized that rewards for regular service were as important as awards for the best performance for motivating their sales staff. Rewarding every woman who made five new sales calls, for example, with recognition, applause, or the honor of special front-row seating at the sales meeting made every woman feel like a winner.

Spreading rewards around was not an exclusively female response, however. McConnell Sr. had begun the tradition of recognizing a representative's average performance. The award structure in the early California Perfume Company often featured prizes for achieving certain wholesale order goals. Unlike the company in the early years, however, Avon's success under the city sales system was built on the enthusiasm and dynamic nature of group recognition. Small or inexpensive prizes, such as special seating at a meeting or a "$100 club" pin meant even more when receiving it in front of one's peers. Distributing rewards throughout a broad section of representatives encouraged rivalry but recognized achievements that focused on the individual's performance or improvement that did not come at the expense of others. The territory system also reduced competition between women in which the success of one might come at the expense of another. For example, in protected territories where only one representative was allowed to work, if that representative sold to five new customers, they were not customers that any other representative could have gotten. And everyone who sold to five new customers got a prize. Therefore, a representative was not "beating out" a coworker, a fact that managers emphasized when explaining the sales contests, setting goals, and handing out prizes. Avon Ladies therefore, learned to encourage each other and to take an interest in one another's progress.

Some contests, however, did engage representatives in direct competition. In 1941, Mrs. Parnell of Dallas, Texas, for example, divided her sales organization into two teams, the Blues and the Silvers. The team with the highest sales over nine weeks (three campaigns) earned a dinner provided by the losing team. Soon most sales offices offered "grand" prizes to the individual with the highest quarterly or annual sales.

In November 1941, the sales promotion department headed by Robert Feeley and Wayne Hicklin started tracking successful managers to try to determine why their meetings were so popular. About twenty men from headquarters traveled around the country and attended various meetings headed by their female managers "to see how the programs are put over after they are presented." They then sought to coordinate mailings and exchange city sales meeting bulletins between managers. In the end, Avon executives could not determine how or why some managers were more successful than others and frankly admitted that the women in charge of the offices knew how to motivate women better than they did.[25]

Sales training remained key to creating a successful city sales office, which managers provided on a regular basis to all representatives. Avon could not rely on representatives to read through their *Outlooks* magazines every month and apply the sales tips contained in them, but if a city manager could persuade her representatives to come to a sales meeting every Monday she could instruct them in a variety of selling techniques. As Gladys Lathom had told Lela Eastman in 1939, even long-term representatives still had things to learn about the company and its products. Managers taught new representatives the fundamentals while also explaining seasonal campaign specials, contests, and compensation information.

Early on, most managers brought new representatives into the office to talk about various manuals, explain Avon's system for soliciting sales and providing follow-up service, and check on representatives' progress every few days or weeks. Managers met with new representatives individually, usually in the hour or two before the regular sales meeting, and then invited representatives to stay afterward to meet other Avon Ladies and ask them about their work. In cities where representatives regularly attended training sessions, average sales per representative were higher, as were overall sales in city markets: "There are approximately 8,000 people attending meetings every Monday morning," Wayne Hicklin reported in 1942. "We know our sales in any city are almost directly in ratio with the attendance."[26]

With so much effort being dedicated to building the urban markets and organizing the city offices, Avon's executives put the restructuring of rural districts on hold. Regular traveling agents continued to work throughout the country recruiting and serving active representatives spread out across sparsely populated territories, just as they had before Avon began its conversion to branch management. Creating a separate City Sales Division had highlighted the need to create a Field (or District) Sales Division, and the lessons learned in city management experience were applied to these rural divisions as well. Executives had realized that rural women, too, could benefit from weekly sales meetings and ongoing training, and slowly they started requiring the remaining traditional traveling agents to concentrate their efforts on smaller districts.

Avon began altering the traveling system used by rural district managers in 1941, with Illinois serving as an experimental state. As Russel

Rooks described at the annual meeting, "The idea is to take eleven District Managers [a.k.a. traveling agents], keeping them in the state of Illinois all year. This would enable us to fill open territories more quickly, place better Representatives, [and] have less mortality [representative turnover]. We would place more responsibility on the district manager than just making appointments. The Manager would help us get sales as well as getting appointments."[27] The Illinois recruiters provided follow-up training and support to weak representatives and, overall, cultivated a better pool of representatives.[28]

By 1945, Avon had established 116 rural districts (91 in the east, 25 in the west). Managers' average earnings grew from $1,485 in 1942 to $2,328 in 1945.[29] These district sales managers, like those in city sales, concentrated their recruiting efforts within a state or region, and like city managers, held sales meetings, drawing representatives from within a forty-mile radius to learn about Avon products and services. However, organizing the rural Field Sales division (renamed Division Sales in 1946) presented more problems for Avon officials than organizing in cities. Managers had difficulty finding centrally located spaces for sales meetings. As a result, Field Division representatives consistently posted lower earnings and shorter tenure rates than their city sales counterparts. While less as efficient than city ones, field representatives continued to earn the bulk of Avon's overall sales, garnering 75 percent of total sales in 1939 and 65 percent of sales in 1943. As the Manual for Avon field managers put it, there was opportunity for career advancement within the ranks at Avon. A field manager who was "willing to work and prove her capacity for leadership" could continue her career with Avon as a city manager. "And the outstanding Field Manager—the one who proves her willingness to think and plan, to carry out the company plans and policies, to really work, and who shows that she has an understanding of people and a true desire to influence them—has a splendid future awaiting her in the management end of the cosmetic business."[30]

Wayne Hicklin, Russel Rooks, and David McConnell Jr. had turned first to the traveling agent staff when they started placing women as managers in city offices because they relied on their experience and business knowledge. As more agents left long-distance, long-term traveling, new positions opened up for women closer to home. Avon first appointed new city managers in the 1940s from this group of travelers and from assistant city office managers. They offered the door-to-door representatives the opportunity to learn the business as assistant managers. In this way, it created the first career ladder for women within the company. In turn, those managers sought individualized deals for salary, commissions, travel, and reimbursement. One example was hinted at during the 1942 annual conference. Willard Callahan, a division manager in Kansas City, suggested using a bonus and commission plan "similar to that under which Mrs. Zada Norris of Michigan is working," but no further details were given as to her situation. As women entered the ranks of management, they had to negotiate the most important terms of compensation individually, ensuring that they would have little opportunity to bargain collectively for better rates or benefits as their sales grew.

City managers relied on assistant managers to recruit, staff the office, and answer phones. Managers also divided the responsibility for filling territories among a team of assistants, giving each control over a defined district of the city where the assistant would be responsible for recruiting and following up leads that came from recommendations and responses to advertising. Assistant managers made all initial visits to new representatives and, according to sales management statistics, did most of the recruiting work in city offices. In 1941, for example, 16,175 new representative appointments were made in 128 city offices; 138 assistant managers made 71 percent of those appointments in the field.[31]

City managers appointed most of their assistants from the ranks of successful representatives. According to the city office guide, when a manager appointed new representatives, one of her objectives was to find women "who can be promoted from your organization as a City Manager."[32] Once a representative had earned more than $250 in retail sales, a city manager could recommend her to the division manager for a position as full-time assistant in the office, where she would earn a salary and commissions and become a full-time employee. After an intensive six-day training program, recruiting took up the bulk of an assistant's time which she spent cold calling, canvassing neighborhoods, and knocking on doors, much the way traveling agents had done, following up on inquiries and recommendations of potential representatives, and providing initial sales training.

City managers selected their assistants and trained them, but the division managers at headquarters frequently re-assigned assistants to other offices and ultimately had the power to promote them to the manager rank. Avon asked city managers to continually encourage prospective candidates to ask about the possibility of advancement within management: "This should serve as a stimulant for the Representative to do her best to show she is worthy of further consideration."[33] From the very first day assistants were assigned, city managers were "to point them in the direction of higher aspirations, creating within them a desire and an ambition to strive for advancement in the Avon organization."[34] On average, assistant city sales managers earned an average of $128 per month (for example, $80 per month between January and September 1945, and $157 per month October through December 1945).[35] A successful assistant could be promoted to head her own city or district office, just as Washington, DC, manager Gladys Lathom was advanced after being trained by Lela Eastman in Los Angeles.

Avon men expected that assistants, like city managers, would be mobile and have enough flexibility to work full-time. Avon characterized its ideal city manager as a woman "not over forty-five years of age" and "free of home ties in order to devote her full time and attention to the efficient development of a District." Furthermore she would exhibit "congeniality" and "leadership," and be a "good advertisement for Avon in a managerial position." A woman with "potential," Avon claimed, had both an aptitude for selling and a home life conducive to holding full-time job. Avon expected managers to work six days a week, which did not entirely rule out married women from management positions, but left women with children and family responsibilities little opportunity to advance within the Avon organization.

Nationwide, women occupied less than 6 percent of all corporate management positions in the 1940s and 1950s.[36] In white-collar work, they were concentrated in clerical positions, as typists and stenographers, but career ladders did not exist for women to rise through the managerial ranks in the way they did for white men. That Avon defined and maintained management positions for women is noteworthy, especially because male executives created such positions for women almost without comment. Indeed, it never occurred to them that men might manage city offices, in part because of the tradition of nearly half a century of employing women exclusively as recruiters and trainers.

On the other hand, Avon executives did not think about employing women in upper divisional or regional management posts. A "glass ceiling" did exist, and it was different for single or widowed women than it was for married women with children. The latter were tied to their homes and had family responsibilities, and both the female city managers and male executives would not recognize or encourage their promotion, assuming that a male breadwinner at home held higher status in the family. Early in the city management program, women needed to be mobile. Avon might assign an assistant manager in Chicago, for example, to open a new office in Seattle and did not want to waste resources training a manager who might not be available to go where she was needed. For widowed and single women, their restricted opportunities to move higher up in Avon's corporate ladder did not have to do with family-free mobility. The men of Avon were perfectly comfortable requesting that a woman move from Los Angeles to Dallas or Washington, DC, and for more than sixty years they had sent women traipsing through the country for months on end. Surely, Lela Eastman could have relocated from Pasadena to the regional headquarters in Kansas City or New York to become Western Division City Sales Manager, or even Vice President of City Sales, if it were not for the fact that she was a woman. Just as city and district management positions, by Avon's definition, belonged to women, corporate offices at the New York headquarters were the province of men.

While men's prejudices kept women from upper management jobs, they also made women eligible for certain specialized management positions. Women's background as representatives became part and parcel of their management knowledge. They used it to emphasize points of sales etiquette to new representatives, a type of tacit knowledge that translated into supervisory authority. Other direct sales leaders would convert this into a management pattern that followed what they believed was a uniquely female "feel, felt, found" emotional logic. A sales manager at the Mary Kay Corporation later modeled using emotional logic for her recruits who expressed reticence about asking customers to become representatives: "I know how you feel about approaching new customers, I always felt that if they turned me down that I was a failure, but I found that so many welcomed me into their homes that I actually owed women the opportunity to purchase these fine products." Women's difference, in this case an alleged heightened emotional responsibility and corporate commitment, could be marketed as part of Avon service, and it could also be turned into management material and knowledge.

As Avon's market grew and the company adopted mass advertising and higher production levels, the role of the city and district sales manager became more standardized in order to coordinate closely with sales campaigns and market forecasts. Tighter control of the market translated into more precise control of both branch offices and the women who managed them. Soon after the creation of the city sales office manual in 1942, Avon began providing specific promotion and training pieces that coordinated with the three-week campaign cycle for city managers to use in their meetings. During the first week of a three-week campaign, Avon sent charts and flyers on how representatives should approach new customers; during the second week, it sent information on how representatives should give additional service to existing customers; and during the third week of a campaign, it reviewed the process of filling out and submitting an order to the company.

The Monday sales meeting agenda, increasingly dictated by headquarters, closely coordinated the three-week sales campaign with new representative training, thereby reinforcing sales procedures for new representatives as well as existing ones. Sample representative/customer scenarios in training literature always included language that featured current sales campaigns. For example, if Avon wanted managers to review how representatives should introduce a "sales leader" (a product that was on special that campaign), then that week's training materials featured the relevant promotional material and products. In this way managers could remind representatives of the steps to a sale, as well as highlighting current campaign information, thereby motivating representatives to go out and sell. Both the sales meetings and the coordinated training and sales campaigns had a direct and positive effect on overall unit productivity.

Although Avon's managers had initially relied on and allowed women to create a sales management program on their own and, in fact, used their experience to create a system that appealed to women as both managers and representatives, Avon's sales and promotion department and division officers eventually took more control over how city managers did their jobs. With every new campaign brochure, contest promotion, or training program that Avon produced, individual managers lost some ability to exercise their own initiative. However, by 1942 not all city and district managers had worked for Avon as traveling agents and so were not familiar with Avon's traditional approach. The process of establishing a standardized format harkened back to the turn of the century when manufacturers and distributors reined in traveling salesmen and molded them into components of brand-name merchandising and advertising campaigns. The method and results were not new, but gender played an important role in the way managers applied the new methods at Avon.

The performance, training, and regulation of Avon's female managers dominated the bulk of the early conference workshops.[37] Annual management conferences served as a clearing house for information on how to manage city sales and coordinate manufacturing, sales promotion, finance, and advertising. Divisional managers monitored the success of each city sales manager and approved basic office issues which she could not authorize, such as the hiring and firing of assistant sales managers and the handling of representatives' complaints. Just as the company's move into city sales created new rungs on a career ladder for women, men too added new levels to their corporate pyramid. For example, with the establishment of individual sales offices, a division manager did not operate with standard guidelines but instead adapted his methods to city managers' unique personalities and situations. Executive and divisional managers gathered together at roundtable meetings to talk about issues ranging from broad topics, such as what individual responsibilities and policies were or should be, to techniques for motivating city sales managers, cutting costs, and coordinating training.

Unlike later conferences, which featured staged presentations and prepared materials regarding regional and district sales statistics, conferences from 1939 to 1942 were organized more like workshops. Everyone improvised, not only with managing individual office performance but also the very nature of their jobs, and this was evident in the roundtable discussion between John Ewald, then Avon's general manager and executive vice president, and his division managers. The meeting minutes were nearly complete transcriptions of discussions, unlike the abbreviated versions typical of such events in the 1950s. Of particular importance was the time devoted to thinking about who their new city managers were, what they needed, and how women's presence forced the men of Avon to define their roles as male managers.

For example, in 1942 Ewald had led a roundtable discussion with his division managers that opened with the question: "What do you think your responsibility is?" It was a genuine inquiry. Each man gave a slightly different answer. Mason Cooper, central division manager, believed his "big responsibility" was to his managers, representatives, and the company itself. "He must lead, encourage and guide city managers and help them achieve success." Maintaining a "close connection" with city managers, Cooper said, ensured that he would always be "on the alert" to ensure that company policies "are followed correctly and in the best possible way." Most other division managers also saw themselves as counselors to city managers, providing them with "leadership, [and] encouragement and giv[ing] them the freedom of realizing their responsibilities," as Paul Reichard, midwestern division manager, put it.[38] Mason Cooper agreed with Reichard: it was his practice to "let his good Managers do their own thinking and let them feel the responsibility which is theirs, . . . guid[ing] them when needed."[39]

Without mentors or established rules, Vice President Ewald and other veterans of CPC/Avon who had a shared memory of corporate culture and David

McConnell Sr.'s legacy, created a new hierarchy with a fluid set of expectations about how to establish and assume corporate responsibility. Division managers had no doubt that their female city managers were capable of independently organizing their offices. However, these men were also fully aware that their managers were women who required or responded better to a special, individualized, paternalistic approach. "[City] managers look for [our] counsel and it is therefore up to [the division manager] to keep closely in touch with them, knowing each individual Manager's problems [thoroughly] and offer advice."[40] "Due to the fact that our Managers are women," Mr. Bell, eastern division manager, continued, "it is important to remember this when dealing with them and if confidence is instilled in them, [a division manager] will derive a great deal more from his Managers."[41] The wartime situation required that even more care be given to female managers. As Paul Reichard noted, women's "special needs" were emotional and not only limited to their business skills, but division managers must be "always aware of the fact that his managers are women, and therefore must give them courage and guidance due to present war conditions."[42]

Significantly, most of the Avon men who acted as division managers, like most of the earliest city sales managers, had worked for Avon while it was a home office operation. In 1942, Avon's executive staff averaged thirty-four years of age and had worked with Avon for an average of fourteen years. Men such as Russel Rooks, Mason Cooper, Wayne Hicklin, Paul Gregory, Paul Madden, O. F. Blattler, Mark Taylor, Willard Callahan, and Paul Detwiler had begun their CPC/Avon careers in the 1920s or 1930s as managers of traveling agents. They had learned to trust women to make independent decisions in the field based on their informed opinions about what worked best for the company. By World War II, these executives were used to women performing unsupervised on a day-to-day basis. They had developed a habit of communicating goals to women with language that empowered them, assuring women that the company "had faith" in their judgment, for example, but that simultaneously allowed male managers to control their activity. In other words, the men of Avon were skilled at using emotional language and motivational and confidence-building techniques to compensate for distance and lack of supervision. While the strategy may have appealed to women, this was not new to Avon in the era of city sales marketing but a continuation of the managerial ideology in use since the early twentieth century.

Stressing personal contact and attention to the details that made managers productive, Avon's executives advocated openly sharing information with women so that they could make independent decisions. Mark Taylor's approach to managing the Los Angeles division office illustrates this philosophy. Taylor brought management prospects to his office for an interview and two-day orientation. "The purpose of this is to show her the reasoning and logic and relationship of organization with Representatives," he said. "It means a lot to a Manager in the field. Then when the Manager goes out, she has a good picture of the organization she will represent and present a good picture of the steps in her work."[43] Other division managers agreed that a personal approach to managing women was key, especially when it came to improving performance. Mark Creason, the Kansas City division manager, added, "When a manager is brought into the office, we can concentrate on her individual problems." [44] John Ewald went even further, suggesting that managers who came to the New York office "should be given undivided attention." In recognition of their privileged place in the organization, "they should be taken to a movie in the evening, lunch or dinner," as well as being introduced to President McConnell and Irene Nunemaker, Avon's beauty editor.[45]

The separation between Avon's male and female managers, not only in physical space but also in corporate culture, was so ingrained in male managers' worldview that it had not occurred to most Avon men that women could share or understand their side of management. It took John Ewald to suggest that Avon's women managers would benefit by participating in the corporate social culture and by seeing the faces of the men who set their office's goals, monitored their performance, and signed their letters of congratulations. In the new branch management format, these socialization activities became critical to indoctrinating managers in Avon's business philosophy. Ewald and other Avon men believed that women's experience at headquarters would translate directly into improving their work in the field. They had asked women to take on a major new responsibility and executives needed their cooperation and energy. Female participation in corporate culture at headquarters and at divisional facilities became a prime component in modernizing and integrating the company in the postwar era. At the same time, women managers were denied admission to most sacred and important corporate rituals, especially the annual management conferences where the men at headquarters made year-end assessments and decisions about the goals and sales plans for the coming year.

"To Be Useful and Lovely at the Same Time":
The Avon Army

As Avon developed city sales offices and opened new urban markets, executives kept one eye on representatives' sales of lipstick and the other on the war. As the US government sent troops overseas, several of the upper management staff in New York, Kansas City, and Pasadena were drafted into the army, leaving their secretaries temporarily in charge of the offices. McConnell Jr. also decided to switch gears at his manufacturing plants. He accepted US military contracts to manufacture and package toiletries kits of deodorant, body powder, toothpaste, and a variety of other items for soldiers to use at the front. The contracts were so large that by 1943, production facilities could not supply representatives' orders and fill military kits at the same time. In order to compensate for the necessary drop in production of Avon's products, McConnell decided to cut back on representative recruiting.

As he reflected on the early 1940s, Wayne Hicklin remembered thinking that Avon was going to be very successful in city markets. "We had 40,000 representatives and were really rolling," he said. "We had what we'd been looking for, [then] along came the war."[46] For the first time in the company's history, executives decided to halt domestic growth. At the time, they had hoped that consumer sales wouldn't decline; fortunately, this prediction proved accurate. Between 1937 and 1942, Avon had opened 128 sales offices, which annually managed a total of nearly 13,000 urban representatives. Sales from city offices nearly tripled, from just under $800,000 in 1937 to more than $4.2 million in 1942. By the time the United States entered the war in North Africa and the Pacific, more than one-third of all Avon representatives reported to city sales office managers and they generated nearly one-third of all sales nationwide.

In 1943, managers reduced the number of sales representatives companywide in order to concentrate their resources in the city markets. They simply eliminated new appointments in towns with populations fewer than 500. Similar efforts swept away the "dead weight" in city sales files, and it was "generally felt that the City organization . . .was undoubtedly in the strongest position that it ever has been." The city representatives were almost all in the active category, although a "number of deadbeats" continued to clutter the files. Norman Chadwick, Avon's general sales promotion manager, offered his assurance "that the necessary action of cleaning house would be taken to adjust this situation."[47]

Managers also tried to streamline the cost of operating sales offices by increasing the efficiency of each representative. In light of the success of the restricted territory plan, rural districts again seemed less attractive to upper management because they were difficult to organize and supervise: operating costs of city offices represented only 9 percent of sales in 1944, compared to 18 percent of sales in the field division.[48] Riley Denny, the New York Office sales manager, later reported that representatives in the largest areas generated the greatest average business, offering "conclusive proof" that eliminating small territories had saved considerable time and effort for district managers.

In January 1943, Avon's executives decided not to open any more new offices and to hold the line on the number of new appointments, but at the same time they hoped to maintain the same volume of business generated in 1942. Some executives optimistically predicted a modest 10 percent increase in representatives' door-to-door business despite the reduced efforts.[49] Companywide, managers reduced the number of new appointments by more than 20 percent, from 33,450 in 1942 to 26,500 in 1943.[50] City sales offices, which had recruited 24,100 in 1942 (or 72 percent of all new appointments companywide), appointed fewer than 16,400 in 1943 (or 61 percent of all appointments that year).

Despite the lower numbers of recruits and active representatives, Avon's sales climbed, and at the end of the year, one-third fewer representatives fueled an 18 percent increase in sales for the company. Their average "sales power" (annual net sales per representative, rural and urban) increased from $329 to $441. The rural representative staff continued to dominate the company, both in sheer numbers and in overall sales. Yet most of the sales increase came from city representatives, whose average sales grew from $446 in 1942, to $628 in 1943, and to $695 in 1944. District sales representatives earned substantially less, although they too experienced overall increases in their average sales, which went from $278 in 1942 to $459 in 1944. In 1944, representative average annual sales peaked at $548 and did not drop below $500 again until 1948. As Wayne Hicklin later explained, "We had those hard core [representatives.] [A]nybody we didn't want to work we let them go (and didn't try to replace them). When the war was over, we had this solid group and we took off."[51] While the male executives at Avon had created the city sales office, mounted a national ad campaign, and reduced the salesforce, the newly minted mid-level managers and the female-devised and driven sales meetings made it successful.

Several factors accounted for the steady increase in the productivity of representatives during the war, including an improved training program, longer tenure rates, and the morning sales meetings. Women with more than one year of experience as representatives had higher average sales than new appointments. In 1943, for the first and only time in Avon's history, women with one year or more of experience outnumbered the number of women appointed that year: of 31,000 representatives, 16,550 were Avon veterans, while 14,500 had worked less than the full year. Compare this to 1941, for example, when there were 27,000 new representatives on file, and only 16,000 representatives with more than one year of experience.[52] During the war, particularly between 1942 and 1945, more women stayed with the company for longer than one year than during any other period in Avon's history. The allure of industrial wartime work drained away many representatives, while others clearly found more potential and perhaps convenience in continuing door-to-door sales.

Longer term tenure correlated directly with higher average annual sales. Representatives with less than a year's experience earned substantially less than their more experienced counterparts. In 1943, nearly 73 percent of first-year representatives earned less than $250 in sales, 19 percent earned between $250 and $500, and fewer than 9 percent earned more than $500. Compare that to representatives on file one year or longer, among whom only 22 percent earned less than $250, while 36 percent earned between $250 and $500, and 42 percent earned more than $500. At the highest sales levels, less than 2 percent of new representatives earned more than $1,000 in 1943, but 12 percent of experienced representatives broke the $1,000 barrier. As the war ground on, the number of representatives earning more than $1,000 increased to 18 percent in 1944 and topped out at 21 percent in 1947.[53] Thus, the longer a representative worked with Avon, the more money she was likely to earn, and the longer Avon could keep a representative active, the more sales they could garner.

Avon decided to recruit fewer women into its sales ranks just as better paying industrial jobs opened for women during the war.[54] At the same time, women may have been discouraged from or unwilling to join direct selling, or may have quit very early. The comparatively sluggish sales of first year representatives probably stemmed from inexperience, and many women probably preferred to take on industrial work, which paid well right from the start, rather than spend time building a customer base. Those representatives who stayed on found customers easily, thanks to women's increased earnings and

Figure 5.1. "War Bond Girls," *Avon Outlook* June 1943. (Courtesy of Hagley Museum and Library.)

a popular culture that glamorized beauty and made color cosmetics more acceptable.

Cosmetics sales industrywide skyrocketed during the war. In these years, Avon's advertisements had featured the achievements of women pioneers in the fields of medicine, politics, reform, and domesticity. The ads were part of a patriotic effort that tied women's beauty into a larger social campaign to improve morale in the country at large and in the army. "Today everything possible is done so that women may readily join the armed services.

They are welcome because they are women, and as such, are lending love-liness and graciousness as well as courage and competence to each job they undertake," one 1945 advertisement said. "Avon's patriotic pledge is to pave the way to new loveliness, a loveliness that becomes an integral part of your charm."[55] Women were now asserting more independence, whether through war work or in "keeping the home fires burning." Avon executives discovered that they could give less attention to coddling and catering to the needs of new representatives.[56]

David McConnell Jr. had proven a very skillful manager. Under his tenure, sales doubled between 1937 and 1940, and overall they increased 350 percent, from $4.2 million in 1937 to $15.8 million in 1944. With more than 30 percent of Avon's production dedicated to filling military contracts in 1943 and 1944, Avon also earned significant income from the government.[57] It came at the cost of comparatively insignificant business that the lowest-performing individual representatives gener-ated. Although Avon executives could not have anticipated the war's sig-nificant impact on Avon's management and sales, they recognized that implementing the city sales plan and developing the new management hierarchy it required would take time. Furthermore, as 75 percent of Avon's representative sales continued to come from rural areas (before 1940), not all of the company's energy or resources could be dedicated to building city markets.

Then, in August 1944, David McConnell Jr. died suddenly of a heart attack at the age of forty-two. When John Ewald was appointed his successor, someone other than a McConnell assumed leadership of the company for the first time in its nearly sixty-year history. With the exception of bringing in outsiders for a brief time from the Fuller Brush Company, Avon executives had not sought assistance from other direct selling companies. Avon's managers knew they could not follow the examples of dominant cosmetics and toiletries retailers such as Revlon or Maybelline because they had no intention of converting to a "modern" mass-market, mass-distribution system. Instead, Avon managers (divisional and district) worked independently within their organization to create the territory plan and the accompanying programs that supported city sales and that reinforced the central tenets of Avon philosophy. They com-mitted to distributing their product via an army of more than 30,000 individual sales representatives who remained the sole outlet for Avon products.

Although World War II represents an important era in Avon's corporate history, it did not affect Avon's women or business in quite the same ways it did business and labor in the country overall. The representative sales force

Figure 5.2. "Honoring a Wave," Avon advertisement (1943). "Be Hostess to Loveliness" campaign and the "Medallion of Honor for Women of Achievement." During World War II, Avon created a patriotic and historical focus on women's contributions to American life. These three advertisements honored women in the American armed services. Each woman featured also received an award and recognition at Avon headquarters. (Courtesy of Hagley Museum and Library.)

did shrink by one-third, from 35,000 in 1940 to 26,000 in 1944, but there is no evidence to suggest it was because Avon experienced difficulty with new recruits. Rather, Avon consciously restricted recruiting in order to focus production efforts on filling military contracts. If anything, Avon was glad to let poor producers leave the company and made little attempt to replace them;

Figure 5.3. "In Praise of a Cadet Nurse," Avon advertisement (1945). (Courtesy of Hagley Museum and Library.)

as a result, it retained a serious and solid sales corps, as evidenced by door-to-door sales growth. The greatest impact of the war, then, was not on Avon's ability to recruit, but on its reduced desire to do so.

Similarly, women's presence within the corporation should not be exaggerated. Corporate expectations of managers and their work, more directly related to what it meant to be a "company man" than to what women might be capable of in business, restricted women's climb into the white male preserve of upper management. Overall, fewer than 1 percent of all Avon women

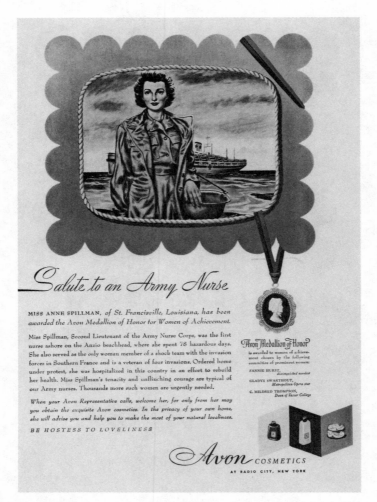

Figure 5.4. "Salute to an Army Nurse," Avon Advertisement (1945). (Courtesy of Hagley Museum and Library.)

worked as managers. In 1949, for example, there were 168 women city managers, approximately 500 assistant managers, and 300 rural district managers who together trained upward of 300,000 representatives.[58] Male managers continued the exclusive hold on corporate power, and rather than share it, consciously presented a representative's business as an even better business opportunity than being in management.

6

"Ding Dong! Avon Calling!"

Selling Women's Economic Personality in the Era of *The Feminine Mystique*

In 1952, business analyst Victor Buell authored a five-part series in *Fortune*, "Selling in Today's Economy." Part Two, "Help Wanted: Sales," reported on the "depreciation" of salesmanship and social status of the salesman in the United States, or as the accompanying illustration labeled him, "Salesman Americanus (Extinct)."[1] The art of personal selling, Buell concluded, had died. Interviews with executives, salesmen, and mothers revealed that the commissioned sales job no longer seemed desirable in the 1950s. Indeed, selling was downright distasteful for men, especially when compared to salaried managerial positions in large corporations. College-educated men had come to regard a sales career as unstable, Buell said, and lacking future potential. Moms agreed; *Fortune* polled a group who said that of the career choices presented to them, they hoped their sons would become "professionals." Their first preference: dentists. Store owners came in second, followed by teachers and then bank officers, while real estate men and insurance salesmen vied for last place. "Anything but selling!" one exclaimed. Mothers' reasons for shunning sales, the editors suggested, came from a "natural feminine distaste" for men working late and traveling far, combined with a belief that salesmen did not do "anything really worthwhile." Selling, they said, was not creative, and the income available through commissions, while conceivably higher than a salaried position in a corporation, paled in comparison to the security and stability a big company provided.

Business had also changed in the post–World War II era, *Fortune* editors explained, and sales no longer needed or relied on the personal relationships a salesman developed to market products. Indeed, the "art" of salesmanship of an older order, marked by persuasion and the ability to size up, react to, and manipulate the consumer, seemed quaint and vaguely pathetic in an age of advertising and mass merchandising. Only door-to-door selling clung to the old methods, but *Fortune* regarded it as an anomaly in the larger economic picture of decreasing sales and a changing merchandising strategy. "By every rule of scientific marketing, direct canvassing is so patently uneconomic that it has no place in the new era," *Fortune* concluded.[2]

Far from being economically untenable, however, door-to-door selling after World War II was about to hit its stride. Indeed, direct selling had entered a period of significant structural and ideological reorganization in the late 1940s and 1950s as new companies and management methods redefined the form and function of the industry.[3] The corpse of "Salesman Americanus" walked, but he was not his proverbial self: he had traded in his familiar guise—a hat, tie, and sample case—for high heels, lipstick, and a beauty showcase. The story of direct selling in the postwar era is the story of the feminization of the direct selling industry. Avon's long history gave it a powerful edge in the rapidly increasing postwar direct sales industry. Women came to dominate the industry sales force, and direct selling management, particularly in companies owned and/or managed by women, created strategies that recognized, mirrored, and exploited women's social networks.

Rebuilding after peace, both increasing the numbers of representatives and rededicating the company to door-to-door selling showed Avon to be a leader and innovator in both cosmetics and direct sales. Taking full advantage of the consumer boom at the end of the war and meeting the needs of thousands of women who lost their war industry jobs, Avon reemerged at the cutting edge of the postwar industry as a business leader for women. In 1947, it recruited the largest army of women representatives ever in company history and in the history of direct selling.[4] The growing suburban market, coupled with the conservative resurgence that forced women out of World War II factory production and into the service economy assured Avon's success in the postwar period.[5] Avon Products, Incorporated, and Avon Ladies destabilized the postwar stereotype of the white middle-class housewife and woman business owner even as they helped to construct it.

The demographics of direct sales representatives nationwide shifted radically in the postwar era. According to sociologist Nicole Biggart, before World War II, women represented less than 15 percent of all direct sales agents in the United States; by 1980, women represented more than 80 percent industrywide.[6] This transformation coincided with larger social and corporate developments in the postwar era: a jump in the number of college-educated men wearing gray flannel suits in white-collar positions, a growing suburban market, increasing family size, and a booming economic and manufacturing rate that outpaced demand. In the thirty years following the end of the war, the social status of sales jobs and salesmanship continued to decline for men, but skyrocketed for Avon women.

Throughout its history, Avon's strength lay in its ability to justify itself and re-create its image in response to the larger social and community environment, and for the most part Avon's leadership moved the company forward, at times even providing an example of how corporate America could adjust and make positive changes on certain social issues. The company's progress was uneven and markedly conservative, and Avon long downplayed, or at worst ignored, women's rights issues long before supporting them in any meaningful way. In the 1940s and 1950s, a woman who "owned" an Avon business participated in a unique entrepreneurial arena: Avon created an economic opportunity that assumed that women needed to combine business and home life. It targeted a huge pool of suburban consumers, newly redesigned and reorganized in convenient, prefabricated neighborhood blocks, staffed by women at home.[7] Here Avon recruiters found a ready and accessible market for new representatives, who in turn found consumers already lined up in neat little rows.[8] Straddling corporate and domestic interests, the Avon Lady would become an icon of white, suburban America, symbolizing both postwar feminine beauty ideals and feminized economic behavior. This positioning of Avon Ladies as both economic actors and domestic women challenged some of the internal contradictions of postwar domestic ideology that saw women passively ensconced in nuclear families, especially as it morphed into and through the civil rights era and the women's liberation movement of the 1970s.

The Avon image that the company presented in its national advertisements during the Cold War era continued to incorporate a general ambivalence about women's economic efficacy. The women who joined Avon in this period experienced an economic space outside the home. They attended weekly sales meetings where they met with other like-minded business women. They learned the basics of running a direct-sales business, managing their customers, planning for a financial future, and instructing women in beauty culture. At the same time, the vast majority of Avon representatives conducted their Avon business as a hobby. Like the women who came before them, they tended to restrict their customer base to a circle of familiar family, friends, and acquaintances, and they dropped in and out of sales activity based on seasonal needs or short-term goals. Female sales representatives found in selling Avon products a way to express their economic and social personalities within the domestic settings acceptable to postwar America.

Judging from those whose stories were highlighted in Avon publications, most relished the camaraderie and fun of the meetings, sales class, jubilees, and contests as emotional rewards on par with commissions. Hobby sales became a hard habit for the company to break.

As the 1950s morphed into the 1960s and 1970s, Avon also had to grapple with the changes that civil rights and women's liberation had on its internal corporate culture. Both movements shifted the priorities of Avon's executive staff, moving the company toward a more racially inclusive representative corps and making them more mindful about increasing the diversity of management and staff personnel, suppliers, advertisers, and consumers. The company achieved sound and measurable results through a careful and sincere effort in the 1970s to achieve the formal policy goals outlined in affirmative action by both the federal government and civil rights groups. However, Avon put much less effort into achieving parity for women in management, and the company's efforts to modernize representative recruitment and to re-envision representatives and consumers as full-time workers, as opposed to being full-time housewives, took decades longer than it should have given the company's identity as a company for women. Corporate paternalism, rooted firmly in the immediate postwar period, remained management philosophy well into the 1980s.

Postwar Conservatism: Championing Avon Men and Courting Little Mrs. Smith

Celebrating the company's sixtieth anniversary in 1946 at their annual management conference, the "men of Avon" raised their glasses to toast themselves, their company, and the 29,000 women who made their success possible. John Ewald, Avon's new president, extolled the virtues of Avon Ladies to a sea of men in white tuxedos before their dinner at the Waldorf Hotel and reminded his men of their obligations in helping women succeed in business. "The needs of the Representative should always be paramount," he said. "She is the very thing that gives you and me our bread and butter."[9] When Ewald assumed leadership of the company in 1945, Avon Products, Inc., was the largest direct sales company in the industry, by both sales and numbers of representatives. With Ewald at the helm, Avon reached its peak of power in the postwar period. The Avon sales force grew more than 600 percent during his fifteen-year tenure: from 26,000 representatives in

1945 to more than 162,000 in 1962. Sales, too, climbed an average of 17 percent each year, from $16 million to more than $242 million in those years. The company's success in the post–World War II period rested on three strategies: the development of a national advertising campaign, starting in magazines and moving into the classic "Ding Dong! Avon Calling!" television commercials that debuted in 1953; the continued development of city sales offices and penetration of suburban markets; and the standardization of sales management and consumer relations that finally made Avon a mass distributor serving a mass market. Under Ewald's leadership, Avon captured 5 percent of the cosmetics market overall and accounted for nearly 70 percent of cosmetics sales within the direct sales industry.[10]

Avon rode a wave of prosperity as the cosmetics market as a whole expanded at a quick pace in the postwar period. Leading companies such as Revlon and Max Factor targeted segmented markets and expanded their consumer base; they marketed to teenagers and college women (creating the Cover Girl brand of "clean makeup," for example), blacks, Latinos, and other ethnic groups. Some companies even renewed their interest in promoting men's products, such as the Elizabeth Arden for Men line.[11] Avon, however, remained steadfastly committed to a white, middle-class, married market. Maintaining its conservative strategy in marketing, Avon followed beauty trends just as it had in the early twentieth century rather than setting its own course.

Like most businesses following the declaration of peace in 1945, Avon did not immediately respond to the new business environment of the postwar period but instead reacted slowly to issues of labor, management, and marketing. Within three years of the end of the war, more than 170,000 women, some ousted from their jobs in the war industries sector, walked through Avon's doors looking for work. Avon recruited 42,000 new representatives in 1946 (14,000 more than in 1945), 53,000 in 1947, and nearly 74,000 in 1948. Still, sales and profits stagnated.[12] In his keynote address at the 1947 "Better Business" management conference, John Ewald emphasized two main challenges facing Avon's postwar leadership: maintaining discipline and enthusiasm within the management staff, and healing the "calloused attitude" Avon had developed toward representatives during the war.

Avon had reached a crossroads. It could continue on the path set during the war that made Avon a major manufacturer and supplier of cosmetics and toiletries, or it could return wholly to individual home sales. Despite the relaxed restrictions on packaging and shipping and the return of key personnel from war responsibilities, Avon had faced its least profitable year in 1946. The military contracts had brought in huge sums of cash, but with more than 50 percent of Avon's production going to fill military contracts in 1943 and 1944, attention to the comparatively minuscule business of individual representatives suffered. By 1945, the size of the sales staff had shrunk by one-third, from 35,000 in 1940 to 26,000 in 1944.[13] When McConnell Jr. died, the company was fast moving away from its history as a mass distributor and had started to build a new financial base as a mass producer. Avon's manufacturing plants supplied the products for its military contracts and through its parent company, Avon-Allied, produced soaps, perfumes, cosmetics, and skin care items on private contracts for companies such as Yardley of London, Prince Matchabelli, Maybelline, Colgate-Palmolive, Charles of the Ritz, Tussy, and Lyman's Limited, which made Chanel's "Irresistible" perfume.[14]

The relatively easy money of government and private brands contracts apparently had wooed Avon's managers, who no longer seemed interested in supporting the business of individual women. As Ewald said in his keynote address, he worried that the representative staff had become far less attractive to management as the company's main source of revenue. Indeed, in 1945, sales increased only 5 percent, the lowest gain in company history. "We are not kidding ourselves, fellows; you know what we did during the War," he said. "We did a lot of extravagant things. It was no secret ... [and] Uncle Sam was paying 90 percent. ... Today we need to ask ourselves if a lot of things are necessary or are they in the realm of wartime operations. ... Those days are over, and now business requires better management."[15] Ewald recognized that Avon's government contracts would not serve them during peacetime, and so he recommitted to marketing Avon brand of cosmetics.

To set the tone for his annual meeting recommendations to help get the company on track, Ewald fell back on a trope Avon executives would copy well into the twenty-first century—a retrospective look at the ideals and practices of the company's founder, David H. McConnell. Invoking McConnell's memory and the history of the California Perfume Company, Ewald suggested that they read the recently reprinted booklet "The Great Oak," "that great piece of philosophy that Mr. McConnell himself wrote."[16] McConnell's 1903 autobiographical history set a recognizable goal for a company that had its roots in "imagination, faith, hope, growth, [and] progress."[17] Avon in 1947 was more than five times the size of the CPC in 1903, and many challenges that the company faced in the postwar era, Ewald said, stemmed from the impersonal attitude Avon men had assumed as it grew larger. The challenges could not be glossed over.

Ewald based his plea to stem the tide of corporate impersonality in a postwar ideal of manhood. "Obviously, it is not my intention to strike a negative note at the beginning of a conference," he said. "But we are men and we have to speak from the shoulder." The first challenge of the corporation, he said, was to create a brotherhood among the management staff, to treat new men as worthy individuals. Following the war, many new faces appeared in Avon's buildings, men who did not know about Avon's heritage, as Ewald and Hicklin and Rooks did, who were tutored in the 1920s and '30s by McConnell himself. It was dangerous, he said, to hire a new man and assume that he would learn "the business" from others, that there was not time to spend training and teaching, that someone else would answer his questions, to pawn him off onto "typists and secretaries" who would explain the bonus plan and show him his work space. Instead, Ewald wanted his managers to talk to those new men, morning and night, ask them how they were doing. Recently he heard of a manager interviewing a young person for a higher position, and what he found was a person with eight year's experience who knew nothing about the business. "Eight years of experience out the window," he said.[18] "In the old days we could get people and they knew the business and stuck with it." Ewald wondered if Avon was still treating employees the way they did ten years ago, before the company had grown too large and size had become a deterrent to developing a family approach.[19]

Ewald taught his men, too, about Avon's heritage and highlighted the company's unique position as a marketer—as a company that held onto an older tradition of personalized service, smaller orders, and an emotional and charismatic approach to management. Seeing Avon's marketing and distribution system as female driven, Ewald insisted that the company continue its exclusive woman-to-woman sales method to build a competitive advantage in the cosmetics industry. His decision had strong implications for Avon's postwar management style. Avon men, as Ewald's words suggested, would measure their success by the sales of the representative staff. But Avon men were in a unique and frustrating position as managers: unlike traditional retailers who closely controlled the daily activities of their sales clerks, the independent contractor status placed Avon in a position from which managers would only cross their fingers and hope that women would work.[20]

Victor Buell, the *Fortune* writer who wrote the obituary for Salesman Americanus, was not far off in his analysis when he branded direct selling "patently uneconomic." Even at the strongest direct sales company in the industry, dissension in the Avon ranks forced Ewald to make strong pleas to keep the company's seventy-five-year commitment to individual sales and personalized service. The company's success from 1943 to 1945, Ewald suggested, had posed some serious problems and instituted some bad habits in the way managers thought of the representative staff. "I dare say that during November and December almost everyone in this room, if they didn't say it, had sort of a halfway idea, 'I wish those orders weren't so large, they take so much merchandise.'—'I wish there weren't so many letters to answer, they are all the same, they are all about complaints.'" But, Ewald warned his executives, "The needs of the Representatives must always be paramount." "She is everything," he said, "but during the War we got calloused—we tried to cut down Representatives. We tried, in a sense to say, 'Do not take any more business.' A year ago we cut our Sales Campaigns just so people would *not* sell, and it was all planned months ahead."[21] Managers in 1946, he said, still acted as if the war was on—when they could afford to let low-producing women go because they had retained a solid staff of full-time, high producers. As a short-term strategy it had worked, but it could not continue in peacetime without detrimental effects. "We are on the minus side right now because of the way we treated her," he warned.

Ewald urged his executives to think about what motivated women and about how to address women's needs. "Keep in mind for a few moments Avon's little Mrs. Smith," Ewald said. "Have a heart; engage her sympathies. Do we give consideration to that little Mrs. Smith that we should? . . . Fellows, it is a challenge to us, to our thinking, our planning, the execution of our daily work. Let's get back closer to the things that have really built this business—consideration, sympathy, understanding and feeling for our associates." As Ewald's words made clear, turning a profit with a system that relied on motivating women required a cultural mindset that deviated from now-standard corporate practices. "Keep in mind that little Mrs. Smith, who can be anywhere throughout this entire country, is depending on us—not just for service, but for a helping hand, for a kind word, for encouragement, and for leadership ability, which we hope you will get out of this Conference."[22] Teaching men "the business" meant teaching them how to treat "a Lady." Ewald's words highlighted the paternalistic relationship between Avon and the Avon Lady; conservative gender roles and the feminization of business practices were both paramount and necessary in Ewald's equation.

Courting "Little Mrs. Smith," the woman whom Wayne Hicklin called the "highest in caliber, appearance and sincerity of purpose" of any sales staff in the history of Avon, became a "science" at the company.[23] Norman Chadwick, Avon's general sales promotion manager, and Robert Feeley, Avon's advertising manager, set a trend for the postwar era, coordinating the sales programming—recruitment, training, and management—with national advertising. The Avon Lady of the late 1940s was younger than she had ever been. In 1950, Avon research had shown that 80 percent of representatives were between the ages of twenty-five and fifty-five, most of whom were twenty-five to thirty-five. However, Avon also found that the next largest subgroup, those between thirty-five and forty-five years of age, produced the highest sales and stayed with the company longer.[24] So while more women worked with Avon than at any time in history, sales did not rise at the same rate as the numbers of new recruits. The lag was not a function of representatives' age, however, but of tenure, a trend consistent with Avon's history, for the relationship between long tenure and higher sales, or in this case, short tenure and low sales, fed on itself. In 1949, for example, Avon recruited more than 74,000 new women to the sales force ranks, of whom 49,000 stayed for at least a year (the mortality rate of 61.6 percent had reached its highest point in company history); the average annual sales per representative fell to its lowest point since 1942, hitting only $433, down from $499 in 1947. [25]

According to an internal 1946 analysis, less than 70 percent of all "active" representatives sent in an order during a campaign. On average, they sold to fewer than one in ten homes in their territories, and individual customers ordered fewer than three items at each sale. The average sales per representative also diminished from the high levels of 1943 and 1944. Starting in 1946, Avon's executives learned that it was just as important to train consumers about how to buy and join Avon as it was to train representatives on how to sell it. However, a high turnover rate in both the representative staff and in city management positions meant that fewer women could rely on their firsthand experience with Avon. Whereas women like Lela Eastman and Louise Fogartie had sold Avon products and recruited Avon representatives for more than twenty years, most managers and assistants in the postwar era had only one or two years of experience with the company. Avon managers responded with more elaborate recruiting and sales materials, presented in a way that they believed "spoke to women's needs."

Feeley called his plan for pandering to "Little Mrs. Smith" and the representative staff "The Pink Ribbon Touch." It informed Avon's recruiting philosophy as well as its advertising and merchandising strategies, and was embedded in a system of rewards and incentives in which race, gender, and class continually occupied center stage of the workplace and work process. What Feeley intended was an attention to detail that spoke to women's desires, as he saw them, from developing products with pretty packaging, such as a lipstick sample case lined with red velvet, to creating sales incentives and prizes, such as jeweled service pins that symbolized representatives' success by placing them in diamond, ruby, pearl, and sapphire categories. In effect, the "Pink Ribbon Touch" packaged the Avon "opportunity" literature that managers used to sell the Avon business to both new recruits and longer term representatives and keep them active.

In order to stimulate more customer buying, Chadwick suggested that Avon focus on "pre-selling" the customer through advertising and offering more demonstration aids, such as catalogs, portfolios, lipstick sample kits, and perfume samples, to representatives. It led to a concentrated effort on sales training. Moreover, Avon tied its products to its commitment of old-fashioned, personalized service, which it advertised as heavily as it promoted the product lines. When a woman purchased Avon, she bought both the lipstick and the service of her representative. Given that most Avon representatives started as Avon consumers, marketing campaigns always targeted consumers as potential representatives.

By 1946, Avon had been producing national advertising campaigns for only ten years. In the postwar era the company shifted away from advertisements touting women's patriotism. They would instead develop long-standing advertising themes about women and business and highlight the desirability of hygiene, glamour, and beauty in its product promotion. In the late 1940s, Avon featured advertisements, produced and coordinated by the Monroe Dreher advertising firm in New York City located two floors below Avon headquarters in Rockefeller Plaza, that focused on the product itself—a lipstick, rouge, or nail polish, for example—placed in an artistic, hand-drawn motif. Glamorous leggy models lent an aura of class. Virginal wasp-waisted brides "Sparkling Enchantment" waited their turn, smelling sweetly of Avon's White Moiré perfume, to "Be hostess to loveliness!" as each ad in *Vogue, McCall's, Good Housekeeping, Ladies Home Journal,* and *Cosmopolitan* urged.[26]

Soon, the advertising agenda also reflected the "pink ribbon" strategy to support and inspire representatives. Avon and Dreher designed monthly spots that gave more attention to the service of the Avon Lady. Little Mrs.

Smith, Avon executives said, needed to see how advertising would "help" build her business. In 1949, Avon sponsored a new campaign featuring celebrity endorsements. Movie and theater stars, such as Irene Dunn, Loretta Young, and Claudette Colbert, were used to enhance Avon's "quality" image and promote Avon's distinctive, personalized selling method. Other "high society" women also adorned the ads. Mrs. Byron Harvey Jr., "gracious and charming leader of Chicago society," claimed "I fell in love with Avon's creams . . . when the Avon Representative called at my home in Chicago." Mrs. Harvey appreciated the "capable, courteous advice" of her Avon representative: "Welcome her when she calls at *your* home." Every ad included an inset of each celebrity purchasing Avon products from her local Avon representative.[27]

The advertisements soon became incentives for top producers. Representatives who were lucky enough to serve a celebrity also appeared in the national campaign. Specific products or product lines were accompanied by images of selling situations—usually an Avon representative and a customer in a home-selling situation. When Claudette Colbert promoted Avon lipsticks, her representative, Mrs. Nelle Ginthner, appeared in an inset, seated in Colbert's parlor, holding out a powder puff sample over a coffee table arrayed with lipsticks, fragrance jars, lotions, and a gift set. All advertisements featured Avon's skin care and glamour products and highlighted the convenience and ease of shopping in the privacy of one's own home. Mrs. Ginthner, a white woman of stout bearing and a head of gray curls, likely resembled the vast majority of Avon Ladies; by the 1950s, mature representatives would appear only in in-house publications, while younger models became the face of Avon in national ads. Markedly, no person of color was included in their advertising. Avon was strictly white women selling to other white women.

In 1951, Dreher began work on the company's first television commercial. It ran for one full minute and dramatized the service call at a private home. One of Dreher's models, dressed in a conservative gray suit with gloves and a hat, festooned with one long feather, rang a doorbell, introduced herself and asked to step inside. Then, seated in a parlor and directly facing the camera, she explained the purpose of her visit, demonstrated two products, asked for an order, and thanked the customer. Although it is not clear whether this exact commercial ever aired, its function carried over into the advertising campaign that featured the two-chime doorbell and the slogan "Avon Calling!" The television commercials taught consumers about the Avon Lady, what she would say and do when she came to the house, how she took

Figure 6.1. "I think Avon lipsticks are sensational!" Actress Claudette Colbert featured here alongside her Avon Representative, Mrs. Nelle Ginther (1951). (Courtesy of Hagley Museum and Library.)

an order, and when it would be delivered. In the third television commercial, Avon used its time to recruit women to the company. The products appeared as props while the "business opportunity" occupied center stage. It was perhaps the first time that women's entrepreneurship and independent business ownership appeared on television as part of a mass-marketing campaign, recasting women's solitary domestic image. Dreher replaced the original

Figure 6.2. "The Right Lipstick" featuring Ann Sothern and her Avon Representative Mrs. Claire Mathews (1952). (Courtesy of Hagley Museum and Library.)

model in the pilot commercial, who also appeared in the "story book" for Avon recruitment, with model Connie Johannes who played the Avon Lady in both television and print advertisements for the next twenty years. The Ding Dong! Avon Calling! commercials were so successful they became an icon of American consumerism. For an entire generation of Americans, the two-chime doorbell remains the signature impression of Avon.

Figure 6.3. "I Am Your Avon Representative" fragrance advertisement featuring Avon model Connie Johannes as sales representative (1959). (Courtesy of Hagley Museum and Library.)

After 1953, Avon's national print advertising campaigns focused on two themes—representative service and beauty products—and all used models as Avon Ladies, creating a uniform image of the company that on average was much younger than its actual representatives. Recruiting ads targeted potential Avon representatives by highlighting "career" aspirations as opposed to a "work" opportunity, independence, skill, femininity, and privilege. The 1953 "Career for Women" series featured four ads, where model Connie

Johannes appeared in a sharp suit, coordinating accessories, gloves, hat, and sample case. Ads highlighted the rewards for selling Avon as "pleasant and profitable." Avon Ladies worked in welcoming neighborhoods where women were literally waiting for her to call. Social rewards often out-classed financial rewards—reinforcing the idea that women would work for emotional satisfaction even more than for money.

Figure 6.4. This "I bring beauty wherever I go," (1953) advertisement featured the Avon representative in a suburban neighborhood. (Courtesy of Hagley Museum and Library.)

Similarly, ads targeting customers in the "I Bring Beauty Wherever I Go" campaign were designed to both instruct women on what to expect during an Avon Lady's call and to reassure them that the Avon Lady was a trustworthy and ladylike carrier of products. Countering any stereotype of pushy or aggressive salesmen, the Avon Lady in these ads spoke in submissive language. "I have the privilege," the ad began, "of bringing Avon's fine cosmetics and toiletries directly to you in your home." The sample case she carried "permits me" to show "luxuriously soothing and softening creams and lotions." "I am happy to help you make all your cosmetic and toiletry selection in the quiet of your living room," the ad concludes. "I will call on you," the final line in the ad copy, stands out as the most assertive promise that Avon made.

The image of the Avon Lady in the 1950s embodied a feminine business personality, classy and deferential, seeking emotional rather than independent financial reward. Self-fulfillment, therefore, worked in both directions. Ads presented direct sales as an economic venue for women helping women, either by suggesting colors and skin care treatments to help them look beautiful or by supporting women's entrepreneurship through the support of a neighborhood business owner. Women who viewed the ads could see themselves as a consumer of Avon, and some women, the company hoped, would choose to become part of Avon by signing on as representatives.

"I Bring Beauty Wherever I Go"

With expanded national advertising campaigns, Avon wanted their representatives to be experts in beauty and cosmetics and offered new representatives an optional nine-week training course to learn the basics of skin care and color cosmetics. An investment in training materials, Avon promised, would build each representative's expertise and was part and parcel of owning a business. In 1954, Avon sold its beauty book, *Beauty Counselor*, to representatives for $5 to use along with product samples in sales calls. It featured detailed descriptions of all the products, instructions on how to use them, what each item felt and smelled like, and how they would improve customers' hair, skin, and appearance. *Beauty Counselor*, compiled by Products Director Irene Nunemaker, sought to improve representatives' knowledge about beauty and skin care products and their use. "Your success in selling Avon is dependent to quite a great extent on how well you know the products

APPEARING JUNE 20, 1953, THIS IS THE SECOND OF A SERIES OF RECRUITMENT ADVERTISEMENTS TO RUN IN THE CHRISTIAN SCIENCE MONITOR TWICE A MONTH. ONCE A MONTH A 1,000-LINE AVON ADVERTISEMENT, DIRECTED TO CUSTOMERS, ALSO APPEARS IN THIS PUBLICATION.

Figure 6.5. "A Career for Women" recruiting advertisement ran alongside Avon's product ads in magazines such as *Christian Science Monitor* (1953). (Courtesy of Hagley Museum and Library.)

you offer," Nunemaker said. "When you can truly help the people you call on—when they get full value in product satisfaction from every dollar they spend with you—then you can build a fine-paying career for yourself." The *Counselor* promised to make every Representative an "expert advisor," and by sharing the advice, "your business will grow."[28]

The bulk of Avon's beauty advice was directed at white women over the age of twenty-five. The first fifty pages of the book featured step-by-step instructions on everything from washing the face and shampooing hair to applying lipstick, eye shadow, mascara, and foundation makeup. Each stage was accompanied by several photographs of young models performing the steps to illustrate proper use of products. Good skin care was a "fundamental" part of living, Avon suggested, and something about which everyone was "extremely interested." "This is a fact because the urge to be well groomed is felt more and more for reasons that include business, success, and happy social and family relations." Lipstick and makeup, it claimed, were "sheer delights" to a woman because "they make her beautiful and lift her spirits high as the sky."[29]

At a time when the cosmetics industry's awareness of a huge new teenage market grew, Avon devoted just two pages to the "Teen-agers' Beauty Care," featuring just a five-step beauty routine consisting of a daily bath, the use of deodorant, pushed back cuticles, clean teeth, and help for blemished skin. "She keeps her make up simple, a light film of Avon Cake Make-Up and a touch of lipstick," is all *Beauty Counselor* recommended for teen girls. Special attention, it said, should be paid to using soap and water to "penetrate sufficiently the oily film on the skin." And it advised using deodorant after every bath, because "under-arm odor can ruin a teen's chances of having friends, being liked and being happy."[30]

Two more pages were devoted to men's grooming products, including the use of "Dr. Zabrieskie's Soap" for skin blemishes, and after-shave lotion. Men could also "take pride in the appearance of their hands" with the use of Avon's Hand Cream and Cuticle Softener. And for men's hair, *Beauty Counselor* recommended "weekly shampoos, daily brushes and scalp massage, diet with fruit and vegetables, covering the head when taking a shower, and dry cleaning the insides of their hats." *Beauty Counselor* noted no specific advice for teenage boys other than suggesting that boys who were just beginning to dress their hair preferred Avon Cream Hair Lotion. Sadly, Avon issued no dire warnings about social stigmas borne by teen-aged boys who did not wear deodorant.[31]

Despite the best efforts to make representatives experts in beauty and the application of cosmetics, most representatives retained limited knowledge of Avon products. In 1958, the company's new cosmetics and beauty counselor, Patricia Neighbors, noted the serious disconnect between Avon's vision of what its representatives offered customers and what representatives actually did. "It's amazing," she wrote, "how many representatives do not know how to use makeup and don't use cosmetics except lipstick."[32] With a tone of half-frustration, Neighbors reminded managers that they should urge representatives to invest in training guides and color charts in order to stay current with new products and trends. "This is an important part of training Representatives to sell," she told her sales managers. "After all, they are in the beauty business and customers expect them to be experts in make-up."[33] The gap between what Avon wanted its representatives to act like as business women, what customers expected of Avon representatives as cosmetics experts, and what Avon representatives actually did continued to vex the company throughout the twentieth century.

"The Doorway of Opportunity"

In the 1950s and 1960s, Avon continued to hew a conservative line about gender roles. Despite the language of independence, Avon always envisioned women in stable nuclear families. A woman's power, Avon literature suggested, rested in both her connection to her family and her ability to earn money. That Avon's managers chose to tie up their opportunity with pink ribbons hid the fact that Little Mrs. Smith's respectability in business rested on the support of Mr. Smith, the curiously ubiquitous yet absent partner. Her Avon earnings contributed to the family's needs but would only supplement, not replace, his income. Sometimes Avon said women could "earn a living"; more often, though, they simply said "earn money." Money was a dream; "a living" would have been a delusion. While in the company's advertisements Avon women seemed in charge of their households, even the highest level of earnings projected in recruiting literature would have never provided enough resources to support a home and family on their own. In the sample earnings chart of the recruiting book, Avon estimated that each customer gave a $1 order. If a representative made just six sales calls a day (the lowest figure on the chart) and worked five days a week ($30 in sales) she could keep $12 as commission. Based on the highest projection, with fifteen sales calls a day or $75 dollars in sales, a representative could keep $30 in weekly commissions. If a discerning recruit were to ask how much Avon Ladies made, she would have been told that there was no way to extrapolate such information, that each individual reaped as much as they sowed. In this way, the opportunity was "limitless" and achieved entirely at the discretion of each woman.

The 1952 recruiting book, "The Story of Avon," presented the business-owner with a consumer theme: "Avon offers you Money to buy the things you want." The accompanying illustrations suggested a wide array of consumer "dreams" women might have: a modern kitchen, education, a new car, a new home, clothing, furniture, and a stock of bills stamped "paid." The work was always touted in literature as "pleasant," "helpful," and useful to the community; the language of women's self-sufficiency and independence also appeared in recruiting talks. The corporate message emphasized that women's character was never sullied by an Avon business: "Using a friendly greeting, call at every home and present a FREE sample. And then, by just being your normal, friendly self, you make the acquaintance of the prospect and proceed to introduce your Catalog and Demonstration Goods."[34] Whenever "The Story of Avon" book pictured money, only perfectly manicured hands handled oversized $1, $5, and $10 bills, while coins often floated in the air. The dreamlike aura of an Avon business lent a Cinderella-like quality to women's lives; "The Avon opportunity makes it possible for a woman to earn as much as she wishes," it said.[35]

Women, Avon attested, were both bound to their families and homes, *and* free to develop individual businesses. Ironically, while images of family pervaded Avon literature, husbands never appeared in the text or the illustrations of recruiting and training pamphlets. Visual images featured Avon representatives with other women, usually a female customer, although occasionally women appeared as co-workers, too. Representatives lived in single-family houses where small smiling children watched as mom filled in order sheets and balanced her checkbook. Daughters always appeared older than their brothers—the promise of girls' initiative and power illustrated in height, at least, unprotected by and not needing the strength of their male siblings.[36]

Through Avon, women received encouragement, motivation, and an invitation to join an economic organization that went out of its way to provide a therapeutic alternative to their contained suburban world, where words like money, earnings, work, ownership, possessions, power, and management rarely entered their vocabulary. Rather than engage women in a discussion about economic rights, Avon portrayed the Avon opportunity as one where women realized freedom through consumption.[37] Women at Avon, however, were not merely pawns of the corporation nor victim to its pie-in-the-sky predictions. In fact, Avon's legal power to define and direct the representatives' work remained tenuous at best. Avon Ladies, working under the cloak of independence—whether real or imagined—also set personal business goals, and in their daily business transactions they operated under a wholly different business structure centered in their homes and neighborhoods.

Figure 6.6. "Out to Win," *Avon Outlook* (1954). As the Avon Representative steps onto the corner of Prize Avenue and Earning Street, she turns to wave goodbye to her daughters before beginning her day. (Courtesy of Hagley Museum and Library.)

While some women did earn a decent annual income on Avon sales, the opportunity was not in fact "unlimited." Earning on a straight commission, a woman was bound by the amount of time she could work. Avon compensated its representatives only in direct proportion to their sales results, so even working full time and at maximum efficiency women were hard pressed to earn a decent, independent living from personal selling. Flat-rate commission structures, which most direct sales company offered before the widespread adoption of multi-level marketing in the 1970s, severely limited how much an Avon woman could make. In truth, an average representative's annual sales (approximately $450 per representative) was barely half of the lowest earnings projection in the recruiting manual. Furthermore, the costs of operating an Avon business, including samples and office supplies, and gas for a private automobile, came directly from the representative's pocket. At a very quick pace, a representative could make four sales calls an hour, and even if she took a $3 order from each customer, she would still earn less than $200 a week before expenses. Women's "potential for success" was unlimited primarily in Avon literature and achieved by only a tiny percentage of representatives. Most women found instead that the potential for failure was more likely.

Given the independent nature of direct selling, Avon Ladies found a wide variety of ways to use the economic and social opportunities the company made available to them. Avon promised commissions, which served as financial rewards, and neighborhood leadership and fellowship, which served as social and emotional rewards. Avon used the Monday morning sales meetings, for example, as a space to train women in their business, but women also used it as a social space where they exchanged advice on how to earn money, build larger orders, and manage their families to free up more time for selling. Years before feminist author Betty Friedan published *The Feminine Mystique*, an exposé of the white suburban housewife, Avon's regional managers spoke openly about using the feminine mystique to their

Figure 6.7. "The Story of Avon," Sales Representative Training Guide (1959). Beautiful manicured hands held the money earned by selling Avon. (Courtesy of Hagley Museum and Library.)

advantage. According to historian Lindsey Feitz, Avon advised its regional managers to present direct selling as a "possible cure for housewives who might be bored, a condition that a psychologist in one article cited as 'one of the most destructive of our emotional states.'"[38] Editors of *Direct Line*, Avon's monthly newsletter for city sales managers, also reminded women that "anything that influences your emotions helps counteract boredom," including "recognition, praise, rewards, a goal, bonuses, changes in environment, deadlines, and social strivings."[39] In the June 1957 newsletter, editors had reassured Avon sales managers and recruiters that busy and organized mothers already embodied the characteristics of a successful representative. As another manager noted, "give a busy woman a job and she'll do it well."[40] In other words, working as sales representatives could actually make women happier.

Representative Dorothy Mizer's might have agreed. Her poem, printed in *Avon Essence* magazine in 1964, breezily disregarded the toll that her Avon-generated happiness took on her husband and highlighted the social and emotional benefits of business. Her desire for money and prizes fueled the small steps Mizer took toward liberation; developing a busy Avon business meant that she would leave her husband to fend for himself if he needed clean dishes, ironed clothes, groceries, and supper.

> "The Avon Lady"
>
> The house is full of Avon.
> The clutter makes me sick.
> But then I'm making money,
> And that's what makes me tick
>
> The dishes aren't washed dear,
> There's ironing to be done.
> But I'm the Avon Lady,
> I'm having lots of fun.
>
> Go raid the ice box, honey,
> I've deliveries to be made,
> Until I get them done, my pet,
> You know I'll not get paid.

Flip the dust mop for me—
I must be on the run,
'Cause I'm an Avon Lady
And there's so much to be done.

The prizes are fantastic,
I must have some of those.
You'll have to wash and iron, dear,
Because you need fresh clothes.

When I'm too old for hurrying,
I'll sit and reminisce
About the Avon friends I've made
and the visits I will miss.

I'll smell again those lovely smells,
Dream the pleasures that each sends,
But what I'll most recall, I'm sure,
Will be my many, many friends.[41]

The domestic ideology of the 1950s that Avon's advertising and promotional literature espoused was part and parcel of a larger trend to place women in nuclear families, secure their energy in care of children, home, and domestic work. Historian Elaine Tyler May called the efforts to contain white women's ambition and vision into the nuclear home a domestic version of Cold War social containment and conformity. The cost to women was a loss of personal independence, job loss, and financial insecurity. But the effort, fueled by images in popular culture, the advice of psychologists and self-help specialists, and the direction of child care advisors, was not monolithic. Women in the postwar years witnessed more than a straightforward retrenchment back into a mythical past. Mass media supported a variety of conflicting messages about women and the nuclear family. Many women, obviously, did not fit the mold of the white, middle-class, married, and suburban stereotype. "Neither wholly domestic nor quiescent," historian Joanne Meyerowitz writes, working-class women, black women, and various radical groups all posed significant challenges to the dominant, white, suburban gender ideal. Women in politics, labor, the arts, and civil rights worked to resist the power of postwar cultural constraints.[42]

Avon women, too, were part of this fractured landscape. On the surface, the Avon message was steeped in conservative domestic principles, but it also highlighted contradictions within postwar gender ideology. Avon talked about women as business owners and participants, not just as consumers, and the company justified women's place in the business world, not as support staff but as entrepreneurial and independent actors. Furthermore, Avon literature promoted, without sarcasm or apology, women's managerial skills and economic potential. Its message did not exist within a vacuum, of course, and within recruiting books and sales manuals Avon drew heavily on domestic ideology that positioned women as subjects of patriarchal control. While not projecting exactly a feminist message, Avon was also neither anti-feminist nor anti-elitist.

"The Better Way"

In 1960 Avon stood as a leader in both the cosmetics and direct sales industry. The company had gone public in 1947, selling shares on the New York Stock Exchange. A 1960 stock valuation report by the firm McDonnel and Company (not to be confused with McConnell) valued Avon as a $170-million-dollar business, characterized by a substantial portion of repeat sales and an "unusual resistance to general economic slumps." It forecast strong growth "at a rapid pace of 20%" predicated on Avon's "continuous program of new product development and backstopped by diligent sales recruiting, advertising, and promotion campaigns." According to McDonnel and Company, every single American home represented Avon's potential market, "a vast unsaturated area for house to house selling."[43] Citing industry statistics from the Toilet Goods Association, house-to-house sales of cosmetics was increasing. In 1950, such sales accounted for just 14 percent of all cosmetics sales; in 1959 it was 20 percent. At the same time, sales in chain stores and department stores decreased; cosmetics sales in chain stores fell from 37 percent in 1950 to 27 percent in 1959, and sales in department stores fell from 27 percent to 18 percent in those years. The report also noted a sharp increase in cosmetics sales at food stores, which accounted for just 6 percent of sales in 1950, and 23 percent of sales in 1959. The valuators remained positive about direct selling because they believed the nature of the product was better suited to the personalized service of Avon's "lady sales reps."

The average representative in 1961, Avon said, was thirty-seven years old, married, and raising two children. She was also white. That the company had always created and worked within a white, middle-class ideal was reinforced again in a marketing analysis case study by the Harvard Business School (HBS). "Avon attempted to select women who 'wore well,'" it said, "as opposed to aggressive 'high powered types.' All representatives had to live in or close to their territories and preferably their husbands owned their own homes. Personal appearance, an impression of judgment and maturity, and time available for working were the main criteria for selection."[44] Home ownership was a key indicator of white, middle-class status, which Avon assumed of both its sales staff and its customers.[45]

Lured by the belief that the company could continue to grow by increasing market saturation, the New Jersey–based stock valuation assessment firm, McDonnell and Company, forecast a new and expanded level of growth for Avon in the decade ahead. This was based on the natural increase in its market in both scale—the sheer number of representatives and customers—and the increasing number of different products it offered for sale. The "sales representative[s] occupy the apex of the pyramid," the report explained. "As one retires, usually a customer assumes the job and adds her circle of acquaintances to the pool of customers. And so the circle ever broadens, producing an acceleration after an extended period of relatively slow growth." The report identified several unusual features and opportunities in Avon's philosophy that accounted for its popularity even in a sea of big brand names. Victor Buell had called direct selling "uneconomic" in 1952; McDonnell and Company on the other hand explained how Avon's counterintuitive methods resulted in stronger repeat sales. Far from encouraging high pressure, high volume sales, Avon expected its representatives to strive for relatively small orders. "A modest order of a few dollars in a three-week period was preferable, because the sales approach was aimed at building an Avon image of low-pressure friendly expertise" where representatives made personalized suggestions in the privacy of the customer's "own living room and free from the distraction of competing products." Avon's strategy focused on getting representatives to spend more time selling. Most of Avon's 165,000 saleswomen in 1963 spent two to four hours a day on sales, serving about thirty-five regular customers who purchased from this representative on nearly every call. The company estimated that another fifteen customers might purchase sporadically, six to eight times a year. "A woman who worked effectively for 15 hours a week could expect to make about $1,500 a year, give or take $300."[46]

Avon increased its market share in direct proportion to the growth of its sales staff. And it owned the house-to-house market; its closest competitors, Beauty Counselors, Stanley Home Products, and Fuller Brush, together were less than a quarter the size of Avon. A 1960 survey in *Redbook* magazine showed that among women who purchased cosmetics from direct sales companies, 80 percent purchased from Avon. Profitability rested in cultivating the goodwill from personal relationships between representatives and customers where most of Avon's commercial clout was generated. "In contrast to standard retail and wholesale margins of 40 percent and 10 percent respectively, that were prevalent in the cosmetic field," the HBS case study explained, "Avon paid a 40% commission. Further, in contrast to the usual advertising expenditure of 15% and 20% of sales, Avon spent 3% of sales."[47]

Avon also expanded its product line and developed continually changing sales campaigns. The frequent addition of new products was well received "because one thing a woman never accepts is the status quo of how she looks." Some estimate that the company developed more than 1,000 new products a year, complete with new copy in the campaign sales books and specialized national advertising.[48] In 1962, Avon introduced its first line of Skin-So-Soft products—a line of skin care products that later developed a cult following as a bug repellent—and in 1963, Avon's packaging again became a focus with its storied line of decorative perfume decanters. These distinctive novelty glass decanters included various sized and colored bottles with stoppers and a large array of figurines that changed from campaign to campaign.[49]

Then, in 1969, Avon quietly introduced its "Better Way" sales campaign structure, replacing the old three-week sales cycles with a new one every two weeks. With little fanfare from the company and no input in the matter, representatives were told to canvass their territories every two weeks rather than three. The shorter sales cycle would provide representatives with "greater sales and earnings opportunities," the company said. But essentially, the "Better Way" was a work speed-up for representatives. Predictably, sales volume increased, but still Avon took few risks on other new markets. Teenagers, the drivers of advertising, mass media, and music in the 1950s and 1960s, would only be acknowledged as a special market by Avon in the 1970s. Avon placed some ads in *Seventeen* in the 1950s and instituted a "Teenage Good Grooming" educational campaign in schools in 1962, but it did not create independent product lines until a decade later.[50]

Never ahead of the curve of marketing trends and seemingly immune to the radical social changes happening in the world around them, Avon's executives prided themselves on their old-fashioned approach to business. Significantly, an entire generation of corporate leadership retired in the 1960s. John Ewald, president of Avon since 1944, stepped down and was named chairman of the board in 1961. His thirty-five-year career at Avon had started in the mailroom in Kansas City. He had taken the helm as Avon's first non-family CEO following the sudden death of David McConnell Jr. in 1944, opened city and suburban markets following World War II, rang the bell at the New York Stock Exchange when Avon opened as a publicly traded company in 1946, and oversaw the "Ding Dong! Avon Calling!" television advertising campaign in the 1950s. During the first seventy-five years of the company's history, only three men had held the reins, but in the ten years following Ewald's retirement, four more executives, three of whom began their careers with the company in the 1930s and '40s, took brief turns in the president's chair. Russell Rooks, Wayne Hicklin, Free Fusee, and David Mitchell continued new television advertising campaigns in the "Ding Dong! Avon Calling!" story-line but neglected to change anything about the company's recruitment strategy or sales management program.

Top leadership in the 1960s needed help to see beyond the strategies that had brought the company so far. For example, as Avon's popularity and presence grew nationwide, especially given aggressive marketing campaigns in magazines and on television, the direct sales method presented an obvious limitation for consumers: the products were available only by representatives, and if a potential customer did not know an "Avon Lady," she had to first write to Avon for a contact. Avon's marketers had always known of this bottleneck problem, and managers often discussed the advantages and disadvantages of making Avon available in retail venues. But when the company received more inquiries than usual about finding a shade of lipstick featured in a *Vogue* ad in April 1962, the company sought the advice of the Harvard Business School in analyzing what could be done to fill unsolicited orders more efficiently. Unfortunately, their new strategies missed the mark.

Analysis showed that the average representative sold to thirty-six to forty-two customers per campaign, so in the quest to place more representatives on more doorsteps, Avon piloted the "Hidden Customer" campaign in 1967.[51] Avon mailed flyers to potential new customers in representatives' territories telling them that they would get free merchandise when their Avon Lady called. The program showed interesting results. "Low performing" representatives liked the program, presumably because it introduced them to new customers in their territories. Cold calling, or approaching strangers, remains one of the most distasteful and terrifying aspects of sales, and the advance flyer offered representatives at least a nominal introduction to new customers. The Avon analysis of Hidden Customer, however, offered no testimonials from representatives who liked the program; instead, the analysis focused on the "high performing" representatives who strongly objected to it. "The people I would normally not call on are a few who will not use Avon and are very rude and hostile or buy from other Avon Reps at their jobs and do not want to be bothered at home and have told me so," one representative noted. Another said, "I do not like this Hidden Customer campaign because I feel it puts undue pressure on you and I don't like calling on houses who have told you very strongly they do not want to be called on."[52] Another noted a visceral response from an angry customer. "My hidden customer hates Avon with a passion. She was very insulting to me," she wrote. "I feel I cover my territory very well and those who do not like or want Avon I do not bother." Another representative said she didn't like the program "because I had more doors slammed in my face than I care to ever have again." Highlighting the personalized service that made Avon popular, another representative lamented that the Hidden Customer program mailings degraded Avon's reputation. "We all receive some of this sort of advertising every day and most of it doesn't leave the Post Office," she wrote. "Why put Avon in this class?"[53]

Another problem Avon could not solve lay in the limitations of large city markets. "The problems of representative turnover and marginal production were viewed by company officials as particularly acute in urban areas," the marketing report noted, "having a large number of apartment dwellings." Representatives complained that they had trouble accessing apartment houses monitored by doormen or with locked doors at street level. They also found intimidating the "relative impersonality of the [apartment] dwellers as opposed to the atmosphere in the suburbs, and the uncertainty as to who would be answering the door." Significantly, Avon reported that representatives were frustrated by "the high frequency of night call-backs required because many women who lived in apartments held day-time jobs."[54] Representatives who found that friends and neighbors were unlikely to buy quit soonest, and on average about 45 percent of representatives were new, hired within the year, leaving managers to spend most of their time on recruiting and training. Tellingly, Avon could not figure out how to meet the needs of either representatives or customers who worked outside the home and so, for the most part, it didn't try.

Still, sales and revenue remained strong at Avon thanks in no small part to the international business it had built in the postwar era. An analysis of the full scale and character of Avon's international operations is covered by other historians. In short, Avon had first reached across the shores to Cuba in 1954, exporting wholesale the company sales pitches, recruiting strategies, advertising, and product line-up. Within fifteen years Avon had expanded into more than sixteen countries and, thanks to its success on the world stage—including operations in Puerto Rico, Venezuela, Mexico, Brazil, the United Kingdom, Germany, Italy, Spain, and France—Avon's sales topped more than $1 billion through the work of more than 600,000 representatives worldwide in 1972.[55]

Civil Rights and Women's Liberation: Avon's Slow Corporate Makeover

Clearly, Avon's leadership decided the best way for Avon to grow domestically was to continue doing exactly what it had always done. When measured by sales, corporate profits, and the increasing numbers of representatives worldwide, the strategy worked, even though major developments in the 1960s and 1970s—the civil rights movement, the feminist movement, and innovations in multi-level marketing from within the direct sales business world—all challenged Avon's business philosophy. Avon actually embraced the goals of the civil rights movement and government support of affirmative action programs, which came along at the same time that Avon had dedicated itself to writing a corporate responsibility plan. But feminism, ironically, seemed to be a non-event at both the corporate and marketing level in the 1970s. Avon had, perhaps, counted too much on its identity as "a woman's company" to believe it would need to defend or adjust its practices. The company would not make significant changes either in how it viewed potential representatives or the way it pitched its earnings opportunities until the 1980s. The third challenge came from within the industry; the explosion in the number of new direct sales companies, most of which used multi-level marketing formulas for recruitment and selling. While often likened to pyramids, multi-level marketing is (usually) not illegal but allows for exponential expansion of representatives' potential earnings. Multi-level

marketing describes those companies that encourage their sales representatives to recruit more representatives—called a down-line—and reward
them with percentages of their down-lines sales. Some of the more famous
multi-level marketing companies (MLMs) formed in the 1960s, such as
Amway and Mary Kay, were characterized by enthusiastic and evangelical
sales meetings, and they offered representatives dramatic earnings potentials
beyond dual marketing companies like Avon that paid a recruit commissions
based solely on their personal sales. While thousands of new multi-level
marketing companies developed in the 1960s and 1970s, Avon executives
took the lead in writing a voluntary code of ethics to regulate member companies of the Direct Selling Association. Feeling secure in its position as a
dual-marketing system, Avon ignored the implications presented by the
popular new multi-level marketing organizations in the 1970s which offered
recruits the potential for exponentially higher commissions. Avon eventually
adopted a more-forward looking language that combined liberal feminism
and business, but otherwise simply discounted the recruiting competition
presented by Mary Kay Cosmetics. They believed Avon spoke to a different
market from the one Mary Kay addressed, and Mary Kay was not to be taken
seriously. Avon acted as if the two companies existed as separate industries.
However, each of the three challenges in the 1970s did affect Avon's policies
for managing its staff and representative corps.

David Mitchell, who became president of Avon in 1972, made stronger but
reluctant steps to modernize policies and personnel by addressing two key
areas: consumer rights and civil rights. In 1972, Avon boasted nearly 300,000
US sales representatives. It was an established industry titan and assumed
leadership in the Direct Selling Association, the trade group formed at the
turn of the twentieth century for securing the reputation of direct selling.

Consumer rights legislation, including product safety requirements and
truth in advertising, were enforced by the Consumer Protection Agency and
the Federal Trade Commission. Avon had already begun addressing issues
related to representative sales contracts when vice president of sales and
marketing, James Preston, helped draft the Direct Selling Association (DSA)
Ethical Code of Conduct in 1970. While corporate membership in the Direct
Selling Association and adherence to the code was purely voluntary, Avon
recognized the public relations value of supporting it during the Nixon administration. Designed to protect consumers, the code called for a twenty-
four-hour cooling off period on all sales over $25, meaning that an individual
who purchased $25 worth of products from a representative could cancel the

transaction within twenty-four hours without penalty. It also required that companies provide written contracts with new representatives and guarantee all products sold to their customers.[56]

Some direct sales companies challenged the DSA Code of Conduct, noting the limited legal responsibility companies had over the activities of independent contractors, yet Avon and other established companies like Fuller Brush, Tupperware, Regal, and Home Interiors and Gifts wanted to maintain their good reputations. Representatives for companies like Avon and Tupperware rarely collected individual orders that exceeded $10 or $20; therefore, the $25 floor was actually designed to target companies that sold high-ticket home improvement, appliances, vacuums, and encyclopedia sets. Aggressive and unscrupulous companies like Holland Furnace and Amway had been under legal scrutiny since the 1950s. Multiple lawsuits had been filed against Holland Furnace for targeting the elderly and other vulnerable people and using hard sales techniques and fraud to sell expensive furnaces. In one case, a salesman sold nine furnaces to the same woman in seven years, each time disassembling the furnace, claiming it was dangerous, and refusing to reassemble it.[57] Amway also fought off claims that it was a pyramid scheme, arguing in 1970 that its "70/30 rule" requiring all representatives to sell 70 percent of inventory to non-Amway customers, and the "10 rule" requiring representatives to sell to ten new customers a month proved it was not a pyramid. The federal courts agreed, but Amway remained under close scrutiny. New allegations of fraud in 1979 remained uninvestigated, but Amway's agreement to settle a 2010 case with $150 million for consumer restitution and reforms shone a light on the entire industry.[58]

Avon executives and lobbyists at the Direct Selling Association and the Federal Trade Commission were also at the center of the process in designing a Code of Ethics for Representatives and member Direct Sales Companies in the 1970s. Avon even designed the new logo for the DSA and made hundreds of thousands of copies of the code that smaller companies distributed to their sales representatives and new recruits.[59] Avon supported a three-day cooling off period applied to new contracts, allowing individuals the option to cancel agreements to sell and, significantly, to return unused merchandise for a 90 percent refund. It served Avon's interest to support the direct selling industry during a period when consumer confidence about salesmen was particularly low. But Avon was not in the direct sales industry in the same way that newer companies were. Far from the hype and promises of instant wealth offered by salespeople by companies like Amway, Avon's reputation with its representatives was entrenched, as was the company's commitment to the rules that they were instrumental in writing. The consumer's rights to return products and the representatives' rights to a written contract outlining their legal relationship with the company had been a tradition at Avon for decades. Avon also generated positive public relations and complied with federal regulations; its "Avon Cares" program was designed to communicate more effectively with consumers and highlighted its positive relationship with the Food and Drug Administration about product safety and quality control. Avon began voluntarily listing ingredients on all its packages in 1973.

Most important, when the federal government required all corporations to abide by affirmative action rules, Avon quickly complied. Avon was part of a trend in the 1970s to codify plans for corporate "responsiveness," writing new personnel policies and procedures for its manufacturing and distribution plants' employees as a good-faith effort to improve race relations within the company and to its community. Internal memos as early as March 1968 had called for plans to demonstrate Avon's socially responsible business practices, all of which dovetailed with Avon's work in the Direct Sales Association Code of Ethics.[60] David Mitchell commissioned a review of the corporate policies and issued a "Statement on Corporate Responsibility" in August 1970 with suggestions for improving policies in the workplace, in consumer relations, and in the environment.[61] Mitchell also created a new Government and Public Relations Department that coordinated information about Avon's relationship with community civil rights organizations.

Avon's public relations and corporate outreach, as outlined in its internal "Plans for Progress" bulletin, promised a robust equal opportunity approach to "minority group problems" that would both demonstrate Avon's moral commitment and generate more sales. Avon's plan, according to historian Lindsay Feitz, was a "proactive policy" that "changed Avon's internal and external relations with the American public."[62] Avon's legal relationship to its independent contractors in fact exempted the company from formal regulation by the federal government; therefore, Avon's efforts to increase the number of African American representatives were made to both satisfy internal affirmative action targets and to bolster Avon's marketing plan. The company's efforts to meet the spirit of affirmative action requirements took place in the context of an increasingly data-driven marketing environment that showed that the black community's purchasing power represented significantly increased revenue; market researchers estimated that black women spent 40 percent more on beauty and luxury items than white women did.[63]

Avon's approach to the African American market had been limited in the postwar period. An advertising campaign in *Ebony* that started in 1961 targeted a middle-class audience, and the content of the ads, derived almost wholly from the scenarios and text copy from Avon's campaigns in *Ladies Home Journal* and *McCall's* that assumed a white audience, was a "separate but equal" version of advertisements to sell both products—especially lipsticks and fragrances—and the sales opportunity. The ads spoke, Feitz writes, "to a limited audience of black women whose [middle-class] cultural tastes, values, and lifestyle" Avon expected minority women "to emulate." Black Avon Ladies, the ads implied, called on middle-class women in their homes, in the middle of the weekday, despite the reality that most black women worked outside their homes.[64]

Good intentions, however, stumbled over deeply entrenched racist prejudice. In January 1972, Avon produced an amended selling program for "Low Income Markets" featuring training brochures with brown-skinned Avon Ladies and customers, offering lower start-up fees to representatives. Avon had associated "low income" with African American and assumed a population with "limited book-keeping and clerical experiences" unaccustomed to submitting orders and collecting money. Instruction booklets targeting new African American representatives used extra graphic illustrations and minimal text to describe both the customer's experience and the representative's business process. In an attempt to be mindful of start-up costs, Avon divided new representative fees into two separate payments, but it also scaled down the traditional Avon showcase to a tote-bag "to reduce theft."[65]

By 1973, Avon had appointed more than 35,000 black women representatives, 12 percent of its sales force, and approximately 200 full-time black district managers and several black division managers.[66] Despite its blundering approach to recruiting African American women, Avon's commitment to improving diversity in its supply line, contractors, and corporate and manufacturing staff was more laudable. Avon's leaders embraced affirmative action, determined that a commitment to civil rights would pay off both internally for its corporate culture and externally in improved sales and public relations. In 1974, Avon contracted with Uniworld Group, a black-owned advertising agency that specialized in promotions and advertising for minority consumers. Their work touted Avon's special products for brown skin and hair. This brought the image of the Avon Lady in the context of a 1970s urban black experience, reminding viewers that "There's more to Avon than you think. "[67] Avon's public relations department also ensured that Avon maintained relationships with the NAACP, the United Negro College Fund, various college scholarships, the Black Miss America Pageant, and Jesse Jackson's grassroots organization PUSH (People United to Save Humanity). PUSH worked with Avon's purchasing department to expand the number of minority-owned suppliers, contracted with twenty-five minority-owned banks to serve the branch offices across the country, and advertised with minority agencies to help recruit African Americans for full-time professional positions.

The partnership with PUSH, together with Avon's strategic use of African American market research and advertising agencies, resulted in what Feitz called "the beginning of a new, racially inclusive corporate identity [Avon] would later export around the world."[68] Although Avon began its efforts to improve diversity and meet the needs of African American representatives and consumers in a paternalistic fashion, the company successfully increased the numbers of African American corporate and manufacturing staff, representatives, and customers. Avon could afford to implement its program; profits had exceeded $1 billion for the first time in 1971. A more cynical reading of Avon's reasoning, that what was good for diversity was good for business, could have stopped at the profit motive. Instead, Avon was fairly "forward-thinking" in its training, outreach, and marketing to an African American audience. While acknowledging the potential profits of opening a new market, President David Mitchell promised that "Avon would accommodate its moral obligation and 'covenant' with Operation PUSH as long as it helped Avon meet 'real business goals.'"[69] As a result, "economic uplift and social responsibility were both possible and profitable." Avon's strategies "repositioned Avon's corporate image to a socially responsible and progressive company [attuned to the] changing racial climate in the United States and the increasing economic power of black consumers."[70]

Avon had embraced the demands of civil rights reform and affirmative action and made substantive changes that improved the diversity of its staff and sales organization. The less organized women's movement and social demands of women's liberation, however, made only a cursory impression on Avon's leadership. The 1960s and '70s were marked instead by a continuation of Avon's paternalistic sales policies, management style, and consumer relations that had built the company into a direct sales leader. Avon then adopted the earnest language of big-tent feminism supporting women's equality, but ultimately it stuck to making non-confrontational statements that echoed the company's long history of defining women as mothers with economic

Figure 6.8. "Avon Calling: Eighty years of Personal Service to the Home" (1966). Avon began marketing to an African American audience in the late 1960s. (Courtesy of Hagley Museum and Library.)

goals limited to improving the lifestyle of their families through part-time work. Incremental changes to this perspective, which shaped how the company recruited and motivated representatives, left Avon sitting on its hands in the 1970s and 1980s while more and more women found full-time work and careers outside their homes and fewer women opened their doors to the Avon Lady.

Perhaps Avon's long history of promoting women as business owners blinded its leadership to the entrenched sexism and racism that functioned both within the corporation and in its relationships to representatives. Inside the corporation, efforts to embrace some of the language of liberation resulted in more women being appointed to management positions. But like the Men of Avon who toasted themselves in 1946 for thinking of the needs of Little Mrs. Smith, the men of Avon in 1972 still could not get beyond the

Figure 6.9. "If you can change your mind, why can't you change the way you look?" (1967). Avon obliquely referenced feminism in the 1960s. (Courtesy of Hagley Museum and Library.)

idea that it was their prerogative, a male prerogative, to bestow economic opportunity on women. As outlined in its Corporate Responsibility Statement, Avon did commit to fighting discrimination throughout the company, but its efforts regarding women specifically were less enthusiastic and used fewer outside consultants than the programs it developed for African Americans throughout the corporation in the same period. For example, in 1972 Avon held a "Women in Management Awareness Training Program" to help them understand the changes for women in the workforce nationwide and to examine their own attitudes about women in-house. Internal memos about recruiting and training female managers utilized the patronizing voice of the male institutional "We"—"Our concerns should be that we are doing all we can to promote the development and success of all individuals in Avon, including women," read one 1972 training overview titled "Managing a Woman Effectively."[71] Even Avon's most forward-looking attempts ended up treating women as objects to be managed.

Progress, as a result, was discernible but slow. Avon did not have any women serving as managers in its 100 divisions in 1969, but by 1972 there were thirteen, most of whom had been promoted from within.[72] Patricia Neighbors, the highest-ranking female manager in Avon at the time, orchestrated a surprise one-woman wake-up call for Avon's regional sales managers, all men, at a meeting organized by Jim Preston, Avon's vice president of sales and marketing. Without disclosing her plan, Neighbors asked permission to begin a meeting on her own to make a point about sexism in the workplace. "I thought, what moxie!" Preston recalled. By Preston's account, Neighbors worked the room, complimenting each of the men on their suits, their hair, and how wonderful they looked. It made them "embarrassed and red faced." When eventually Neighbors took the podium, she told them, "This is the way 75 [male] district sales managers start meetings every month with the [female] sales associates. Don't think for a moment that the emotions you just experienced aren't experienced by these women every month."[73] Ten years later Preston noted that Neighbors had tried to teach the men of Avon an important lesson—"I would like to say it was a watershed moment," at the time, he said, "but all it did was make the men angry." Neighbors wasn't punished, however, and in 1974 she was named one of the first female vice presidents at Avon and continued pushing for more women in management and female-friendly policies.[74]

Part of Avon men's reluctance to tackle sexism in their company culture may have been due to individual personalities and cultural prejudices, but one could also argue that sexism was a byproduct of working for a company that was dedicated to and prided itself on "understanding the needs" of women. For the better part of a century, Avon's male executives and managers were rewarded and promoted on their perceived knowledge of women and their ability to translate this knowledge into profitable programs and policies. Many of these same men took genuine pride in knowing that they worked for a company described as "committed to bettering women's lives and engaging a discourse of service and uplift that permeated Avon's internal culture," even while undercutting the advancement of the few female executives in their own ranks.[75] Not until Jim Preston was named CEO in 1988 would Avon examine the culture that required women and minorities to adapt to the business instead of vice versa. Preston vowed that Avon's culture would "change to accommodate and value diversity in the workplace."[76]

In the meantime, substantive moves to improve gender equity in the Avon staff, including naming two women to the board of directors in 1972 and 1973, slowly changed the attitudes and assumptions in management about women as business people. On the one hand, Avon's leadership was ahead of the curve in corporate management; prior to the 1970s, only a handful of Fortune 500 level companies had any women on their boards, and most of those were wives or daughters of their companies' founders.[77] McConnell's daughter, Edna, controlled more than 10 percent of Avon's stock, but she never held a seat on the board; her husband, Van Alan Clark, however, did serve as chairman. Their son, Hays Clark, began his career with Avon at the end of World War II as an engineer at the Suffern, New York, manufacturing plant and eventually led Avon's international division through a period of far-reaching growth in the 1960s and 1970s; Hays, too, served as an executive vice president and eventually on the board.[78]

Avon named Cecily Selby as the first woman on the board of directors in 1972, exposing the board's first-draft feminist intentions. Both the way Selby told her own story and the way Avon introduced her to the company and representatives show several major characteristics of token female representation in corporate America. Selby came to Avon with exceptional qualifications. A graduate of Radcliffe College, she earned her PhD in molecular biology from the Massachusetts Institute of Technology. She had taught histology at Cornell Weill Medical School in Manhattan, specializing in skin and muscle, and was a research associate at Sloan Kettering Memorial Hospital when she was named to the Avon board. But it was her position as national executive director of the Girl Scouts and her previous service as headmistress of the

Figure 6.10. Women in Management. "Women Hold Key Avon Management Positions." Avon Annual Report (1974). The offices in Avon's new corporate headquarters on 9 West 57th Street in Manhattan overlooked Central Park. (Courtesy of Hagley Museum and Library.)

Lenox School, a private all-girls school on the Upper East Side in New York City, that initially attracted Avon's attention. Selby, who also served on the board of directors for RCA and General Electric, described herself in a 1997 interview with the *Harvard Crimson* as a "safe choice" to diversify Avon's board. She had relished her tenure with RCA, Selby said, because with her background in science "I could understand all the mumbo-jumbo about microprocessors." By her own account she had the strongest technical background of the whole RCA group. Avon, on the other hand, wasn't even aware that Selby was working on skin research when she joined the board, "so that was a pleasant surprise" for the company, she said.[79] Selby had also worked in management at the Girl Scouts of America. Did board members somehow think there was a parallel between 4,000,000 Girl Scouts selling cookies and Avon Ladies that made Selby valuable to Avon? Perhaps, but Selby also knew her worth at the Girl Scouts. " 'I'm a corporate manager,' she said pointedly. 'I have a staff of 720 in New York and six branch offices. I have 12 departments and a $12 million budget. We publish three magazines. I'm running a big business here. Avon and RCA are much bigger, but the problems are all the same." [80]

Even once Avon discovered her science background, Avon continued to focus on Selby's family life in all its publicity. In her interview for Avon's *Newsletter* article introducing her to the company, Selby's feminism shines through, but like most women in the early days of the movement, she couched her work history in the context of her family obligations. Efforts to balance career, motherhood, and family obligations, Selby explained, shaped her choices. "My professional life has been conditioned by my family," she told her interviewer. "I have been trying to find activities that correlate with the children's schedule and needs. When the children were young, I was a researcher. I found, however, that research was such a creative artistic thing that it was taking too great a part of me. I didn't want to be the kind of mother that children couldn't bother because she was working. I wanted to be able to leave my work at the office at the end of the day." Selby put her scientific career on hold as her sons approached adolescence, and she became head-mistress at Lenox School, a job that she surely did not leave at the office door at the end of the day. By 1972, noting that her sons were in college when she joined Avon's board of directors, Selby described herself as being in "the third phase of my life. . . . There was the academic, then the education, and now the world community service and effort that encompasses the entire national picture," she said. As the executive director of the Girl Scouts, she was busier and traveling more. "I have a very active husband who works 12-hour days through the week. He's happiest when I'm just as busy. . . . I believe very much in quality over quantity," she concluded. "Over the years I may not have been washing clothes or cleaning the house for my children and my husband, but when I was with them, I was free to give them individual and undivided attention." [81] Like most successful women in business, Selby developed a carefully crafted image of strength and confidence, tempered by savvy discipline. Her goal, it seemed, was to both assert her skills and yet not ruffle too many feathers.

Selby chose to play to masculine boardroom culture to ease her way into the process without threatening the men. The press had some expectation that women on corporate boards would use their influence to shape corporate policy for women. Selby acknowledged as much but opted for a soft touch. "It's hard for a man who's been conditioned by his mother, his sister, his wife and his secretary to treat women as peers," she explained. "I sometimes light up a cigar as a gag and it relaxes everyone," she said, "with an impish smile." Whether tokens or non-tokens, one commentator noted, women can "turn the board room into a classroom for corporate chauvinists."[82]

White privilege also shaped the way Avon presented their female board members. Ernesta Procope was the second woman named to the Avon board of directors in 1974 when Avon's collaboration with PUSH was strong. Avon publications treated Procope's personal life or philosophy with much less curiosity than they did Selby's. Procope had founded the Bowman Company in 1953, which by 1973 was the largest black-owned insurance brokerage company in the United States. Her husband, John Procope, was publisher of the *Amsterdam News*, a newspaper for the African American community in Brooklyn. *Black Enterprise* magazine ranked Bowman as the seventeenth largest black-owned company in the nation, and Catalyst, a non-profit company dedicated to supporting women in business, honored Procope as an Outstanding Woman in Corporations in 1977.[83] Both Selby and Procope emphasized the importance of encouraging corporations to build more space for women in management and executive level jobs. Procope's voice, however, is not as present in the extant Avon archive as Selby's, and her opinions about women in the corporation can only be extrapolated from brief comments in other publications about Avon's marketing push to capture black and other ethnic markets. Compared to Selby, Procope came off as decidedly less chummy and more focused on the opportunities and roadblocks faced by black business. For example, the *Amsterdam News* published an article on Procope's inclusion as one of four female corporate directors in which she described the corporation as an entity built on networks of other corporations, all of which presented an opportunity to build and support black business. The $62 billion consumer market, Procope noted, resulted in an increased use of black media and "Black oriented advertising, consulting and public relations firms." [84] Progress was frustratingly slow, and when asked at the Catalyst Awards dinner for her opinion about whether national priorities were changing to respond to minority constituencies, Procope offered a lukewarm assessment: "It would be heartening indeed to be able to give a resounding 'yes' in answer to the question," she said. "However, I would say that in reference to our national administration, each President has assumed a trifle bit more since the Truman Administration."[85] Without commenting specifically on Avon, Procope instead talked about the overall picture of African Americans in corporate America; "Blacks have made strides," Procope said, in consumer relations and affirmative action, "but there are far too few Blacks in finance, administration, marketing and line operating positions."[86]

In 1975, the year before Procope joined the Avon board, approximately 35,000 black women worked as Avon representatives, constituting nearly 12 percent of its domestic sales force. There were also about 200 full-time black district managers and "several" division managers.[87] Avon's initial approach to developing multiculturalism rested on the twin assumptions of black women as "either future Avon representatives in untapped urban markets, or as impoverished persons in need of job training and economic uplift."[88] Avon retained the Uniworld advertising agency to create a robust multicultural approach to both selling and recruiting. Marketing products were designed with the needs of black consumers in mind, and a recruiting strategy developed television and print ads in an urban context.[89] Still, Avon occasionally lapsed back into a homogenous approach prioritizing a white standard of beauty and professionalism. In 1976, Uniworld created a new recruitment campaign to attract working women, white and black, to the ranks of Avon Ladies. The text copy of the ads was identical, as were the

Figure 6.11. Avon Board of Directors, 1986. Cecily Selby, standing *center*, and Ernesta Procope, seated third from *right*. Avon Annual Report, 1986. (Courtesy of Hagley Museum and Library.)

sales situations illustrated by photographs—an Avon Lady with her sample case over one shoulder, a one-on-one sales demonstration, a customer using Avon products in her home. One brochure used white models, its twin used black models.

Times were changing, and despite Avon's successful programs to offer more employment opportunities to African Americans, Avon remained behind the curve. Management and marketing conferences in 1970 and 1972 had both tried to forecast changes in American demographics and their effects on Avon sales.[90] Avon predicted that by 1975 the number of families would increase owing to the number of young adults forming new households, but decreasing family size would mean that sales per household would also decrease with fewer members to supply. Interestingly, Avon initially looked to changes in women's work patterns only with an eye toward marketing, not recruitment. The number of working women would increase, the report suggested, from 25 percent of women over the age of fifteen in 1968 to more than 40 percent in 1975. "Working women will decrease potential at home calls. Alternate ways to day-time in-home selling will be required." Avon apparently did not feel a need to adjust to this reality right away. "Non-working women still represent a large and growing segment and continued servicing of these traditional in-home customers will provide a viable pace of growth."[91] Indeed, Avon's marketing department could not envision a sales strategy other than face-to-face or at-home solicitation. Avon could not meet the challenge of servicing working women in part because the company remained wedded to protecting representatives' sales territories built around residential neighborhoods rather than encouraging office sales, open market transactions, or the elimination of sales territories altogether. So committed was Avon to the in-home sales call that it did not officially "allow" representatives to sell at the workplace until 1986.

Avon saw itself competing for women's labor with other corporations and developed an all-or-nothing approach to recruiting working women. Avon believed it had to sell Avon as a full-time job that women would choose instead of other work. In 1983, it created a new advertising campaign "If You're Serious, You're Avon" to bolster the career of the Avon Lady, the reputation of the product and the company, and the desirability of an Avon career. It convened focus groups to test the waters. It ran two ads, with identical copy except for the headlines, one of which focused on Avon as actual work, "Avon. Not Sort of Working. Working," and one that presented Avon as a business, "Avon. Not Just Business. Your Own Business." The ads promised representatives a "New Avon" that offered "greater earning opportunities, more professional sales training, and full-time career potential unlike any-thing Avon has offered in its 97-year history" and described its representa-tives as "professional," "independent," "elite," and "proud." It also promised greater earning opportunities; "We're talking about real money," it said, "not pin money." Sales training had "become more professional than ever," with "full-time career potential." Representatives could choose to work full-time or part-time, the ad said, but then it belied its older assumptions about why women joined the company and touted the line about limitless opportunity. "The harder you work, the more you will be rewarded," it said. "Not just emo-tionally, but financially and even professionally within the Avon system." Throughout its efforts to build women's career aspirations, emotional rewards continued to outplay money in the Avon system. Toward the end of the ad, Avon's bad habit of patronizing women rose to the surface. "Sure it's going to take work to make your Avon career work for you," it said. "You'll learn to organize your time. To keep appointments. To run your own business. To familiarize yourself with the many products Avon offers." As the language in the ad suggested, Avon was not targeting the established career woman who was seeking to transfer her knowledge and skills. She was not the target audi-ence; rather, Avon spoke to the hesitant and inexperienced woman who still needed guidance in the most basic business operations.

Focus groups composed of Avon customers and non-customers, working women and "non-working women" were assembled to test the effectiveness of the ads, which homed in on the language of work.[92] Managers who wanted to know how women would interpret the recruiting pitch focused on phrases like "being independent, keeping your own hours, having your own business, not having a boss." "What does that mean?" they asked. Interviewers were told to focus on what women thought was surprising, important, and mean-ingful in the ad. "Does knowing that all products are guaranteed matter"? What does having a "career opportunity mean"? Was $30 considered a very small start-up cost? What is "unlimited" earning potential? "What effect does not receiving a guaranteed weekly paycheck have on your attitude?" "Doing business in a relaxed social environment," it asked, "how would this fit/not fit with your desire and need for self-respect, challenge, recognition, social fulfillment, social development? Feeling a sense of affiliation? Being part of a "sisterhood?"[93]

In the end, Avon wanted to know if the headlines were too stern. "Is the mood of the advertisement believable? Is it too serious? Taking the fun out of the job?" These fears underlay nearly forty years of recruiting and training complications. In its key findings, the focus group analysis showed that Avon's "overall image is positive (good company, quality products) and would not appear to be a deterrent to Representative recruitment." On the other hand, "Perception of the job of the Avon Representative is another story." The main drawback was financial. "The job is seen as offering disproportionally little money relative to the amount of work." Focus group participants also hedged on the emotional work of Avon. Many were uncomfortable with the door-to-door sales format. "In many instances," analysts said, "this is compounded by fear of rejection and the conviction that they cannot sell." Focus group participants overall preferred the headline "Not Just Business. Your Own Business" because it didn't include sub-headlines like "Pin Money" and "Sort of Working" which "were felt to be demeaning and actually reinforced negative associations."[94]

Avon had always hoped that the trimmed-down, full-time sales force of World War II could be replicated again when the high individual sales of full-time seasoned representatives pulled the company through the Depression. But as they moved through the recessions of the 1970s and 1980s, Avon could not compete against the draw of the paid labor force and a new feminist ethos that encouraged women to enter corporations as equal partners. Perhaps Avon could not fully commit to the notion that direct sales was, in fact, as serious to individual representatives as it was to the corporation. Or perhaps it knew this all along and only half-heartedly expected Avon Ladies to treat their business as something other than fun.

Ever-increasing sales figures made dealing with low-producing representatives bearable. Consider Avon's progress in the long view. In 1945, sales hovered around $15 million. In 1953, when Avon launched its first international markets, sales climbed to nearly $55 million. By 1965, 250,000 representatives worldwide generated $351 million in sales. Avon crossed the $1 billion mark with more than 600,000 representatives worldwide in 1972 and reached $2 billion in sales with 1 million representatives just six years later. Just as the company had thrived during the Great Depression, the recession of the 1970s presented more opportunities for direct sales, until Avon reached a high of $3 billion in sales in 1982. Avon had finally opened its management and board to women and taken their advice. The corporate culture had changed significantly, but at heart it was still a business run mostly by men.

7

Women of Enterprise

Avon and the Women Who Wanted It All

In 1986, the National Park Service unveiled a newly restored Statue of Liberty to commemorate the monument's centennial. Lee Iacocco, chairman of the Chrysler Corporation, had led a two-year million-dollar fundraising effort to update the aging statue and Ellis Island facility; the bulk of the $174 million raised came from nineteen corporations, including Avon Products, which had been granted licensing rights to use the Statue of Liberty in advertising and promotion. By happy coincidence, 1986 was also the 100th anniversary of Avon. Avon sold Statue of Liberty shaped perfume decanters, painted the image onto its beer-stein shaped decanters, and minted Lady Liberty coins, lapel pins, and brass stamps. Avon's print ads claimed that they sponsored the Monumental Makeover because Lady Liberty "has encouraged us to make opportunity a reality for millions of women."[1] At the same time, the company launched a new effort to refresh its public relations programs and to boost its image as a company for modern women. In the last two decades of the twentieth century, buoyed by its strong economic growth, Avon Products showed its strongest commitment yet to sustaining a focus on national issues facing women in business, both in corporate offices and as entrepreneurs.

Society was changing and Avon wanted to respond in a positive way in support of women. The company positioned itself as a corporate leader on social issues and leveraged its reputation as a company for women in furthering its marketing and recruitment goals. The company was not without fault; in 1986, Avon still had not named its first female CEO, but a fascinating feminist experiment played out at Avon as it engaged a national conversation about women and work. The company had some credibility for taking a leadership role on these issues. *Working Woman* magazine consistently named Avon as one of the top ten employers for women, recognizing Avon's success in building "a company by and for women."[2] The Catalyst organization, a non-profit group dedicated to promoting women in business and management, had twice recognized Avon for its record in employing and

Monumental Makeover.

How else could we describe it? Especially considering that now, in celebration of her forthcoming centennial, she's about to receive what may be the most massive makeover in history.

As an Official Sponsor, we at Avon are proud to lend a hand. For this lady called Liberty has encouraged us to make opportunity a reality for millions of women. In business, sports and life.

So, as the world's #1 beauty company, how could we not help the woman we find most beautiful stay that way.

AVON Helping keep the face of America beautiful.

Figure 7.1. "Monumental Makeover" (1986). (Courtesy of Hagley Museum and Library.)

promoting women. The company did not take its dedication to women's issues for granted, and during the 1980s and 1990s it led a number of initiatives that served to legitimize its status as a corporate role model for women and business.

What the predominantly female Avon workforce thought of these policies, initiatives, and focus is difficult to discern. The archives from the 1980s and '90s are lacking substantive profiles and accounts of representatives as individual voices in the company. In fact, the Avon representative herself becomes increasingly anonymous in this period. We can piece together some information from sales figures, the size of the workforce, and Avon's financial status, but missing are the personal narratives we were presented with earlier in the company's history as legal obligations to maintain privacy shaped how Avon collected and preserved its records.

Avon faced two existential challenges, one from outside the walls of the corporation and another from within the direct sales industry. The ongoing feminist movement made it possible and desirable to address women's issues in business, and it provided a language and set of goals for women's economic parity and for addressing issues of discrimination in the workplace. The substantial backlash against those efforts was never far from the conversation about how to achieve those goals, and for the most part Avon's public relations voice consistently sided with the determination to change women's lives for the better. Avon sponsored a splashy awards program, called the Women of Enterprise, which sought to understand the challenges of women's entrepreneurship and to celebrate those who achieved success. Their stories provide one avenue for assessing Avon's success in the 1980s and '90s. The company could talk-the-talk of feminism, but it faltered in key decisions, namely, in taking so long to name a female CEO.

Avon faced its second major challenge in these decades from within the direct selling industry and the competition presented by multi-level marketing. Companies like Amway and Mary Kay Cosmetics, Avon's largest rivals, had changed the commission structure for their independent contractors, allowing for exponential growth to accrue based on the productivity of one's recruits. Representatives could earn commissions both on their own personal sales and the sales of the person they had recruited. An independent contractor would recruit a new person, and then encourage that person to recruit, and so on, until they had built a cascading tier, or downline, that could result in substantial bonuses. Both Mary Kay's corporation and Amway had drawn criticism of their intense focus on recruiting to the point that many people regarded them as cults or Ponzi schemes. Amway (but not Mary Kay) had been hauled to court, and lost, several times for dubious practices. All of this attention had made multi-level marketing seem like a practice far outside the preferable staid and sober culture at Avon. But the biggest problem arose in the stark disparity of earnings advertised by Mary Kay's unit leaders who seemed to regularly earn checks that paid thousands of dollars in commissions every month, and Avon's representatives who earned their 30 percent commission on personal sales. In 1980, Mary Kay boasted that more women earned $40,000 with Mary Kay than with any other corporation in America, and she was not exaggerating. At the very time that Avon had invested in recruiting campaigns that characterized selling as "not sort-of working," multi-level marketing promised not just pin money but earnings that could support a family. This is not to suggest that multi-level marketers actually earned that level of income—in fact, most didn't. The "hobby" representative was just as prevalent at Mary Kay as she was at Avon. But as the 1980s and '90s wore on, it became painfully obvious that Avon's flat commission structure was simply not set up to allow those superstar sales representatives nearly as much potential as the tiered earnings of a strong downline did. In the end, Avon's monumental makeover of the late twentieth century was only skin deep and could not save it in the end.

The 1980s became for Avon, an opportunity to rebrand the company while strengthening its reliance on a female workforce, women's consumer power, and the rise of feminism in the workplace. A national conversation about women's opportunities and experience in business focused on the problem of women's under-representation in management. The direct selling industry and companies like Avon were uniquely suited to engage both sides of the conversation about women's role in corporate America. As an international, Fortune 500 company (in fact, Avon liked to remind people that they were actually a Fortune 250 company), Avon could develop management strategies to serve its corporate employees, and it could also extol, advise, and celebrate the efforts of individual entrepreneurs building their own businesses.

Popular magazines, academic departments, and government initiatives asked what corporations could provide in mentoring and training to pull women up through the corporate ladder. Others urged individual women to push through corporate barriers on their own.[3] A 1986 *Wall Street Journal* article, "The Glass Ceiling: Why Women Can't Seem to Break the Invisible Barrier that Blocks Them from the Top Jobs," exposed the structurally sexist policies that truncated careers of women in business. The term "glass ceiling" had originally been used by Marilyn Loden, a mid-level manager at New York Telephone. Loden had participated in what she described as an impromptu presentation at the 1978 Women's Exposition in a panel titled "Mirror Mirror on the Wall." Loden said she had originally intended to blame women themselves for their own negative self-perception and lack of advancement in business. But uncomfortable with placing the burden on women, she instead pointed to men's networks as barriers that actively kept women from top offices. The glass ceiling quickly became a shorthand explanation of women's lack of advancement in nearly every industry. By 1991, President George Bush ordered the US Department of Labor to create a "Glass Ceiling Commission" to study the barrier and create a series of recommendations for shattering it. Robert Reich, secretary of labor in the Clinton administration, published the commission's findings in 1993, featuring several of Avon's multicultural and diversity programs, ongoing since the 1970s, that had increased the numbers of women in management.[4]

Changing the management protocols and cultures that had hard-boiled discrimination in even the most well-meaning corporations required top-down determination, which at Avon, came from the leadership of President Jim Preston who spearheaded the efforts in the 1980s that led to Avon's having more women in powerful positions than did any other Fortune 500 company.[5] But while Avon's corporate culture had become more female friendly, there were still formidable barriers to women in Avon's corporate ranks. Under Preston's leadership, Avon had succeeded in promoting women such as Christina Gold, who served as head of Avon Canada in 1989 and the North American Division in 1993, and Susan Kropf, who served as director of US Operations. Despite these achievements, when Preston retired in 1998 the Avon board still passed over both Gold and Kropf to be CEO of Avon International. Instead they chose Charles Perrin, who at the time was serving as CEO of Duracell Batteries. Perrin had limited experience in the cosmetics industry and none in direct sales, a track record that led many Avon loyalists to lament a lost opportunity to prove itself as a company of and for women. As a result, talented women left the company soon after Perrin's appointment. Christina Gold immediately resigned and accepted an offer to lead Excel Communications, a direct-sales company specializing in long-distance telephone service, and later took on leadership in industries such ITT Defense. Andrea Jung, who was serving as president of Avon's global marketing and new business, was named the fourth woman on the Avon board of directors. In an interesting twist, Sheila Wellington, president of Catalyst, defended Avon's decision to hire Perrin. "To render Avon a pariah because of this decision strikes me as a bit much," she said. "Avon is such an outstanding company for women. Any way that you look at their achievements for women, they are absolutely stellar. The fact that they did not choose a woman as their chief executive strikes me as picking on the good guys when there are 120 companies in the Fortune 500 who have no women officers at all."[6] That Catalyst publicly went on record defending Avon was significant and likely generated some dissent within the organization it-self, given its founder's long-established warnings to businesses about losing female talent.

Felice Schwartz, business consultant and CEO of Catalyst, had founded the organization in 1962 to promote women in business. Schwartz had fo-cused on working with corporations to promote and retain women in man-agement. The demographics of the 1980s, she noted, was rapidly changing, and corporations would need to recruit and invest in women in order to re-main competitive in a world market. In a 1989 annual review, eight years before the shake-up at Avon, Schwartz urged corporate leaders to imagine a scenario where a manager would be hamstrung by losing female employees. Short-sighted policies cost businesses both talent and investment, she said. If the fictitious manager "had provided flexibility to those who had worked in his company for six or eight years before they'd had their first child—those women in whose training and experience he'd invested heavily and whom he knew to be good—he could have retained them and amortized his in-vestment in them." If barriers to women's advancement were not removed, Schwartz warned, "women will leave—particularly the best of them, who will seek and find other career opportunities, perhaps with competitors."[7] Still, most corporations, even Avon, did not prioritize keeping their best female executives.

Then, in 1989, Schwartz authored the article, "Management Women and the New Facts of Life" for the *Harvard Business Review*, advancing her life-long mission to convince corporations to utilize and expand the extraor-dinary intellectual and creative women in their pipelines by advocating concrete changes to corporate culture. She had been warning businesses for nearly twenty years that they avoided accommodating women at their own peril. In the competitive world of management, Schwartz said, business simply could not afford to lose good workers. Major shifts in corporate cul-ture were necessary to attract and retain the best talent available, she said, including creating an environment where business made it less difficult to talk about gender discrimination, harassment, or alternative management solutions. Corporations also needed to change their culture and honor the multiple personal priorities that women and men wove into their adult lives. Schwartz had argued for more than a decade that the male manager proto-type, which assumed that men were supported by wives who took care of homes and children and family, could not continue to undergird modern human resources policy.

Two things shocked the business world in Schwartz's article. First, she flatly asserted that business must accept the fact that "the cost of employing women in management is greater than the cost of employing men."[8] Corporations, she said, would need to pay for family-leave time, invest in developing female mentors who could speak about strategy and balance, and accommodate non-traditional work schedules. A longtime advocate of flex time, job sharing, onsite child care, and extended maternity leave, Schwartz emphasized the value of corporate loyalty that these policies would engender. "What we need to learn is how to reduce that expense, how to stop throwing away the investments we make in talented women, how to become more responsive to the needs of the women that corporations *must* employ if they are to have the best and the brightest of all those now entering the workforce." The payoff, she noted, would come in the long term as corporations could reap the benefits of retaining their investment in women's training and talent.

"Can you hear the collective gasp?" Columnist Ellen Goodman asked. Goodman feared that saying out loud what every manager already knew would be an opening to stop looking for ways to employ women in the first place. Schwartz defended herself by saying that in fact she had intended to shock corporate front offices. Her intended audience, readers of the wonky *Harvard Business Review*, was not the general public, and so the second part of her claim was followed up on: "The greater cost of employing women is not a function of inescapable gender differences. What we need to learn," she wrote, "is how to reduce that expense, how to stop throwing away the investments we make in talented women, how to be more responsive to the needs of women whom corporations must employ if they are to have the best and brightest."[9]

Schwartz's attempt to remind management that not every person who joined a corporation could be expected to work long hours or be promoted and relocated. It may have been true for young men fresh out of college, but women, she said, were individuals who existed on a continually changing curve throughout their working lives where work and family would be prioritized differently. For shorthand, she said, she distinguished two types of women, "career-first" and "career and family" categories. "Under these circumstances, there is no question that the management ranks of business will include increasing numbers of women," she wrote. "There remains, however, the question of how these women will succeed—how long they will stay, how high they will climb, how completely they will fulfill their promise and potential, and what kind of return the corporation will realize on its

investment in their training and development." For laying bare this opportunity cost, Schwartz was lambasted in the press and accused of advocating a
two-track system for women.[10] Detractors, many of whom apparently never
read Schwartz's actual article, quickly derided her recommendations for
managing and promoting—or as they saw it, not promoting—women with
families. Feminists, business leaders, and pundits feared that "the mommy
track," a phrase Schwartz never used and often refuted, would dead-end
women in middle management, while pushing women in the upper management track, they said, would turn women into childless automatons.

Schwartz was by no means so rigid in her recommendations, as the bulk of
her article asked corporations to rethink the outdated cultures that suggested
people would "be happier if we could turn back the clock to an age when
men were in the workplace and women in the home." "Career-primary
women," she wrote, served as role models for younger women, giving their
companies "significant advantage in the competition for executive talent."
Schwartz questioned the gender stereotype and double standard of the aggressive, "masculine" woman—"it is clearly counterproductive to disparage
in a woman with executive talent the very qualities that are most critical to
the business and that might carry a man to the CEO's office." She reminded
corporations that women faced special difficulties in corporate life precisely
because they were a minority. "The male perception of talented, ambitious
women," she wrote, "is at best ambivalent, a mixture of admiration, resent-
ment, confusion, competitiveness, attraction, skepticism, anxiety, pride and
animosity." Excluded from lunch, golf outings, and locker rooms, women
missed key career and business opportunities. Women, Schwartz said, never
felt secure in the business environment, uncertain "whether they should
speak out or grin and bear it when they encounter discrimination, stereo-
typing, sexual harassment, and paternalism."[11]

Betty Friedan, the feminist leader and author of *The Feminine Mystique*,
attacked Schwartz's categories, calling them "dangerous" and a kind of "retro-
feminism." "There are not two types of women," Friedan said. "All women
must have real choices. . . . How they put it together, their priorities at different times, is a matter of individual choice. The so-called Mommy Track,"
she said, "is really the Mommy Trap. It says to women that if they choose to
have children, they pay a permanent price. It's another word for sex discrimination."[12] Schwartz remained adamant. "I watched as a tornado of public
opinion began to spin farther and farther from my intention and from my

ideas," Schwartz wrote. "Over and over again I was challenged for things that I not only did not say, but do not believe and find abhorrent."[13]

Regardless of Schwartz's objections, the "mommy track" nomenclature stuck. "Should women have to choose between a career and family?" *Time* magazine asked in 1989. "The plan suggests relegating most working mothers to a gentle career path. . . . Only women willing to set aside family considerations would be singled out for the fast lane to the executive suite."[14] Such misrepresentations—namely, that male corporate managers would be the ones identifying women for the tracks—flew in the face of Schwartz's lifetime mission. "I think it inexcusable that the current corporate environment makes it so tough for women to have children *and* high-powered careers," she wrote. "The kind of time commitment that is, in reality, required in the very top jobs—the eighteen-hour day, the ten-hour day, or even the chock-full eight-hour day—almost always precludes a concomitant intense involvement in the life of one's children. This holds as true for men as it does for women. I don't believe that one can both be a CEO and regularly pick up the kids after school at four o'clock, or even be home for dinner every night."[15] Schwartz was frequently guilty of essentialism, of assuming all women as mothers or potential mothers. If she can be criticized for anything, it seems, it is not extending her focus to issues like paternity leave.[16] In an ideal world, Schwartz had noted, women would not have to make career-family choices. But in the real world, "I'm saying neither men nor women can have everything. There are trade-offs."[17]

"Having it all": the phrase had been bandied about throughout most of the 1980s, and largely it was used by the media to fabricate yet another feminist cat-fight about who was responsible for women's exhaustion in trying to balance work and family. In 1982, Helen Gurley Brown's *Having It All: Love, Sex, Money Even if You're Starting from Nothing* had appeared on the best-seller list for only a month but fed into a debate among feminists and anti-feminists alike that has lasted for decades. Feminists, and Schwartz was certainly one, had long argued that the terms of employment must change to accommodate women's needs: flex-time, job-sharing, child care, extended maternity leave, and working from home. Second-wave feminism had held workplace equality as a goal and women were urged to expand their careers, climb higher up management ladders, and reach for new responsibilities at work. Many women in business knew the cost to both their long-term careers and earnings of taking too much time off for maternity leave; furthermore, increased availability of child care meant more women were bringing their small children to daycare, returning to work sooner after childbirth, and sacrificing family time for career. Backlash from all sides emerged, both chiding women for even believing they could "have it all," or blaming women for emasculating the workplace in an effort to make corporate culture more female friendly.

Avon's 1986 "How Good You Look" advertising campaign appears to have been inspired by such public discourse. In the ad, a model of color is seen in a business suit and enters an office building accompanied by the lyrics, "You have that confidence and you have that style," creating the impression of a successful executive. But, of course, she's an Avon representative, taking busy phone orders at a pay phone while happily juggling her address book, order book, catalogs, and a grocery bag. You can have it all and look good too, the ad suggests. The campaign continues with another 1986 ad that features a quick montage of a model jogging through a busy urban street and grabbing a quick ice cream without stopping, another model kissing her son good morning, then another at a typewriter. The Avon product is delivered, and the ad ends with the confident model representative striding along a street followed by yet another model in her robe primping in front of a mirror before the final shot of that model at dinner in a dimly lit restaurant. The message seems clear. Career, family, and a fine dinner to cap off a busy and productive day.[18]

The national commercials Avon launched in the 1980s demonstrated yet again the Avon lady visiting the home with the catchphrase "You never looked so good." Avon also promoted the women's new corporate personality in a retrospective ad campaign implying that it was time for women to ditch "cookie-cutter" looks and define their individuality as consumers of cosmetics. A sampling of the commercials from the 1980s presents white middle-class women in their early thirties selling to other suburban middle-class women of the same age group. One exception was the 1987 Avon Christmas commercial that featured African American women and their admiring men in a montage of delighted Avon customers at the holiday season. Curiously, the only woman's occupation highlighted was nursing.[19]

Self-help magazines made the image of a feminist, according to historian Ruth Rosen, into a "Superwoman, hair flying as she rushed around, attaché case in one arm, a baby in the other."[20] "Having it all" quickly moved from being a serious quest for women looking to combine family and career to a media scolding of feminists for wanting it in the first place. "Blame for even raising the desire to do so was laid at the feet of feminists who had promised women a 'false dream,'" Rosen argued. An alternative antifeminist position had emerged in the 1980s to counter the feminist message. A new generation of women separated themselves from the movement that begrudgingly acknowledged the desirable goals of feminism—equal pay, non-discrimination, and end to sexual harassment—and rejected the stereotype of the "angry feminist." "I'm not a feminist, but . . ." became an unofficial slogan of younger women who tacitly appreciated select goals of feminism through a divide that was in part a generation gap and in part a self-fulfilling media prophesy. A feminist became cast as selfish and repellent, a "narcissistic superwoman who embraced the values of the dominant culture." Working women fought to defend themselves against a popular perception in the media that cast them, according to Rosen, no longer as a loyal mother and wife who would care for the community, "but a dangerous individual, unplugged from home and hearth . . . the female version of America's ambitious but lonely organization man."[21]

The Superwoman invariably appeared in the media as a hardworking career woman who learned to multi-task and hyper-organize her family and time to never miss out on a career move, soccer game, school play, or professional development opportunity. Both mocked and applauded, the Superwoman was, on one hand, a selfish feminist who made life difficult for ordinary women by setting unrealistic goals. On the other hand, she was a sad and overwhelmed mother who lost track of her children's lives, her marriage, and her own life, all to follow a career. As for individual women, there was no shortage of advice on how they could organize their personal lives, achieve career goals, and manage their families.

Fueling the fire at Avon was a direct competitor, Avon's most vocal critic, Mary Kay Ash, the founder of Mary Kay Cosmetics. A dynamic and motivational corporate innovator, Mary Kay, the pink, multi-level marketing company, had steadily challenged Avon, appealing strongly to direct sales representatives through its promise of exponential earning potential and a cult of personality. Mary Kay fashioned herself as the Superwoman, although the term wasn't yet much in use in popular culture when her first autobiography appeared in 1981. Mary Kay added a complex layer to the Superwoman debate. Ash was many things—pro-woman, pro-business, evangelical, and distinctly anti-feminist—and what she said mattered in both the direct selling industry and in pop culture. Politically conservative, Ash in effect legitimized the feminist critique about corporations as bastions of sexism. "It seemed to me that women's brains were worth only 50 cents on the dollar in a male-run corporation," she wrote in her 1981 autobiography. Her faith in women's business acumen and her ability to marvel at the modern changes to women and family around her seemingly knew no bounds. At the same time, her advice to the women in her own corporation was also steeped in conservative traditions about husbands and wives. But having grown up poor, Mary Kay never faulted women for the choices they had to make to keep their families running; she assumed the role of the Superwoman not out of feminist arrogance but rather in celebration of scrappy self-reliance.

Mary Kay's self-styled rags to riches success story outlined in her autobiography featured extraordinarily detailed and intimate advice for women seeking financial success and independence. "Our daughters and granddaughters do not think of *supplementing* their lives with a career," she wrote in 1981, "because having a career and being a woman are now seen as naturally equal parts of the same role."[22] Ash herself was a single mother for much of her life though she tended to marry quite frequently. Her advice to women, whether married, divorced, or single, was to organize, decide priorities, and "subcontract elements of your work" with a housekeeper or cleaning service, regardless of income level.[23] A housekeeper was an essential investment, especially for a poor woman, who would benefit more by using all her energies to build her business. New social attitudes in the 1970s brought "time-saving and woman-saving innovations," she said. High-quality daycare, extended public school hours, fast food restaurants, permanent-press clothing, dishwashers, and microwaves made managing home and career easier. A new generation of "modern men," Ash claimed, showed greater acceptance of women as social and professional equals and were more likely to pitch in on housework. Of course, most women knew full well that the exhausting routine of the "second shift" was not going away any time soon, but the goal of direct selling was to sell extraordinary dreams to women seeking answers on making life easier.

Mary Kay also counseled that career women needed the buy-in and support of their families, however those families were structured. Much of her advice to women revolved around the women's selling their business potential to their families who might otherwise see a new job as competition for their needs. This problem, she said, could be solved by considering "the feelings and opinions of everyone around you" and getting them to see how "your career will benefit everyone" financially and personally.[24] She counseled women to spend quality time with their children and not to feel guilty about working long hours. "I found that when I was away from my children for a few hours each day, I was a better mother than when I was home all day long," she wrote. "The children seemed to appreciate me more, and I know that I was more patient with them."[25] The rewards of a career, Mary Kay said, were extremely fulfilling, allowing women to discover strengths and resolve weaknesses they never knew that they had. "But if you lose your family in the process, then I believe you will have failed. . . . It's no fun to come home and count your money by yourself."[26] Ultimately, Mary Kay developed a sheen of cartoonist proportions. Artist Berke Breathed's depiction of her in "Bloom County," *Attack of the Mary Kay Commandos*, highlighted the potential of mocking the fully embraced caricature of her appeal. Avon had embraced the family as a motivating factor in its recruitment but had downplayed the significant emotional aspects that Mary Kay now exploited. "You can have it all," Mary Kay told the hundreds of thousands of women who worked as Beauty Consultants for her business.

In May 1989, the direct sales company Amway made a bid to buy Avon for $2.1 billion. Amway is a multi-level company that sold household and beauty products and was a strong competitor of Avon. Amway's attempted hostile takeover was roundly rejected, but then a week later, Mary Kay herself showed interest. Dallas-based Mary Kay had taken her company private in a leveraged buy-out and could show $400 million in sales. Her interest may have been as much public relations as it was a true takeover offer. Avon's sales for that year topped $3 billion. Avon executives naturally declined.[27] The self-proclaimed Superwoman had, however, made a very public statement about her ambitions. Significantly, Mary Kay also extended her advice to corporations that did not want to lose out on women's talents in her 1984 book, *Mary Kay on People Management*. Peppered throughout the book was also a hint that corporations weren't really all that interested or capable of changing their profit and loss mindset quickly enough to accommodate modern women. Occasionally Mary Kay slipped in some advice for those women employees who didn't have time to wait for male managers to become less sexist, essentially recommending that women leave corporations that showed no signs of genuine reform.

In this larger context of recognizing women's economic challenges, particularly "limited advancement opportunities within a typical 9 to 5 workplace," and the difficulty of finding quality time to spend with family and children, Avon, together with the Small Business Association (SBA), chose to highlight women's entrepreneurship as a way out of corporate sexism. Avon tied its own business model to women's desires for liberation. The awards program was first and foremost a public relations strategy to draw attention to Avon's business model. Like Mary Kay, and like the vast majority of direct sales companies, Avon believed that self-employment promised women "flexibility, control and financial reward." But in addition to joining a direct sales organization, Avon identified other career options from which women could choose. "Among these is a strong and growing interest to go it alone—to become entrepreneurs." Avon chose to celebrate and "support women as they face and meet their personal challenges" through a program called "Women of Enterprise."[28]Building on its solid reputation as a leader in direct selling and as an international corporation that promoted gender equity, Avon officially turned its attention in 1987 to a nationwide conversation about women and business ownership.[29] Avon created a major public relations program called "Rediscovering the American Dream" that attempted both to create greater awareness of the direct selling business model for women and to recognize women-owned businesses. Women of Enterprise, the prize program for independent business women, was the centerpiece of this program. Part public relations plan to support Avon's efforts to attract new recruits and part directive to address women's issues, the Women of Enterprise offered a new window on women's experiences in business at a time when the nation's attention was focused on discrimination, harassment, equal pay, and women's career ladder.

Partnered with the Small Business Administration's Office of Women's Business Ownership, the program sought to draw attention to the achievements of women entrepreneurs across the nation. "The average man fantasizes about learning to fly," one call for applications proclaimed. "Women dream of being self-employed."[30] The Women of Enterprise program was the first to "recognize and support the grassroots entrepreneurial spirit of American women."[31] Women were starting their own businesses at twice the rate of men, Avon noted: "In the last decade, the number of women-owned businesses rose by 69 percent, five times the rate of businesses owned by men," and it was predicted that by the year 2000 "half of all the businesses in the country would be run by women." Echoing Felice Schwartz, "For years, men in business have relied on a well-established support system—the 'old boys' network,'" Avon wrote. "Unfortunately, no 'old girls' network exists for women, especially those starting a business. They need role models and solid information on how to succeed."[32]

Together, Avon and the Small Business Administration conducted a nationwide search for women from all ethnic groups who "demonstrated great resourcefulness and initiative in creating their own financial opportunities." They opened the first competition nationwide in 1987 and selected five awards winners from a field nominated by Chambers of Commerce and SBA chapters across the country. The first five winners represented a carefully chosen cross-section of women from a wide range of age, ethnic, geographic, and family categories, reflecting Avon's commitment to diversity. The award winners shared obvious success in business, but Avon and the SBA also favored women who built businesses in traditionally male dominated fields—such as construction, real estate, and financial planning—and in keeping with the spirit of the awards, women "who made it against the odds." The Women of Enterprise program also featured the language of uplift and motivation, the staples of direct sales literature.

The Women of Enterprise Program advertised in *Ms.* magazine, looked for women who had been self-employed "profitably" for at least five years and who had achieved their business goals by "surmounting a difficult personal challenge or economic circumstance." In its first year, Avon and the SBA received more than 100 applications from women around the country. The winners included M. Charito Kruvant, who formed Creative Associates International that created educational materials for dyslexic students; Mary Winston, the "eldest of 25 children born to an Alabama sharecropper" who founded Winston Janitorial Services, the largest in the country; Laura Balverde-Sanchez, who turned around a bankrupt Mexican sausage company, and Sydney Stoeppelwerth, a blind teacher turned motivational speaker who became an oil wildcatter.

Alongside the awards announcements and ceremonies that featured hallmark Avon glamour and shine, the program's focus remained on the achievements of women entrepreneurs from the nation at large. The award winners had "overcome tragedy, prejudice and professional hardships or personal handicaps to achieve business success." "With vision, spunk and an indomitable spirit, they turned their lives around. Like America itself, these exceptional women represent a variety of ethnic and racial backgrounds, and their businesses encompass everything from engineering, to trucking, to gourmet foods."[33] Publicity was the main reward from Avon's $300,000 budgeted program, and winners were prepped for media exposure on the major television network's morning shows. Each winner was flown to New York for an awards luncheon with other entrepreneurs, business women, and the media. For example, Avon arranged with talk show host Phil Donahue to moderate an entire episode with the winners to talk about their accomplishments and the needs of women in business more generally, and it hosted an elaborate awards dinner attended primarily by the press. Winners also received a Tiffany crystal trophy and a $1,000 cash award, but "the real award," Avon noted, was "the conferring of public honor on the winners who Avon promised would serve as role models for other women."[34]

Avon had good intentions in encouraging all women to follow their en-trepreneurial dreams, which were no doubt driving the awards program, but of course Avon also sought to reap the opportunity to sell its own brand of entrepreneurialism. Before their selection by an independent advisory panel of "outstandingly qualified women (and some men)" the winners were screened for their "favorable attitude towards Avon" and their "ability to serve as a spokesperson" for Avon's "commitment to American women."[35] The Avon public relations department, which oversaw the program, believed it created awareness among a sizable segment of American women of Avon's "flexible and versatile" earning opportunity, bolstered their fourth-quarter recruiting numbers, and "enhanced Avon's image as a company which 'cares' about its customers."[36]

As a public relations program, the Women of Enterprise Awards placed Avon as a sponsor of women business owners everywhere. The application process and awards gala targeted potential recruits who, Avon hoped, would see an element of themselves in the stories. The contest requirement that applicants show both a profitable business and significant personal hardship built on and perpetuated a popular trend in women's corporate culture and highlighted a theme long familiar in Avon's corporate ethos—the narrative of the extraordinary individual who found financial success or social meaning in business.

To its credit, Avon intentionally sought to create a diverse pool of finalists. The 1987 award winners included two women of Caucasian descent (in-cluding one immigrant from Germany), one Hispanic woman, and two African American women. Initially, Avon did not shy away from choosing women who used the program to voice hard-hitting analysis and complaints about the twin obstacles of racism and gender discrimination. Many ap-plication questions were specific to the business, seeking figures on sales, investments, market reach, and operating costs, but for the most part, the applicants and Avon strongly emphasized the personal narrative. Full applications, many handwritten, highlight the applicants' assumptions that their personal story, particularly of hardship, would be weighed more heavily in the awards process. Avon, too, with its long history of evangelical testimonies of women's business success, prioritized the emotional, rather than the economic, rhythm of entrepreneurship. The questions asked and individual answers given on the 1987 applications show how deeply embedded both Avon and the program applicants were in the larger conversation about women, business, and "wanting it all."

Marie Jackson-Randolph had earned a PhD in education and English and had already received more than 300 awards, including mention on the list of "100 Outstanding Black Business and Professional Women" in Detroit. She had opened a chain of black-owned day-care centers, the Sleepy Hollow Educational Centers, in 1978 for children from age two and a half weeks to fourteen years. Her centers operated twenty-four hours a day and reached out to more than seventeen neighborhoods in Detroit, including one in an "Arabic neighborhood" and another that catered to handicapped children. Jackson-Randolph's story met the award standards for overcoming hardship—in 1979, she lost three of her four children in a house fire. As a family business, she employed her husband, mother, father, brother, niece, and two cousins. Her self-reported sales and profits increased from $3.4 million in sales in 1985 to $4.6 in 1986; profits increased from $130,000 to $224,000 in the same period—a testament, Avon noted, to the number of women entering the workforce. Like most women in the awards program, Jackson-Randolph faced substantial financial challenges. Without venture capital to invest in 1977, Jackson-Randolph said she turned to her own savings and used start-up money from friends and relatives. Business and family were never separate, Randolph said, not in management and not in everyday obligations. "As a woman entrepreneur," Randolph wrote, "I am challenged by the reality of a man's world and by the task of being the boss at the office and my husband's wife at home."[37]

The second winner, Mary Ann Padilla of Denver, Colorado, was the owner of Sunny Side, a temporary office personnel service that she began in 1973. The daughter of Mexican immigrants who worked in the fields picking onions and peas, Padilla worked for ten years in temporary employment, but in 1975, in the midst of a recession, she had a difficult time finding work. She had few clerical skills, she said, and no degree, but decided to start her own company to generate money for rent. "Because of my extreme naiveté and ignorance of starting a business," she wrote, "I blindly plowed ahead never thinking that I might not succeed." Like Jackson-Randolph, Padilla relied on family help. Her husband was a CPA, and they invested all profits back into the business. Padilla credited her strong ethic to her family background. "My inner strength comes from being one of nine children. I was always aware of who I was and where I came from (poor Hispanic female). I was never allowed to use this as a crutch for not achieving," she wrote.[38] Later in her application she claimed that she was not aware of any special challenges she encountered as a woman entrepreneur. Other applicants were not so quick to dismiss the racism they encountered, unlike Padilla whose strategy to reassure her potential benefactors led her to internalize the problem as one that didn't affect her.

Like Jackson-Randolph, Padilla had also been recognized by her local business community. She was selected by the US Hispanic Chamber of Commerce as the 1986–1987 Hispanic Business Woman of the Year, an honor that earned her a phone call from President Ronald Reagan, and she was recognized by the Council of Women at Work and the Minority Business Award. When asked why she wanted to be an Avon Women of Enterprise Award winner, Padilla wrote, "Given my education, social and ethnic background it is important to me to be recognized as a role model for the many youth of similar background. With the high school dropout rate and the under achievement within the minority community, I would want these youth to recognize that life really can be a series of choices, not chances."[39]

Sharlyne Powell of Yakima, Washington, started Women at Large, a company with nine fitness "salons," a $39 physical fitness video for working out at home, and a clothing line for larger women. Like Padilla and Jackson-Randolph, Powell came to her business knowing "absolutely nothing" about either business or exercise. Powell spoke of the extraordinary humiliation experienced by large women from both the public and their doctors who considered overweight women "health risks who couldn't and wouldn't exercise." Powell initially followed some "bad business advice," she said, to hire "svelte" instructors, but when she realized that large women felt more empowered by heavier ones, Powell quickly accommodated. A thin instructor, she wrote, was a "role model" for women who wanted to be fit, but not necessarily one for women who wanted to lose weight.

Like the other winners in 1987, Powell didn't begin her business until her children were older. When asked about the effects of her business life on her personal life, Powell noted "the loss of time I spent with my family has been the hardest. Wife and mother was always there. Now she is an independent business woman. My family is all grown and all believe strongly in what I am trying to achieve, therefore they support my efforts 100 percent. They also see changes in the women's lives who come to Women at Large and fully understand the impact this program has in every community we have a salon in." Powell's Women of Enterprise application included a dozen testimonials from clients about her program, echoing the enthusiasm of its founder. Like her co-winners, Powell believed the importance of a woman's business extended out into her family and community. The pressure to be a role model encouraged women to succeed in their business.

Heida Thurlow of Houston, Texas, was nominated by Barbara Tober, editor in chief of *Brides* magazine. Her company, Chantal Cookware, made cookware and serving pieces. Thurlow claimed she was the founder of America's "first and only woman-owned cookware company," and she held a degree in mechanical engineering from West Germany's Essen Institute. She owned patented features on cookware, such as an air pocket design on stainless steel handles to keep them cool. Thurlow's Women of Enterprise award application, which clearly didn't require vetted sales and profit figures, listed her 1985 gross sales as "a few mill" and her 1986 gross sales, "up 5%," as "several mil." She also noted that her sales were "up 63% in the first 3 months of 1987, perhaps as much as many mil!" Thurlow was a breast cancer survivor, and unlike other winners, she began her business in 1971 when her oldest child was an infant and she was pregnant with her second child. She wrote that her children joined her when she traveled to European factories, trade shows, and buying offices. "It's neat," they said, "to see Mom's cookware in catalogs or on TV shows such as *Golden Girls*, *Family Ties*, *Valerie*, and *Perfect Strangers*."

Like the other winners, Thurlow said she learned her business through "trial and error" which "cost more years than necessary." She claimed her biggest challenge was financing. "Only when I found a bank with a female VP did I get a loan for my business without my husband's guarantee," she wrote, "while these same banks never asked for my signature when he borrowed money!" Although the application did not expressly ask candidates for a broader message to women considering an independent business, Thurlow and many other applicants wrote one anyway. She touted the characteristics and skills that women developed every day in their lives and encouraged them to see these as valuable business traits. "Most mature women had to develop excellent organizational talents and the capacity to improvise," she stated. "If they would apply these talents toward building unique businesses, it would not only give them greater fulfillment but it would also give us, the consumer[s], a great wealth of wonderful products and services. I am certain that they would be at least as resourceful as myself, whether I traded my goods at the flea market, climbed with my best business suit onto a flatbed truck to unload the first shipment of lids, donned an outrageous hat at my first housewares show in order to get buyers to notice my tiny booth, or requested a room with a desk during chemotherapy treatments. We as consumer[s] would benefit greatly if women would apply their resourcefulness towards business."[40]

The final winner was May Yue whose family left China in 1949 for Hong Kong. She moved to the United States in 1964 and attended the University of Minnesota where she graduated in 1969 with a degree in education to teach Home Economics and a certificate in financial planning. Later, she worked in a financial services firm, where she developed the idea to work with middle-class and upper-middle-class consumers on financial planning. Like most of the women in the awards program, Yue confessed to knowing very little about the business she hoped to get off the ground; "Everything we did," she said, "was a first time effort with no guidelines to follow." At the same time, her application belied business traditions already established in her family. The business took a toll on her family, she wrote; she separated from her husband for a year "because of lack of time and also both of us were too involved in our own business. The pressures of business do affect one's personal relationships if one doesn't pay close attention to them," she wrote. When asked to identify her biggest challenge, Yue wrote that it was "to prove my credibility. To overcome the patronizing attitude of men and to trust my instinct and intuition." Also in keeping with many other applicants in the awards program, Yue devoted substantial time and energy to the cause of women in business. In 1983 she founded the MINN-WE Foundation, also known as the Minnesota Women Entrepreneurs, a think tank for female business owners, which sponsored a three-weekend Training in Excellence program for seasoned business owners. MINN-WE also provided financial capital to women-owned businesses.[41]

In the Awards applications, most women cited persistent sexual and racial discrimination as barriers to achieving their business goals, factors that were notably missing from the list of obstacles to business success in the survey. Women added these to their write-in responses, and given how insistent minority women were about the problems, it's hard to understand why analysts overlooked the importance of these barriers in their final report. Perhaps racism was not talked about as blatantly in the entire applicant pool of 400 as it was in fifteen winners' files, but it's more likely that analysts at New World Decisions didn't believe it was important enough to be categorized.[42] At the very least, analysts did not see how closely linked racism was to the structures that supported business. For example, whereas women may have noted that difficulty securing credit made sustaining their business a challenge, the part that unstated racism played in this difficulty likely flew under the analysts' radar. While noting that many women didn't use commercial credit, analysts may not have realized that many minority women might have considered it futile to even try to secure a bank loan.

By 1989, Avon had received more than 400 applications for the Women of Enterprise program. Recognizing the valuable data they had collected, Avon sent the applications to New World Decisions, an analysis firm, which fed the data into a national attitude survey. The survey company compiled categories of Motivations and Obstacles for business success. Nineteen percent of applicants said "control and flexibility" were major motivations for starting their business; a chance for opportunity logged in at 17 percent, and "economic necessity and personal family crisis" were ranked at 14 percent and 12 percent, respectively. At the bottom of the list of motivations were ambition to earn more money (9 percent), having lost their job (5 percent), and gaining control and flexibility with family (4 percent). When asked what character traits women believed accounted for their success, most marked "optimism," "healthy attitude," "sense of humor," and "some skills."[43]

Women's self-assessment of obstacles to their success presented some difficulties in interpretation. When asked in the open response section of the application about professional obstacles they faced, most women noted their own lack of specialized knowledge, ability to raise capital, difficulty establishing credit, need for a better researched business plan, and training in marketing, management, and other business skills; some also noted the need for a college degree. However, survey analysts, focused as they were on emotional characteristics, did not include women's difficulty in securing financing, which developed as a consistent theme in the awards applications.[44] Applicants were asked about the loans they received, including a special question about whether they had applied for and received SBA loans—few had. "While women say raising capital was a major obstacle they faced in starting or building their businesses," survey analysts found that "it does not rank as one of the most essential ingredients of entrepreneurial success; only five percent believe the ability to raise bank financing or venture capital are among the two types of skills needed by women business owners."[45] In other words, what the survey company identified as obstacles and skills were clearly not compatible with what women believed was necessary to their success.

If women believed that entrepreneurship offered a path out of 9 to 5 corporate America, or that their own business could give them flexibility, control, or the ability to spend quality time with their children and family, they were sorely mistaken. Finalist Linda Alvarado, owner of Alvarado Construction and winner of the US Hispanic Chambers of Commerce Business Woman of the Year award, among others, noted that prioritizing family, even for short periods, "means lost opportunity cost." Alvarado always sought the silver lining of balance; opportunities lost in business mean "opportunity to be with your family at special times." Sometimes, she said, it was impossible to leave her business, so "dad goes to the mother/daughter Brownie dinner." The businesses created by the Women of Enterprise applicants were anything but flexible; they were instead exceptionally time-consuming and exacted mental and emotional energy that left most women depleted. But, considering of course that the Women of Enterprise applicants were a self-selected sample, these women were willing to pay the price. New World Decisions Analysts expressed surprise that most women started their businesses in mid-life when the needs of their families were high; 56 percent of the 1993 applicants were married, 38 percent widowed or divorced, and only 6 percent never married. Eighty percent of applicants had children under the age of eighteen when they began their businesses, and nearly half of these had three or more children.[46] This is remarkably similar to the analysis Avon conducted on their own representatives, which underscored the part-time nature of Avon's canvassers.

Driving women into independent business ownership, however, was not so much the desire for control or flexibility with family, the quality vaunted by the media, but rather a desire for control over career. In order to be rewarded, women needed to demonstrate emotional grit. It was never enough for a woman to simply be a successful business owner or to have recognized and exploited a sound business opportunity. Women of Enterprise applicants needed to have overcome a highly emotional and personal roadblock that would have stopped ordinary people from doing ordinary things. Most applicants described personal loss—the death of a husband, child, or parent—abandonment, prison, alcoholism, bankruptcy or crushing debt accumulated by a spouse or family member. So the question, "could" women have it all (family and career) perhaps should have been rewritten. If women could not have both—which nearly all applicants insisted was impossible—women would have to decide which they would prioritize. And as business owners, the Women of Enterprise applicants emphasized that the choice was theirs to make.

In the first years of the program, Avon and the SBA seemed focused on business success, but later they chose winners whose personal stories evoked a strong emotional appeal. While all the women operated successful businesses, less attention was paid in awards press releases to their business acumen and management skill and more to their dramatic story. Women's success in overcoming a personal or economic challenge quickly became more of a priority to the awards program than their business success. In the first years of the program, applicants routinely understated their personal battles in applications. Interviews with winners revealed even more dramatic details of hardship, which Avon featured in public relations profiles. The tantalizing stories told on morning news programs and in radio interviews complemented the tone of daytime talk shows and human interest stories, but also reinforced a narrative of women business owners carrying emotional baggage. What began as an attempt to talk about serious and systemic issues of women and the economy, and structural support for women-owned business, had devolved into a talk-show style program of women and personal hardship by the later 1990s. In many cases it became difficult to identify the type of business a woman had built, so focused were the award winner biographies on their personal tragedies.

To its credit, Avon continued the awards program for nearly fifteen years. While one Avon representative was included as an honorary award winner each year, cash prizes were reserved for women wholly outside the Avon organization. Eventually the prioritizing of non-Avon women created some tension in the corporation. In 2002, Avon revised the standards for the Women of Enterprise Awards, stopped collecting outside applications, and gave all awards only to women who served as Avon representatives. No longer would the company invest in a commitment to encourage all women to follow their dreams, inside or outside of Avon. Only those inside Avon would be the center of attention.

Avon's public relations rationale for Women of Enterprise had taken an ironic twist. Far from being a vehicle through which Avon could promote its own entrepreneurial opportunities, the awards program instead highlighted the extraordinary depth of risk, time, finance, and obstacles navigated by independent business women. Judged against the prospect of "going it alone" experienced by the Women of Enterprise, the Avon contract once again came across as a pale and one-dimensional version of entrepreneurship in which the corporation provided all the leg-work and made all advertising, design, product placement, and distribution decisions. On the other hand, for women who really wanted no part of "going it alone" Avon offered a circumscribed opportunity, a means of entering business, earning money either full-time or on the side, and with that they could enhance their standard of living. In this key way, nothing had really changed at Avon, not in a hundred years.

In other ways, however, Avon's reputation as a company deeply concerned about women's issues was exemplified by the Avon Foundation. Founded in 1955, the foundation's work moved center stage in 1992 with

Figure 7.2. Susan Kropf, President and Chief Operating Officer, and Andrea Jung, Chairman and Chief Executive Officer, Avon Products, Incorporated. Together they promised to deliver a beautiful transformation of Avon's beauty image, the direct sales opportunity for "career-minded women," and Avon's global commitment to women's issues, particularly the fight against breast cancer. Avon Annual Report, 2002. (Courtesy of Hagley Museum and Library.)

the Breast Cancer Crusade and the yearly Avon Walk for Breast Cancer. The Breast Cancer Crusade began in Avon United Kingdom when the pink ribbon campaign was launched in support of breast cancer research and was quickly adopted in the United States. Since 1992, Avon reports it has raised $321 million for cancer research.[47] The high-profile emphasis on a compelling women's health issues greatly enhanced the public perception of Avon as a company for women. Avon also organized a second program that addressed the needs of women who experienced domestic and gender violence. In 2004, the Avon Foundation branched out to sponsor the Avon Promise to End Violence Against Women and Girls. Addressing issues of gender violence, a subject that had been taboo just a decade earlier, the Speak Out initiative aimed to raise awareness, educate, and develop prevention and direct service programs. Between 2004 and 2016, Avon and the Avon Foundation for Women contributed more than $60 million globally to support these goals.[48] The global outreach echoed the renewed corporate emphasis on expanding Avon beyond the plateauing US market.

Departing from their long practice of tinkering at the edges of the business model, the Avon executive suite made a substantial decision in 1999, hiring Andrea Jung, then president of product marketing for Avon's North American division, to become the first female chief executive officer for Avon in its 113-year history. Two years later at the young age of just forty-two, Jung added chairman of the board to her resumé. Jung told the Los Angeles Times: "We had great products, but women were saying, 'This is my grandmother's makeup brand.' "[49] Jung's vision was followed closely in the business news as she attempted to mold Avon's old-fashioned image into a luxury brand, added retail sales, and created internet-based marketing strategies to support the sales force. Jung's efforts were considered successful at first, but even early on, some business reporters were already worried that her attention to the sales representative staff was waning.

In 1996, Jung had taken the company onto the international stage when it became a corporate sponsor of the Summer Olympics in Atlanta, Georgia, and an accompanying ad campaign featured athletes Jackie Joyner-Kersee and Becky Dyroen-Lancer in the "Just Another Avon Lady" television spots.[50] In a black and white commercial broadcast during the games, Jackie Joyner-Kersee is seen running gracefully along a beach, narrating her proficiency in various events. "I can throw a nine pound shot-put fifty-one feet. I bench press 155 pounds. I jump further than all but 128 men in the world" while the camera focused on the details of musculature, hair, and sweat. Then she pauses, throwing her arms up in victory. "I have red toenails," she states matter-of-factly, the camera showing her bare feet in the ocean surf and the words: "Just Another Avon Lady."[51] The use of a celebrity athlete of color was a step out for Avon, but it was likely a rearguard action.

At the corporate level, Avon continued to name women to the executive suite, and especially in comparison to other Fortune 500 companies, Avon's track record as a company for women was exemplary. As Avon opened more and more international markets, it drew deeply on its 132-year history of empowering women. The 2000s would see the continuing rise of globalization of the Avon opportunity, increasing competition in the cosmetic industry, and the impact of the digital age. Jung and Avon seemed unprepared for this last challenges. Her thirteen-year tenure with Avon (1999–2012), while historic and mostly successful, ultimately did not end well. While the international markets grew, the US share of Avon's sales stalled starting in the 2000s largely because Avon did not make the shift into an internet platform or digital marketplace quickly enough in the first decade of the twenty-first century. Increasingly, when the representative rang the doorbell, there was no one home to answer, and the direct canvassing became problematic. Cosmetics offered by retail stores cut into sales by providing convenience for the consumer. Jung's attempts at a turnaround during this period mostly floundered. One such plan in 2001, after 114 years of direct sales and declining to have a retail presence, Avon created a line of products for J.C. Penney and Sears stores. Yet representative sales figures continued to fall along with profits.[52]

In 2002, Avon tried again to redefine the brand in marketing the new "Becoming" line of products using "ordinary women" in their advertising rather than supermodels. The "The core to what Becoming is all about, is celebrating a woman's personal journey through self-discovery," said Stuart Sklar, group vice president of retail marketing for Avon Products in New York. "We thought it would be very inappropriate to use supermodels to embody the message because it is so personal, it's so real and so intimate."[53] Marketing costs continued to rise as Avon fought to keep the brand relevant in the United States when 60 percent of sales were overseas.[54]

While Jung had expanded overseas operations by opening markets in China and Russia, by 2008 the company's US sales continued to slump, and critics felt she had failed to focus sufficiently on the representatives in the field. It was during this time that Avon's internal audit discovered bribes had been paid to Chinese officials and in 2011, an investigation by the US

Securities and Exchange Commission was opened seeking information regarding the actions of its executives in China. Avon eventually agreed to pay the SEC $135 million to settle the claims against it.[55]

Although Avon never invested in brick and mortar stores, its expenses grew enormously. In 2011 alone, Avon spent $400 million on advertising, another $472 million on brochures and catalogs (although they recouped half of that by charging reps for the materials), and lost $400 million in returns and $131 million in obsolete merchandise. Their net income as a company was just 6 percent of sales.[56] The company's stock price dropped. Jung's uphill battle finally ended in 2012.[57] In April of that year, Avon announced the hiring of Sherilyn S. McCoy, a former Johnson and Johnson employee as chief executive after rejecting an unsolicited takeover offer from Coty, a private beauty products firm. Avon's lead director, Fred Hassan, said McCoy had a "unique combination of strategic and finely honed operational skills, a significant turnaround track record, global experience and people leadership."[58]

In an interview from 2013, McCoy outlined her vision for Avon. "The vision is to restore Avon to an iconic beauty brand and to our leadership position in global direct selling, as well as continuing to ensure that we live up to our mission of empowering women. In terms of the plan, it's really about driving growth—getting the right growth platforms—simplifying and getting our business much more efficient, and in doing that driving costs out, and ultimately to build organizational capabilities and strengths for the future. It's really those three areas."[59] Ironically, McCoy's statement hewed to similar remarks made by Avon presidents decades before.

McCoy's tenure lasted until 2018, but despite numerous strategies to revive the door-to-door sales Avon was so known for, she was unable to solve the basic underlying issues, particularly the expanded digital competition the company faced. Avon's reliance on the door-to-door direct sales model had finally run its course in the United States. In 2016, Avon faced the sad and brutal reality that it could not continue. The company split off its North American operations, which were the least profitable, and moved the Avon Products, Incorporated headquarters to London, where, as a British company, it now organizes its world market in more than seventy countries and the representative staff of nearly 6,000,000 women. The North American operations group was re-formed as New Avon, a separate limited liability company (LLC). In January 2020, the Brazilian-based Natura group, the second largest direct-sales cosmetics company in the world, second to Avon Products, Inc., completed its purchase of New Avon and promised to remain committed to building the Avon Anew, Skin-So-Soft, and Avon Color brands.

Avon's downward decline was more than fifteen years in the making. The manufacturing plant in Suffern, New York, home to the original California Perfume Company facilities, closed in 2002. The loss was largely symbolic at that point and the company's future still looked strong. In 2008, Avon still employed nearly 40,000 people across the United States, but business started to move overseas. Avon's Distribution Plant in Newark, Delaware, its fully automated packaging plant that assembled representatives' orders from across the northeast, closed in 2009. It was followed in 2012, when the Springdale, Missouri, manufacturing plant shuttered. Then, in 2016 Avon headquarters moved to London, leaving the Rockefeller Center offices in Manhattan empty. At that time, New Avon (the North American division LLC) moved to Rye, New York, to set up shop in the lipstick manufacturing plant the company had built right after World War II. It, too, was soon shuttered, along with Avon's last manufacturing facility in Morton Grove, Illinois, just northwest of Chicago, which closed in 2018. The loss of employment to so many thousands of people was devastating.

The corporate makeover that Avon had begun in the 1980s and '90s had succeeded in opening a new conversation about women in corporate America that sought to lift women's status as both business owners and corporate executives. The corporation had put its money where its mouth was, promoting women's issues in the workplace, and slowly but surely opening its executive suite to women in a way that was both visible and substantive. Avon had fulfilled its mission to be a company for women as well as a company of women. The Women of Enterprise program created a stage on which Avon led a national conversation about discrimination and the glass ceiling, addressing both the structure of corporate America and the businesses on Main Street. But try as they might to place the Avon Lady on the same entrepreneurial stage, the individual representative's public persona did not evolve. Selling Avon remained, as it always had been, a means to earn a side income and a social forum where women could talk about sales, products, and their goals for achieving a measure of economic independence. The face-to-face sales call, however, simply could not compete in the internet age.

Epilogue

This history of Avon and Avon Ladies is one story amid a much longer history of women and business in the twentieth century. Coming of age in the 1980s, I grew up in a family in which my mother, a mid-level manager at a telephone company, encountered the glass ceiling in a slow-motion reality show. One by one, men she had trained became her boss, while her ideas and reports were appropriated by others and then used to justify their promotions and pay raises. The experience showed me how a business's assumptions about appropriate gender roles could shape its management philosophy, daily communication, and corporate values. When I learned that Avon had made gender central to its business model, my curiosity was piqued. Its deep-seated language about women and business ownership revealed a company that thought about how women and men might create a corporation that assumed and relied on women's agency as integral to success. Throughout the twentieth century, Avon's championing of women's economic potential was its hallmark contribution to business history.

This history of women and business, and women in business, has followed two major themes, one about women's entrepreneurship and their need for money, the second about the path of women's entry into the corporation and their eventual rise to middle management and executive leadership. The Avon Lady's dual identity as independent contractor and company representative played a unique role in both the corporation's history and in our understanding of women in business. By concentrating on the dynamics between Avon's corporate headquarters and the legion of independent Avon representatives, this book has made women's experience of business and the language of ownership central. In doing so, it has not focused on examining the products themselves or customers' experiences of using them; it has not looked at the ways that Avon designed forty shades of lipstick or competed with other cosmetics manufacturers for market share of anti-wrinkle cream. As a historian, I am leery of reading through a company's advertisements as evidence of a company's motivations and or internal operations. Advertisements can demonstrate how the company markets or envisions a product and shapes a corporation's public image, but they are not a blueprint for reading internal corporate dynamics. The correspondence, conference reports, sales figures, and the voices of Avon's women managers and representatives that are featured throughout this book provide a significant counterpoint to the iconic images of the Avon Lady.

Central to this history was taking the experience of the Avon representative seriously. This meant imagining the isolation of the rural representative in the early twentieth century, the excitement as well as the nervousness with which she carried her catalogs into the homes of her neighbors, the potential awkwardness of trying to collect payment, and the thrill of pocketing a 30 percent commission. It meant imagining the Avon representative of the 1950s navigating a new suburban neighborhood and hoping not to have a door slammed in her face, and the experience of African American representatives sampling perfumes and lipsticks with their friends and neighbors. What were their goals? What was it like for them to attend sales meetings and listen to women talk about marketing and customer service?

When I started this research, I wanted to know more about what it was like to be a representative. As a graduate student I was always looking for ways to earn some cash, so I turned to a friend who sold Mary Kay Cosmetics and offered to sign up. For about three years I held the occasional home party, complete with do-it-yourself facials and product samples. I distributed catalogs to friends and family, supplied cleansers and moisturizers, touted mascara and foundation. I carried and traded inventory with other Mary Kay reps, attended Monday sales meetings, got scolded by my director for wearing slacks and not a dress (because in 1996 Mary Kay wanted us to look like women!). One year I flew to Dallas, Texas, to attend Seminar, the Mary Kay annual extravaganza of prizes and ceremonies where women are crowned Queen of Sales and handed keys to pink Cadillacs. My unit director had just earned her car and several other women wore "red jackets"—representatives who had recruited at least three other representatives and earned their first piece of the official Mary Kay uniform. Back home, I happily accepted a plaque for earning fourth place in sales and stuck cheap colored jewels onto my Ladder of Success pin. All told, I earned several thousand dollars and, I must say, had a lot of fun. In many ways, my Mary Kay adventure helped highlight what was unique about Avon. But it also validated the social experience of being in direct sales, especially the relationships representatives build with one another, which were often more important to women I worked with than the business.

These modern hallmarks of the direct selling industry—charismatic leadership, enticing recruiting pitches that promise wealth and power, the representative's investment in over-priced inventories, and the constant urging to expand the market—were muted in Avon's approach to managing a far-flung network of female representatives. Yet many representatives whose voices appear in the corporate literature emphasized how rewarding the social interactions were to their experiences. Even the early twentieth-century traveling agents, whose work formed the backbone of the company, highlighted the emotional work of sales and recruiting. Throughout the company's history, women often mentioned first the satisfaction they felt in working for Avon rather than monetary rewards. While most Avon representatives earned just a few hundred dollars a year and rarely worked the job as a full-time occupation, the opportunity to own their own business offered a path away from economic dependence.

Ironically, just as Avon provided many individual women with an opportunity to make money, it denied women access to the top managerial ranks for most of its existence. Inside the company, women were afforded few opportunities for leadership and control before the 1980s. Avon's paternalistic and deeply conservative approach to managing representatives, a common theme in the history of women's labor, meant that women's promotion proceeded at a glacial pace. Avon's men remained oblivious to women's latent talent as managers until women themselves carved out new corporate spaces for themselves far away from central headquarters. The traveling agents of the early twentieth century, even though tightly scheduled and in constant contact with their male supervisors, earned a unique managerial status that enabled them, in the post–World War II era, to create a wholly new domain in regional sales offices. Their physical separation, in cities far from corporate headquarters, made women's management opportunities possible. Avon crept further toward a more recognizable feminist corporate philosophy during the advent of second wave feminism and the civil rights movement, and there, as elsewhere in industries, women persisted in poking holes in the glass ceiling of the corporate headquarters during the 1970s and 1980s. In its decades as an American company, Avon served as an early model for how women could succeed in business, even as its board welcomed women into the executive offices of corporate power only on the eve of the twenty-first century.

To the very end of its presence in American culture, Avon has remained steadfastly devoted to both the direct sales business model, which shaped its demise in the age of internet marketing, and to women's economic potential. An Avon Lady no longer appears at our front doors, but worldwide the memory of the Avon Lady ringing the doorbell, sample case in hand, ready with a smile, has endured.

Notes

Introduction

1. For a more complete picture of the industrial organization of direct selling from a business perspective, see Richard Berry, *Direct Selling: From Door to Door Marketing to Network Marketing* (Boston: Butterworth Heinemann, 1997).
2. Alfred C. Fuller, *A Foot in the Door: The Life Appraisal of the Original Fuller Brush Man as Told to Hartzell Spence* (New York: McGraw-Hill, 1960).
3. Fuller, *A Foot in the Door*, 200.
4. Kathy Peiss, *Hope in a Jar: The Making of America's Beauty Culture* (New York: Metropolitan Books, 1998), 245.
5. For a more complete picture of the industrial organization of direct selling from a business perspective, see Berry, *Direct Selling*.
6. Consumption patterns and consumers in the postwar era have received very little attention from historians. It is an odd development, given the central role consumption plays in the ideology of cold war domesticity, prosperity, and the ideology of middle-class life. Joy Parr, in Shopping for a Good Stove: A Parable about Gender, Design, and the Market" in *His and Hers: Gender Consumption and Technology*, Roger Horowitz and Arwen Mohun, Eds., (Charlottesville, University Press of Virginia, 1998), analyzes the sales strategies of consumer durable manufacturers in Ontario, Canada, in the 1950s. Her article speaks both to the way marketers invoked masculinity in salesmanship on the sales floor, and the response, or more appropriately the backlash, of women consumers as they attempted to purchase new stoves and ranges. Lizabeth Cohen, "From Town Center to Shopping Center: The Reconfiguration of Community Marketplaces in Postwar America," in *His and Hers: Gender Consumption and Technology*, ed. Roger Horowitz and Arwen Mohun (Charlottesville: University Press of Virginia, 1998) examines the way women and shopping claimed a new space in suburban New Jersey as shopping malls restructured consumption habits. In these new private, profit-oriented spaces, Cohen sees women's limited role as shoppers (and as the primary source for retail sales labor) as part of a much larger trend in making the mass-consumption economy, and the shopping mall as the new community civic space where political behavior could be circumscribed to fit within the bounds of being citizen-consumers.
7. Alison Clarke, *Tupperware: The Promise of Plastic in 1950s America* (Washington, DC: Smithsonian, 2001), 105.
8. Clarke, *Tupperware*, 85, 88–89.
9. See Nicole Woolsey Biggart, *Charismatic Capitalism: Direct Selling Organizations in America* (Chicago: University of Chicago Press, 1989), 42–44, and Clark,

Tupperware: The Promise of Plastic in the 1950s America, 78–100. Stanley Home Products used the home party plan in conjunction with door-to-door sales. However, only women appeared as representatives in its national advertisements featuring the "Stanley Home Party." Other companies recognized the party form but did not institute it. For example, there are several instances in Avon sales and training literature where women described their sales at impromptu gatherings of women, but neither the saleswomen nor the company seems to have made the connection and translated into a marketing plan that efficiency and success of selling to four, five, or more women at a time rather than one-on-one.

10. Ironically, although sales work may have been losing its prestige (if indeed it ever really had it), some sales jobs remained "men's" jobs, particularly in durable goods and high commission sales. There was a huge variety, however, within the narrow classifications of sales. Automobile salesmen, for example, could be well paid and have posh offices if they dealt with new cars, or crass and always scrounging to make a deal if they worked in a used car lot. On salesmen and the masculine culture honored on department store sales floors, see Alice Kessler Harris, "Women's History Goes on Trial: EEOC v. Sears, Roebuck and Company," *Signs* 11 (Summer 1986): 751–779, and Ruth Milkman, "Women's History and the Sears Case," *Feminist Studies* 12 (Summer 1986): 375–400. Joy Parr discusses salesmen's tactics for selling stoves in Canadian stores in "Shopping for a Good Stove."

11. Biggart, *Charismatic Capitalism*, 2. According to Biggart's reading of the National Association of Direct Selling Companies' records for 1936, women accounted for approximately 10 percent of distributors nationwide in the 1930s.

12. Fuller, *A Foot in the Door*.

Chapter 1

1. Union Publishing records in the Avon archive include personal correspondence from McConnell to his family, business correspondence to McConnell, and from McConnell to his sales agents (AP Series 8, Box 125, David H. McConnell Sr./ Union Publishing Co., 1880–1888).

2. Quotations from "Autobiography of the Founder" (1903) (AP Series 3, Box OS-10); on McConnell as an agent for Union Publishing Company, see Correspondence, David H. McConnell Sr./ Union Publishing Co., 1880–1888 (AP Series 8, Box 125).

3. Ibid. Mr. Snyder's brothers owned a banana plantation in Brazil, into which McConnell, too, tried to invest. Snyder sold McConnell his Union Publishing shares, then purchased them back three times in eight years. While Snyder was away, McConnell supported his own family as well as Snyder's with Union Publishing income. From interview with Mr. McConnell, April 15, 1936. Interviewer unidentified (AP Series 8, Box 125).

4. Quotation from "The Autobiography of the Founder" (1903) (AP Series 3, Box OS-10).

5. "The CPC Idea" (1922) (AP Series 3, Box 113, Recruitment booklets 1918–1937).

6. Quotes from an interview with David McConnell Sr., April 15, 1936. Interviewer unidentified. The company's headquarters were never in California but always in Manhattan (although McConnell's brother, George, did manage a small sales office in San Francisco, which closed in 1912).

7. Judging by the business correspondence and the style of mass-circulation letters that McConnell sent to the entire sales force, it seems that Union Publishing may have employed as many as 100 or more men and women.

8. McConnell's Scrapbook, "California Perfume Company," November 5, 1892 (Bound volume, AP Series 3, Box 114).

9. On products available at the CPC, see "The CPC Story: Autobiography of the Founder" (1903); CPC catalog (1896) (AP Series 3, Box 113).

10. The historiography of itinerant salesmen, especially in the nineteenth century, examines a variety of social and cultural material. The most relevant studies are Timothy B. Spears, *100 Years on the Road* (New Haven, CT: Yale University Press, 1995); Karen Halttunen, *Confidence Men and Painted Women: A Study of Middle Class Culture in America, 1830–1870* (New Haven, CT: Yale University Press, 1982). Peter Wosh, *Spreading the Word: The Bible Business in Nineteenth-Century America* (Ithaca, NY: Cornell University Press, 1994), explores the history of colporteurs, including women, and Bible sales. Thomas Schlereth, "Country Stores, County Fairs, and Mail Order Catalogs: Consumerism in Rural America," in *Consumer Culture and the American Home, 1890–1930*, ed. Glenda Dyer and Martha Reed, proceedings from the Second Annual McFaddin-Ward House Museum Conference (Beaumont, TX, 1989): 47–55, explores the impact of the Sears catalog on rural marketing in Texas at the turn of the century.

11. Business strategies other than the complex centralized bureaucratic forms identified by Chandler have been studied by historians such as Charles F. Sabel and Jonathan Zeitlin, "Stories, Strategies, Structures: Rethinking Historical Alternatives to Mass Production," in *World of Possibilities: Flexibility and Mass Production in Western Industrialization*, ed. F. Sabel and Jonathan Zeitlin (New York: Cambridge University Press, 1997); Philip Scranton, *Endless Novelty: Specialty Production and American Industrialization, 1865–1925* (Princeton, NJ: Princeton University Press, 1997) and Philip Scranton, *Figured Tapestry: Production, Markets, and Power in Philadelphia Textiles, 1885–1941* (New York: Cambridge University Press, 1989). Thomas Dicke, *Franchising in America: The Development of a Business Method, 1840–1980* (Chapel Hill: University of North Carolina Press, 1992), explores the history of the franchise, another alternative distribution method of mass produced materials. His study encompasses the history of Ford, Sunoco, and Domino's Pizza. While the details of how these companies managed their distribution systems and sold franchises varies, the significant difference between franchises and direct selling is that franchises required much higher capital outlays from the distributors, covering real estate, buildings, and equipment; they employed labor and were beholden to corporate distribution of raw materials, be it gasoline, engine parts, or cheese, and were subject to corporate advertising, just to name a few of the constraints.

12. This estimate, which is impossible to substantiate, comes from the Agents Credit Association, a professional conglomeration of direct sales companies. Among the ten companies that formed the Agents Credit Association in 1910, including the California Perfume Company, were textile companies such as Mutual Fabric and Standard Dress (both in Binghamton, New York) and Queen Fabric in Syracuse. With the exception of World's Starr Knitting in Bay City, Michigan, and McLean, Black and Company in Boston, all of the companies were located in or around New York City. The association protected members in credit matters and account collection. In 1914, the group reorganized and changed its name to National Association of Agency Companies. From 1917 to 1920, the group operated as the National Association of Agency and Mail Order Companies, and in 1920, the name was changed to the National Association of Agency Companies. At the May 1925 annual convention, the group adopted a new name: National Association of Direct Selling Companies. They used this identifier until the 1970s when the organization became the Direct Selling Association (February 21, 1964 letter from J. M. George, President NADSC to Norman Chadwick, Avon Products (AP Series 4, Box 117, Affiliations/Direct Selling Association, 1921-1988).

13. On selling soap, perfumes, and cosmetics via mass marketing, see Vincent Vinikas, *Soft Soap, Hard Sell: American Hygiene in the Age of Advertisement* (Ames: Iowa State University Press, 1992). On unbranded, bulk sales, see Susan Strasser, *Satisfaction Guaranteed: The Making of the American Mass Market* (New York: Pantheon, 1989), 35, 365-366.

14. Several companies converted product distribution from direct sales to retail, including those that sold *Encyclopaedia Britannica*, Kirby vacuums, Hoover vacuums, Wearever aluminum cookware, and Wonderbra.

15. On different types of salesmen and their responsibilities, see Strasser, *Satisfaction Guaranteed*: 21-23, 58-88, 193-195, 195-202; Spears also describes the nuances of peddlers, jobbers, drummers, and commercial travelers in *100 Years on the Road*, 51-77.

16. Historians Alfred Chandler and Olivier Zunz, for example, described the history and professionalization of independent salesmen in light of increasingly powerful corporate control. Chandler's seminal study, *The Visible Hand: The Managerial Revolution in American Business* (Cambridge, MA: Belknap Press, 1977) the prevailing history of large-scale corporate growth in the late nineteenth century, analyzed a number of firms, including DuPont, Singer, and the Pears soap company, which initially used independent agents or drummers to distribute products. Olivier Zunz, *Making America Corporate, 1879-1920* (Chicago: University of Chicago Press, 1992).

17. The economic fate of individual salesmen in the nineteenth-century mercantile organization of the economy, as both Chandler and Zunz argue, was one of perpetual decline in the shadow of the ever more powerful corporation. Zunz, *Making America Corporate*, 11-36, 175-198. In his study, large companies (DuPont, International Harvester, Ford, and Metropolitan Life Insurance) took over independent, small, producer-oriented local economies in order to control and manage their growth. As a result, they shifted the local focus of independent agents toward a homogeneous

service economy controlled by corporate-centered values. His analysis looked in part at the more human elements behind the seemingly inanimate corporate mask—the social characteristics and values, particularly of middle managers and salaried workers and their operative role in creating corporate culture. The salesman's ability to make independent decisions and hold cultural authority in his community was reduced, according to Zunz, if not swept away entirely in executives' effort to expand the growing corporation. Both drop the story of salesmen at the advent of print advertising in order to feature the rise of mass consumption, production, standardization, and new management structures and strategies in the twentieth century. Repeatedly, historians will sacrifice individual salesmen and assign them an early death, as Timothy Spears argued, to become controlled instruments of corporate sales offices and departments that reduced their ability to make independent decisions and, therefore, potentially harm corporate profits. Spears, *100 Years on the Road.*

18. The cultural history of peddlers and independent traveling salesmen and the tradition of distrust in the nineteenth century is explored in Spears, *One Hundred Years on the Road*; Halttunen, *Confidence Men and Painted Women*; Joseph T. Rainer, "The 'Sharper' Image: Yankee Peddlers, Southern Consumers, and the Market Revolution," *Business and Economic History* 26, no. 1 (Fall 1997): 27–44.

19. See Richard Tedlow, *New and Improved: The Story of Mass Marketing in America* (New York: Basic Books, 1990). On Sears's development of Texas as a test market for his new catalog in 1906, see Patrick H. Butler III, "Sears in Texas: 1906–1913," in *The Consumer Culture and the American Home, 1890–1930*, ed. Glenda Dyer and Martha Reed (Beaumont, Texas: McFaddin-Ward House, 1989.)

20. "Manual of Instruction" for representatives, 1899 (AP Series 3, Box 113).

21. In 1913, the city of King, Monterey County, California, filed a lawsuit against the CPC in an attempt to ban local representatives. McConnell and the CPC quickly won its right to solicit for sales (AP Series 1, Box 110, "Legal/Tax and Licensing Laws/King, CA 1911, 1913). On the 1922 Green River ordinance, see Nicole Biggart, *Charismatic Capitalism: Direct Selling Organizations in America* (Chicago: University of Chicago Press, 1989), 32. On the Fuller Brush approach technique, see Alfred Fuller, *A Foot in the Door: The Life Appraisal of the Original Fuller Brush Man as Told to Hartzell Spence* (New York: McGraw-Hill, 1960), 55. Some towns lodged informal complaints against recruiters, however, but not against the representatives who did the actual selling. In this regard, McConnell's tactics worked. On community resistance to direct sales agents, see Biggart, *Charismatic Capitalism*, Chapter 2. Fuller discusses the effects of the Green River Ordinance on his sales management in *A Foot in the Door*, 171–172. Local merchants and Chambers of Commerce sponsored legislation that required distributors to purchase business licenses. These laws were fought by the Agent's Credit Association, formed in 1910 by ten firms, including the California Perfume Company, and later known as the National Association of Direct Selling Companies with ninety-one members—both distributors and suppliers in 1925. "In 1927 the NADSC general counsel opposed 164 state and local ordinances and reported 'killing 111 of these bills'" (Biggart, *Charismatic Capitalism*, 32, 183 fn27); *Report and Minutes of the 1927 Annual Convention* (Winona, MN; NADSC, 1927) 4.

22. The titles of the door-to-door representative of the CPC changed frequently, from Depot Agent in the 1890s to Sales Manager in 1900s to Sales Representative shortly after. The "Traveling Agent" also bore various titles, including "General Agent" and "District Supervisor," all of which CPC officials used interchangeably until 1945. I have chosen to use the terms "representative" and "traveling agent" throughout these first three chapters to avoid confusion.

23. Mrs. Albee's tenure at the CPC was probably quite short. She is not mentioned in any surviving memoirs, including Anna Figsbee's unpublished memoir, *My Company and Me* (1951) (AP Series VIII, Box 125, Anna J. Figsbee bound volume). Figsbee joined the CPC in 1901. McConnell probably kept in touch with Albee, either for business or personal reasons, for in the photograph that was printed in the 1903 history Albee appears closer to seventy years of age than fifty (AP Series 8, Box 125, clippings file Mrs. P. F. E. Albee, 1951–1981).

24. "The CPC Story: Autobiography of the Founder" (1903) (AP Series 3, Box OS-10).

25. Ibid.

26. Angel Kwolek-Folland also notes the gendered nature of work and the role of women in corporations as "mothers" to the public and corporate employees in *Engendering Business: Men and Women in the Corporate Office, 1870–1930* (Baltimore: Johns Hopkins University Press, 1994), 2.

27. Albee may have contributed to the 1899 manual. The introduction states that the author was "involved in selling for more than twenty years," which was true of both Albee and McConnell. The 1915 recruiting manual used similar language, and in addition, "A Successful General Agent" signed the final page of the introduction. However, Albee had died in 1911, but given the repetition within the manuals, it does not necessarily imply that Albee had not written all or part of the first edition. Nevertheless, both manuals contained information on company policies and procedures (orders, billing, shipping, etc.) that were assumed by managers in the sales offices and headquarters. Albee would not have organized this information, and most likely McConnell or his staff compiled it. I would not rule out the possibility of Albee's contribution; however, there is no solid evidence that suggests she had made one.

28. On the history of the Bud Hastin's Avon collector group, see Bud Hastin, *Avon Products and California Perfume Co. Collector's Encyclopedia*, 13th ed. (Kansas City: Bud Hastin, 1994).

29. AP Series 8, Box 125, clippings file Mrs. P. F. E. Albee, 1951–1981.

30. Lu Ann Jones traces the peddler well in to the 20th century as a purveyor of goods, but whose wagon also served as a site of consumption where women helped define the terms of trade by barter: Lu Ann Jones, "Gender, Race, and Itinerant Commerce in the Rural New South," *Journal of Southern History*, v66 n2 (May 2000), 297–320.

31. Kathy Peiss, *Hope in a Jar: The Making of America's Beauty Culture*. New York: Metropolitan Books, 1998. 67–69.

32. Information on the Suffern factory and numbers of employees in *Tompkins History of Rockland County* (1902-03): 170–171, in David H. McConnell biographical information file (AP Series 8, Box 125).

33. Billing, packaging, and shipping cycles are detailed in several general CPC catalogs, sales promotion literature, and recruiting pamphlets.

34. McConnell, for reasons that are unclear but probably had to do with customs restrictions, also opened a manufacturing facility and sales office in Montreal in 1915, which supplied the Canadian contracts. The San Francisco office, managed by McConnell's brother George, burned in the city's 1906 earthquake, but was rebuilt soon after and operated until 1923.

35. Interview with Mr. McConnell, April 15, 1936. Interviewer unidentified (AP Series 8, Box 125).

36. "The CP Book: A Comprehensive and authoritative guide to the intelligent selection and use of Milady's Toilet Articles and other Household Necessities" by Myron Leroy (1904) catalog with color illustrations. (All catalogs mentioned here are in AP Series 3, Box 113.)

37. "For Beauty, Health and Home" (1902) (AP Series 3, Box 113).

38. "The CP Book" 1906: 12.

39. Ibid.

40. For the contents of the three separate outfits, see "Manual of Instruction" (1899): 17 (AP Series 3, Box 113).

41. Ibid.

42. California Perfume Company color plate catalogs 1916–1929 (AP, Hagley Museum and Library Imprints collection). Quote from the *Instructions for General Agents* handbook (1915), No. 10 "The Advantages of the Color Plate Catalog," pp. 4–6. (AP Series 3, Box 113).

43. "Outfit" cost estimates in file General Agent Procedures, 1922–1924 (AP Series 3, Box 113, General Agents Cost System).

44. From box F-5, folder Rationale of Direct Selling. IIIC-1 (1959) October 30, 1959, letter from J. M. George, President NADSC to C. J. Terriere, Avon Products. On COD shipping, see Schlereth, "Country Stores, County Fairs, and Mail Order Catalogs." NADSC president (1950) J. M. George claimed that when the post office began offering COD (cash on delivery) shipping in the 1920s, thousands of new companies joined the ranks of direct sales businesses.

45. On the Kardex system, see Joanne Yates, *Control through Communication: The Rise of System in American Management* (Baltimore: Johns Hopkins University Press, 1989), chapter 4.

46. On personalized letter writing, see "Personal Note" CPC Chat, October 20, 1922, and Bulletin No. 55 "Personal Note" in file General Agents Procedures, 1922–1924.

47. McConnell's Scrapbook, New York California Perfume Company April 7, 1897 (AP Series 4, Box 114, Bound Volume).

48. McConnell's Scrapbook, New York California Perfume Company March 1899 (AP Series 4, Box 114, Bound Volume).

49. Ibid.

50. "Privilege Includes Responsibility," *Christmas Bulletin*, no. 121 December 1921 (AP Series 3, Box 113, *CPC Bulletin* 1910–1927).

51. As sociologist Nicole Biggart argues, the direct selling industry did not develop this "alternative form of enterprise as a principled attack on over-rationalized capitalist work arrangements. Rather, [they] pursue[d] these arrangements in order to better control workers." See *Charismatic Capitalism*, 8.

52. If she worked from September 1924 to April 1926 (seventeen months) Guest would have earned commissions averaging $25 per month.

53. "Our Daily Chat," April 28, 1926, bound volume.

54. CPC Special Bulletin, November 1910 (AP Series 3, Box 113, *CPC Bulletin 1910–1927*).

55. Ibid.

56. In addition to the CPC, McConnell owned and operated D. H. McConnell and Co., and among his products in 1894 was a tableware line called "Gold Aluminum Flatware" (AP Series 8, Box 125). See also *Tompkins History of Rockland County (1902–03)*, p. 170. McConnell may also have owned part of or had close relations with other tableware suppliers; all of the silverware and several serving pieces offered as prizes in *Outlook* were manufactured by "Wm. Rogers and Co." Indeed, some evidence suggests that in addition to the perfume business, McConnell managed a wholesale trade as a jobber in tableware.

57. See July 1911 *Outlook*, for contest announcement and photos (AP Series 3, Box 113, Selling Method, incentives/recognition, auto program).

58. I have not found any evidence about the types of prizes other direct selling companies offered in this period. The CPC often suggested that representatives could use their prizes as gifts for friends and family members.

59. March 1917 *Outlook*.

60. "Instructions for General Agents" (1915), 2.

61. "Travel Talks" c. 1920, 3.

62. "Instructions for General Agents" (1915) 2.

63. "Instructions for General Agents" (1915) No. 33, "A Fish Story."

64. "Instructions for General Agents" (1915) No. 43 "Use Grappling Irons."

65. CPC Chat, August 1, 1925 bound volume.

66. "CPC-Avon Sales Representative's Contract" (1931) (AP Series 3, Box 113, Representatives/Contracts 1909-1935).

Chapter 2

1. "Does It Pay?" recruiting booklet, (1922) 10. (AP Series 3, Box 113, Recruitment booklets, 1918–1937).

2. Ibid., 23.

3. Ibid., 19.

4. Jeanne Boydston traces the nineteenth-century roots of women's unpaid labor as consumers in *Home and Work: Housework, Wages, and the Ideology of Labor in the Early Republic* (New York: Oxford University Press, 1990). Direct sales work took place

within a family and domestic structure where women's labor remained largely invisible, and where, by the early twentieth century, women's work increasingly revolved around their role as consumers. On women, work, and consumption in the twentieth century, see Victoria de Grazia and Ellen Furlough, eds., *The Sex of Things: Gender and Consumption in Historical Perspective* (Berkeley: University of California Press, 1996); Caroline Goldstein, *Creating Consumers: Home Economists in the Twentieth Century* (Chapel Hill: University of North Carolina Press, 2012), discusses the role of home economists in teaching women how to use new consumer items and meet cultural standards of efficiency.

5. Susan Porter Benson describes an interconnected triangle of managers, saleswomen, and consumers in *Counter Cultures: Saleswomen, Managers, and Customers in American Department Stores, 1890–1940* (Chicago: University of Illinois Press, 1986). From a perspective of labor history, Benson portrays women consumers and women sales agents more often in opposition to male managers, although occasionally one group could play the interests of the other off managers in order to gain an advantage. Class differences, however, made the ultimate trajectory of each woman's group in the department store follow divergent paths, such that the two would rarely exchange places and the potential for integrating business, or labor more accurately, and domesticity was very low. In direct selling, however, a good customer was and is often the recruiters' first choice.

6. Hundreds of women's progressive organizations and church groups raised money for their programs, but there is no analysis of how women managed, invested, or distributed that money. Kathleen Waters Sander, *The Business of Charity: The Woman's Exchange Movement, 1832–1900* (Chicago: Illinois University Press, 1998), analyzes the voluntary exchange stores and the implications they had on women as entrepreneurs and economic actors. See also Andrea Tone, *The Business of Benevolence: Industrial Paternalism in Progressive America* (Ithaca, NY: Cornell University Press, 1997).

7. Boyden Sparkes and Samuel Taylor Moore, *The Witch of Wall Street, Hetty Green* (New York: Doubleday, 1930).

8. Susan Yohn, "'They Hated Me on Spec': Assessing Popular Attitudes Towards Business Women" (unpublished paper presented to the History Department Workshop, University of Delaware, April 2000); and Yohn, "'You Can't Share Babies with Bonds:' How Americans Think about Women Making Money," *IRIS: A Journal about Women* 40 (Spring 2000): 20–27.

9. Nancy Marie Robertson, Indiana University/Purdue University, "A Room of Their Own: Banking and Women's Departments in the United States," presented at the Business History Conference, Palo Alto, California, March 2000.

10. The perception expressed by both men and women that it was dangerous for women to work outside the home is a product of early industrialization. In the nineteenth and twentieth centuries, it usually accompanied clear class- and race-driven political objectives and goals. For an analysis of home and work dialog pertaining to women in the early twentieth century, see for example Alice Kessler-Harris, *Out to Work: A*

History of Wage-Earning Women in the United States (New York: Oxford University Press, 1982).

11. CPC Chat, January 16, 1925.

12. Nancy Grey Osterud, *Bonds of Community: The Lives of Farm Women in Nineteenth-Century New York* (Ithaca, NY: Cornell University Press, 1991), looks at women's roles in commodity production, their relationship to the economy and their position in formal cooperative farm organizations such as the Grange and mutual insurance, as well as in informal networks of neighborhood exchange.

13. "Handbook for District Supervisors," 1924 (pages unnumbered). (AP Series 3, Box 113, Sales System/Manager's Manual). This section was reprinted from a longer version that appeared in 1915: "Instructions for General Agents" manual, No. 41 "What Your Business Means."

14. Ibid.

15. Ibid.

16. See Angel Kwolek-Folland, *Engendering Business: Men and Women in the Corporate Office, 1870-1930* (Baltimore: Johns Hopkins University Press, 1998): 136. On the transition between the familial traditions of the pre-corporate order to rationalized bureaucracy, see 129–164. Kwolek-Folland also analyzes female imagery in financial industry logos and publications, 130–134.

17. On married women in the labor force, see Alba Edwards *Comparative Occupation Statistics for the United States, 1870–1940*, US Department of Commerce, 16th census of the United States: 1940 (Washington, DC: US Government Printing Office, 1943); Janet Hooks, *Women's Occupations through Seven Decades*, US Department of Labor, Women's Bureau Bulletin #218 (Washington, DC: US Government Printing Office, 1947); Alice Kessler-Harris *Out to Work*; Lynn Weiner, *From Working Girl to Working Mother: The Female Labor Force in the United States, 1820–1980* (Chapel Hill: University of North Carolina Press, 1985); Leslie Woodcock Tentler, *Wage Earning Women: Industrial Work and Family in the United States, 1900–1930* (New York: Oxford University Press, 1979).

18. Nicole Biggart, *Charismatic Capitalism: Direct Selling Organizations in America* (Chicago: University of Chicago Press, 1989), 8.

19. Biggart, *Charismatic Capitalism*: 29–30, discusses census figures for "huckster" wholesale and manufacturer's sales representatives, store clerks, and total numbers of sales workers, noting that the census takes into account only a person's primary occupation and therefore underestimates the numbers of sales people who worked that as a second job.

20. *CP Outlook* [*CPO*] 10, no. 1 (April 1914).

21. The percentage of married and unmarried men is unknown.

22. The classification system is spelled out on the back of the 1925 situation reports in the Lela Eastman correspondence file (AP Series 8, Box 125), and in the District Supervisors' Handbook (1924).

23. District Supervisor's Handbook (1924), "Territory" and "We Can Always Satisfy on Territory," 58–59.

24. "Composite Record of Towns and Districts" (1918–1927) (AP Series 3, Box 113, file Representatives/Sales Statistics, 1902–1928).

25. Osterud, *Bonds of Community*, 12. There are very few historical analyses of rural women in the twentieth-century United States. Most assume that rural women are part of farm families and position them as wives and mothers and as consumers. Farming could be viewed through the lens of business history but is rarely done so. See also Mary Neth, "Preserving the Family Farm: Farm Families and Communities in the Midwest, 1900–1940" (PhD diss., University of Wisconsin, Madison, 1987). Neth examines maintenance of gender integration and participation of women in farm work and barn chores. See also Mary Neth, "Building the Base: Farm Women, the Rural Community, and Farm Organizations in the Midwest, 1900–1940," in *Women and Farming: Changing Roles, Changing Structures*, ed. Wava Haney and Jane B. Knowles (Boulder, CO: Westview Press, 1988).

26. Mary Neth, "Gender and the Family Labor System: Defining Work in the Rural Midwest," *Journal of Social History* 27, no. 3 (Spring 1994), 569.

27. Ibid., 275–288.

28. Walker started distributing her hair care products for black women in Denver in 1905, and like the CPC, sold her products directly to the buyer through representatives, primarily in the South and Midwest. Walker's representatives also recruited others and earned a commission on their sales. See Kathy Peiss, *Hope in a Jar: The Making of America's Beauty Culture* (New York: Metropolitan Books, 1998)\,: 67–70, 73–77. However, Walker's plan should not be considered a full-fledged multi-level marketing plan. It appears that Walker paid an initial commission on new recruits, and like the CPC, paid women for their training services, but her agents' commissions did not build through layered recruit lines, or "uplines" as modern multi-level marketers term them. Blacks were not featured in CPC literature until the 1960s.

29. "Handbook for District Supervisors," (1924), 13.

30. Ibid. Italics in original.

31. Ibid., 15. Italics in original.

32. I gathered the names of all women whose hometowns were published in the CPC *Outlook* and *Bulletin* from 1905 to 1910. I organized them by state and then determined in which county each resided. I tried to locate each woman, starting with those state censuses that are indexed by Soundex, which included Alabama, California, Colorado, Idaho, Kansas, Massachusetts, Michigan, Montana, New Mexico, North Dakota, Pennsylvania, South Dakota, and West Virginia. Soundex is organized by reducing last names to numerical codes in such a way that several last names may have the same four-digit code. Within each code, households are listed alphabetically by the head of household's first name, which was usually a man. Since I often did not know a representatives husband's or father's name, I had to scan all cards within a Soundex code. Therefore, rather than looking for names, I visually scanned first for cards within the proper counties, then for town, then for last name, then for the representative's first name. For states that were not indexed by Soundex, I organized the towns by size of population, and for towns with populations under 1,000,

I manually scanned the entire town census. Ironically, this often proved easier and quicker than trying to locate individuals by Soundex.

33. From "The Permanence of a CPC Sales District: One Hundred Reasons for Becoming Our Representative" (1926), 6 (AP Series 3, Box 113, Recruitment booklets, 1918–1937).

34. Neth, "Gender and the Family Labor System," 570.

35. CPC Chat, January 16, 1925.

36. CPC Chat, August 11, 1925.

37. CPC Chat, November 12, 1926.

38. "Handbook for District Supervisors" (1924), 34.

39. Wendy Gamber, *The Female Economy: The Millinery and Dressmaking Trades, 1860–1930* (Chicago: University of Illinois Press, 1997): 52. On the history of women's business ownership in the nineteenth century, see also: Wendy Gamber, "Gendered Concerns: Thoughts on the History of Business and the History of Women," *Business and Economic History* 23 (Fall 1994): 129–140; Susan Ingalls Lewis, "Beyond Horatia Alger: Breaking Through Gendered Assumptions about Business 'Success' in Mid-Nineteenth-Century America," *Business and Economic History*, 2nd series, 22 (1992): 65–73; Lucy Eldersveld Murphy, "Her Own Boss: Businesswomen and Separate Spheres in the Midwest, 1850–1880," *Illinois Historical Journal* 80 (Autumn 1987): 155–176; Murphy, "Business Ladies: Midwestern Women and Enterprise, 1850–1880," *Journal of Women's History* 3 (Spring 1991): 65–89.

40. On marriage as both an asset and a liability to women's businesses, see Gamber *The Female Economy:* 25–54, and Scott Sandage, "Deadbeats, Drunkards, and Dreamers: A Cultural History of Failure in America: 1819–1893" (PhD diss., Rutgers University, 1995), particularly chapter 5 on nineteenth-century libel suits and the R. G. Dun credit organization's surveillance of husbands' and wives' domestic lives to explain failure. Lucy Eldersveld Murphy also relies on the R. G. Dun credit reports to track women entrepreneurs in the nineteenth century in "Her Own Boss" and "Business Ladies." R. G. Dun stopped chronicling the personal assessments of individual businesses in the 1890s. Individual direct sales representatives of any concern did not appear in these listings; they rarely asked for credit because they sold on commission, maintained low inventories, and their businesses were too small and short-lived to warrant reporting.

41. "Converting Spare Hours into Dollars" (1923–24) 6 (AP Series 3, Box 113, Recruitment booklets 1918–1937).

42. "Manual of Instruction" (1899) p. 4 (AP Series 3, Box 113).

43. Ibid., 5.

44. Ibid., 7.

45. Exhortations to walk and work include "Another Walk Talk," *CPO* 10, no. 3 (June 1914); "Are You a Walker?" *CPO* 10, no. 7 (October 1914); "Like Walking?" *CPO* 10, no. 9 (December 1914); "Walk! Walk! Walk!" *CPO* 10, no.11 (February 1915); "Walking Is Good Summer Sport," *CPO* 11, no. 5 (August 1915); "Walking a Beautifier and a Pastime," *CPO*, 11, no. 8 (November 1915); "Walking as a Lost Art," *CPO* 11,

no.10 (January 1916); "Walking Machines," *CPO* 12, no. 1 (April 1916); "Walking as a Summer Exercise," *CPO* 12, no. 4 (July 1916); "Walking as a Habit," *CPO* 12, no. 5 (August 1916); "Winter Walking," *CPO* 12, no. 11 (February 1917; "Would You Be Strong and Healthy? Then Just Walk," *CPO* 12, no. 12 (March 1917).

46. Quote from "Walking as a Lost Art," *CPO* 2 (January 1916).

47. "Converting Spare Hours into Dollars" (1923–24) 1 (AP Series 3, Box 113, Recruitment booklets, 1918–1937).

48. "Field Notes" *CPO* 10, no. 5 (August 1914).

49. "Does It Pay?" (1922): 5.

50. "Winner in July Talcum, Baby and Elite Powder Sales Contest," *CPO* 10, no. 6 (September 1914).

51. From "The Permanence of a CPC Sales District: One Hundred Reasons for Becoming Our Representative" 1926, p. 5 (AP Series 3, Box 113, Recruitment booklets, 1918–1937).

52. "The Permanance of a CPC Sales District: One Hundred Reasons for Becoming Our Representative" (1926.)

53. Ibid.

54. Ibid.

55. Ibid.

56. Ibid.

57. Another explanation for this statistic is that the number might also include representatives on file early in the year who did not produce, and who were later replaced or their contracts terminated by the CPC. For example, a representative who signed up in October and submitted orders totaling $50 might not submit another order between January and June, at which time she would be replaced. Therefore, her contract would be labeled inactive, but it would not necessarily mean that she had never submitted an order. Unfortunately, it is impossible to check. Another way to measure the correlation between tenure and sales performance is through an analysis of sales representative prize winners. In 1922, fewer than 5 percent of "new" representatives in the New York office earned sales prizes awarded to any representative who sent in orders of $30 or more. In Ohio, only three of the fifty-one representatives earned prizes in 1922 for submitting orders of $30 or more. Overall, Eastern Division representatives earned 186 prizes (twenty-nine by beginners); Western Division representatives earned 159 prizes (fifteen by beginners); and the Southern Division representatives earned 143 prizes (ten by beginners).

58. "Field Notes," *CPO* 12, no. 7 (October 1916).

59. "Field Notes," *CPO* 10, no. 5 (August 1914).

60. Neth, "Gender and the Family Labor System," 569.

61. *CPO* 10, no. 4 (July 1914): 6.

62. Lu Ann Jones, "Gender, Race, and Itinerant Commerce in the Rural New South," *Journal of Southern History* 66 (May 2000): 311.

63. All quotes from *CPO* 5, no. 2 (May 1910).

64. Boydston, *Home and Work*, 113–119.

Chapter 3

1. Quotation from "Travel Talks," California Perfume Company, New York (c. 1920) (AP Series 3, Box 113, Recruitment booklets, 1918–1937). In 1900, McConnell employed 48 travelers; in 1910, 100; and after 1915, more than 150. The number of representatives leveled out at 25,000 by 1925.

2. On the creation of public relations departments, see Roland Marchand, *Creating the Corporate Soul: The Rise of Public Relations and Corporate Imagery in American Business* (Berkeley: University of California Press, 1998).

3. The classic analyses of the self-made man literature include Irvin G. Wyllie, *The Self-Made Man in America: The Myth of Rags to Riches* (New Brunswick, NJ: Rutgers University Press, 1954); John G. Cawelti, *Apostles of the Self-Made Man* (Chicago: University of Chicago Press, 1965); and Richard Weiss, *The American Myth of Success: From Horatio Alger to Norman Vincent Peale* (New York: Basic Books, 1969). On the evangelical tradition and business as a "calling," see Max Weber *The Protestant Work Ethic and the Spirit of Capitalism* (New York: Routledge, 1930; reprinted 1992).

4. "Instructions for General Agents" (1915), section No. 37 "Prospects for General Agency Work."

5. "Our Daily Chat," bound volume, March 25, 1926.

6. "Instructions for General Agents" (1915), section No. 37 "Prospects for General Agency Work."

7. "Instructions for General Agents" (1915), "Preparation for your Work": 3.

8. Ibid.

9. "Our Daily Chat," March 31, 1926, bound volume.

10. Ibid.

11. *CPO* 18, no. 10 (January 1923): 7.

12. Fogartie Diary, February 1, 1930 entry (AP Series 8, Box 125, Fogartie Diary, 1930–1931).

13. Fogartie Diary, February 9, 1930 entry.

14. Lela Eastman interview (1972) (AP Series 8, Box 125), 22.

15. Eastman interview, 23.

16. These figures assembled from monthly appointment reports printed in Daily Chats, 1924.

17. CPC Chat, April 21, 1926.

18. CPC Chat, February 13, 1925.

19. See Claudia Golden. In 1920, $100 per month was percent higher than the average monthly salary of white-collar women.

20. Timothy Spears, *100 Years on the Road: The Traveling Salesman in American Culture* (New Haven, CT: Yale University Press, 1995), 55. By comparison, in Chicago, insurance clerks made about $1,800 per year, lawyers about $4,000, and skilled workers between $500 and $800. See also Jurgen Kocka, *White Collar Workers in America, 1890–1940: A Social-Political History* (London: Sage, 1980),

77. Between 1870 and 1900, traveling salesmen earned an average income of $100 to $150 a month, plus commissions. However, depending on the types of products they sold, salesmen could add more than $2,000 to $3,000 to their salaries each year.

21. "CPC District Supervisors" handbook (1924), 43.

22. Bulletin No. 48, "General Agents' Expenses" (AP Series General Agents Procedures, 1922–1924). Also presented in Daily Chat (find date), and "CPC District Supervisors" handbook (1924), p. 42. Two years later, the CPC added streetcar fare within city limits to the list of allowable expenses.

23. Lela Eastman correspondence file (AP Series 8, Box 125) contains many letters that mention that an advance expense check was included. Holiday meals were offered every Thanksgiving and Christmas according to the Daily Chats.

24. General Agents Expense Bulletin (AP Series 3, Box 113, General Agents Cost System, 1923).

25. Salary information available in Eastman correspondence file (AP Series 8, Box 125). Bonus information on individual agents cited monthly; those discussed here are available in CPC Chats, bound volume, 1926.

26. Eastman correspondence file, situation report August 31, 1927.

27. Bonus reports, Eastman correspondence file (AP Series 8, Box 125).

28. See CPC Chat, September 14, 1927, for contest rules.

29. Eastman correspondence file, May 7, 1928, letter from Bachler to Eastman in Twin Falls, Idaho.

30. Eastman correspondence file, October 6, 1927, letter from Bachler to Eastman in Cheyenne, Wyoming.

31. Eastman interview (1972), 26.

32. According to CPC Chats from September 1925, managers urged women to hire cars if they could find lodging in a central location and work a number of small towns in the area. However, no reimbursement policy existed before World War II for women who used their personal automobiles for business.

33. Eastman interview (1972), 38.

34. Eastman interview (1972), 25--26.

35. "Our Daily Chat," March 31, 1926.

36. Fogartie Diary, May 18, 1930 entry.

37. Fogartie Diary, October 12, 1930 entry.

38. Fogartie Diary, March 16, 1930 entry.

39. Fogartie Diary, March 15, 1930 entry.

40. Fogartie Diary, March 16, 1930 entry.

41. Fogartie Diary, November 28, 1930 entry.

42. Letter #13, "To Our Travelers," unsigned, c. 1908. The letter re-appeared in Instructions for General Agents, "Qualifications of General Agents" by a Successful General Agent (California Perfume Company, New York: 1915), 11, and in "CPC District Supervisors Handbook" (1924), 43.

43. "CPC District Supervisors Handbook" (1924), 43.

44. Ibid., 44.
45. Fogartie Diary, September 13, 1930 entry.
46. Fogartie Diary, May 12, 1930 entry.
47. Fogartie Diary, April 4, 1930 entry.
48. Fogartie Diary, February 24, 1930 entry.
49. Fogartie Diary, May 25, 1930 entry.
50. Fogartie Diary, March 7, 1930 entry.
51. Fogartie Diary, July 10, 1930 entry.
52. Fogartie Diary, January 12, 1931 entry.
53. Spears, *100 Years on the Road*; Susan Strasser, "The Smile that Pays," in *The Mythmaking Frame of Mind: Social Imagination and American Culture*, ed. James Gilbert, Amy Gilman, Donald M. Scott, and Joan W. Scott (Belmont, CA: Wadsworth, 1993): 159–160. Attracting members by the tens and hundreds of thousands, many of these associations built clubs in major cities, worked to protect salesmen's interests, and provided fraternal benefits such as insurance and burial plans, and several also provided religious support. Additionally, they worked to dismantle local licensing laws that did not distinguish people selling by sample from peddlers. In 1872, the Commercial Travelers National Association obtained discounts on railroad and steamboat lines, hotels, and Western Union. In 1910, the *Commercial Travelers Magazine* listed twenty-eight traveling salesmen's associations, fraternal groups, insurance companies, and burial societies. The Travelers Protective Association held a convention in 1892 attracting 7,000 members. Census figures are a very unreliable source for determining just how many men and women worked as commercial travelers in 1890. Many were counted as clerks or salesmen, or missed altogether, which was not unusual for such a mobile population.
54. Strasser, "The Smile That Pays," 160.
55. Mrs. E. Earle Clyde, "Our General Agents," *CPO* 18, no. 7 (October 1922); Miss Flora Prout, "Our General Agents," *CPO* 17, no. 5 (August 1921): 3.
56. "Travel Talks" (c. 1920), 3.
57. This is probably Hattie Goss whom CPC also profiled in *Outlook* 17, no. 6 (September 1921): 3 (w/photo).
58. *CPO* 11, no. 2 (May 1915): 6.
59. Ibid.
60. "Travel Talks" (c. 1920), R.F.O. Texas, 21.
61. "Travel Talks" (c. 1920), Miss E.S.T. Missouri, 21.
62. "Travel Talks" (c. 1920), Mrs. J.H.L., Indiana, 14.
63. "Travel Talks" (c. 1920), Mrs. M.N.W. Illinois: 12.
64. "Travel Talks" (c. 1920), Mrs. M.A.D. Kentucky, 11–12.
65. "Travel Talks" (c. 1920), Mrs. M.A.D. Kentucky, 11–12.
66. "Travel Talks" (c. 1920), Mrs. M.A.D. Kentucky, 11–12. (Italics added.)
67. "Instructions for General Agents" (1915), section No. 37, "Prospects for General Agency Work" (AP Series 3, Box 113).

Chapter 4

1. Fogartie Diary, November 27, 1930 (AP Series 8, Box 125, Fogartie Diary, 1930–1931).
2. Fogartie Diary, May 17, 1931.
3. Fogartie Diary, December 7, 1930.
4. Fogartie Diary, December 11, 1930.
5. See Chapter 2 for signing bonus and quality bonus award information.
6. Quotation from "45 Years of Steady Growth: Do You Really Know What the Great CPC-Avon Organization Represents?" *Avon Outlook* (February, 1931): 2.
7. "The CPC business is better than ever on our forty-seventh anniversary," *Avon Outlook* (May 6, 1933): 2.
8. Lizabeth Cohen argues that the "crucial groundwork" for establishing a mass-consumer society was laid in the 1930s. She examines the role that the state and federal government played in shaping a consumer society, in both its role as an arbiter of the economy and in its political power in shaping consumption as "a new vehicle for delivering the traditional American promises of democracy and egalitarianism." Lizabeth Cohen, "The New Deal State and the Making of Citizen Consumers," in Susan Strasser, Charles McGovern, and Matthias Judt, *Getting and Spending: European and American Consumer Societies in the Twentieth Century* (Washington, DC: German Historical Institute, 1998): 111–125.
9. Victor Buell, "Door-to-Door Selling," *Harvard Business Review* 32 (May/June 1954): 113–123.
10. "Evidence . . . A Depression-Proof Business," W. J. Alley, secretary and treasurer, *Avon Outlook* (January 2, 1933): 2.
11. See Alfred Fuller, *Foot in the Door: The Life Appraisal of the Original Fuller Brush Man as Told to Hartzell Spence* (New York: McGraw-Hill, 1960), 172. On Encyclopedia Britannica, see Herman Kogan, *The Great EB: The Story of the 'Encyclopaedia Britannica'* (Chicago: University of Chicago Press, 1958). On Beveridge's training with Fuller Brush, see Fuller, *A Foot in the Door*, 133–134. On Stanley Home Products, see Joan B. Marcus, *To Better Your Best: Stanley Home Products, The First 50 Years* (Westfield, MA: Stanley Home Products, c. 1981).
12. "Direct Selling Takes a New Direction: NADSC—1910 and After," unpublished manuscript in Direct Selling Association (DSA) archives, Washington, DC. Report closely follows style, language, and format in Avon archives on report to NADSC (the DSA forerunner) by Russel Rooks, "Direct Selling Challenges and Opportunities as I See Them," 1957 (AP Series 4, Box 117).
13. On direct sales expense-management issues, see Buell, "Door-to-Door Selling," 113–123.
14. In gathering data for his 1958 sociology dissertation, Raymond Ries, "The American Salesman: A Study of a Direct Sales Organization" (PhD diss., University of Illinois, Urbana, 1958) sketched out "Tiebolt's" sales motivation and reward structures and its workforce. He sat in on sales meetings, accompanied representatives on their sales routes, and interviewed managers and corporate executives as part of his study. As

such, Ries's dissertation is one of the only "objective" scholarly descriptions available of the internal dynamics of a direct sales organization in the post–World War II era. The company's true identity is unknown. Recruiting information is on p. 58.

15. On post-Depression direct selling company management style, see Nicole Woolsey Biggart, *Charismatic Capitalism: Direct Selling Organizations in America* (Chicago: University of Chicago Press, 1989), 32.

16. On the popularity of cosmetics in the 1920s, see Kathy Peiss, *Hope in a Jar* (New York: Metropolitan Books, 1998), chap. 4, "The Rise of the Mass Market," 96–133.

17. "Daphne" fragrance lipstick appeared in the 1917 color plate catalog (California Perfume Company).

18. Peiss, *Hope in a Jar*, 73–74.

19. On Recordon line, see color plate catalog, 1928; Anna Figsbee, an accounts manager who began her CPC career in 1902, described the Recordon line as a prestige product. Figsbee, "My Life," unpublished bound manuscript (AP Series 8, Box 125, Figsbee file).

20. Color plate catalog (California Perfume Company), 1929.

21. Peiss, *Hope in a Jar*, 196; Avon's trade catalogs, 1932, 1936.

22. For availability of products in rural areas, see Peiss, *Hope in a Jar*, 169–170: "It was not until the end of the 1930s that farm women's use of cosmetics approximated that of urban dwellers."

23. Peiss, *Hope in a Jar*, 103.

24. According to the Princeton yearbook, David McConnell Jr.'s goal was "to become a manufacturer of toiletries and household goods" (Princeton University, alumni records. The clippings file on David McConnell Jr. includes biographical items, news items, and obituaries).

25. On the executive staff's age, tenure, and turnover, see *Outlooks, Bulletins*, company introductory literature, anniversary issues, "Avon Products, Inc.," a study by Hemphill, Noyes, and Co., 1958 (AP Series 1, Box 110, file Stock, Shareholder/Official Data 1946, 1958).

Nepotism also thrived within the CPC executive ranks. McConnell Jr. was, of course, the first son of the founder. W. Van Alan Clark, vice president of production at Suffern, held a degree in chemistry from Cornell University, joined CPC in 1921, and was also married to McConnell's first daughter. Both Clark and his son would eventually serve as chairman of the board at Avon through to the 1970s. Alexander Henderson Jr., vice president of packaging in 1939, joined the CPC in 1916 to work in the shipping department and became an assistant buyer of raw materials in 1921, taking over for his father A. D. Henderson Sr., who was one of McConnell's earliest business partners in the 1890s and who served as secretary and treasurer until he died in 1922.

26. *Handbook for District Supervisors*, "Working Large Cities," California Perfume Company (1924), 45 (AP Series 3, Box 114).

27. October 1965 interview with Wayne Hicklin, president, of Avon Products (AP Series 8, Box 125, Wayne Hicklin, 1964, 1972).

28. "Schedule of City Sales Offices opened during the period December 15, 1935, to February 10, 1941" (AP Series 5, Box 122, Sales System/Field Organization/City Sales, 1935–1941). The CPC organized sales offices in Boston and Philadelphia in 1938 but waited until after 1940 to organize most of the northeast corridor. The company did not even attempt to organize New York City until the 1950s.

29. In 1938, the earliest year for which city sales statistics are available, Avon had organized 4,038 representatives (of 30,000 active representatives) in 54 city sales offices nationwide. City sales representatives generated nearly $800,000 in sales. Operating costs for city offices totaled nearly $140,000, or 17.5 percent of sales, the highest margin in company history (AP Series 7, Box 124, "City Sales Total Business and Cost" in "Avon Round Table: Check of Facts and Figures" management conference, 1943, 30). According to 1947 annual conference report, Avon operated 34 offices and generated sales of $317,222 in 1937; 53 offices and $783,258 sales in 1938; 88 offices and $473,532 sales in 1939, in "Avon Better Business conference, January 1947: 33–34 (AP Series 7, Box 124). In contrast, sales in "small town America" totaled $3,641,348 in 1937; $4,011,362 in 1938; and $5,758,979 in 1939 (ibid., p. 34). As a percentage of sales, therefore, city sales represented 8.7% in 1937; 19% in 1938; and 8% in 1939.

30. See Biggart, *Charismatic Capitalism*, 32.

31. Eastman interview, 38–39 (AP Series 8, Box 125).

32. Eastman interview, 38–39.

33. Hicklin interview transcript 1964, 6 (AP Series 8, Box 125, Wayne Hicklin, 1964, 1972).

34. Two hundred percent turnover is a modest estimate; some analysts claim that direct selling companies may have absorbed turnover rates of up to 400 percent.

35. Hicklin interview transcript, 5.

36. "Our Daily Chats" July 25, 1932, bound volume.

37. *Avon Outlook*, August 1 to August 23, 1932.

38. Hicklin interview transcript, 5.

39. On the employee relationship and the failed salary plan, see Hicklin interview transcript, 1964, quotes from 1–2.

40. Hicklin interview transcript, 1964, 6.

41. Fuller Brush's expectations for their salesmen in "The Fuller Recruiter's and Trainer's Manual" (Hartford: Fuller Brush Company, 1928) and "Making Good, and Making Money" recruiting pamphlet (Hartford: Fuller Brush Company, 1937), copies in author's possession, courtesy of the Fuller Brush Company. See also Fuller, *A Foot in the Door*. See also Walter A. Friedman, "The Peddler's Progress: Salesmanship, Science, and Magic, 1880 to 1940 (Direct Marketing, John H. Patterson, Henry B. Hyde, Alfred Fuller)" (PhD diss., Columbia University, 1996).

42. Biggart's *Charismatic Capitalism* studies emotional control and motivation through the lens of sociology and Weberian theory. Her study analyzes multi-level marketing companies, including A. L. Williams Life Insurance, Amway, and Mary Kay, from about 1970 to 1980. She argues that direct selling organizations fundamentally differ from firms in both their social relations and managerial strategy. Direct selling businesses, in response to their use of independent contractors to distribute products,

rely on alternative, emotional management devices that bind individuals morally and emotionally to the institution. As a result, direct selling companies do not necessarily follow rational decision making, but Biggart argues that in certain circumstances, an alternative, emotional logic can be more economically advantageous than strict rational, dispassionate judgments. Direct sales managers created an alternative form of enterprise in order to better control their distributors (Biggart, *Charismatic Capitalism*, 1–19).

43. In 1940, Avon asked local city sales office managers to survey women who had discontinued their Avon contracts. Whereas less than 1 percent cited their husband's objection to their working, fully one-third said they had lost interest or "didn't like" the work, or had never started. ("City Sales Removals and Reasons, 1942" (for New York and Kansas City divisions) in "Avon Round Table of Facts and Figures" management conference report (1943), 34–35 (AP Series 7, Box 124, Conferences/Reports).

44. "Our President Writes a Stirring Appeal on Helping Unemployment through Capitalizing the CPC Opportunity," *Avon Outlook* (May 1931): 3.

45. Ibid.

46. "No Finer Tribute Could Be Paid Mr. McConnell, Our President." Representative letters on his seventy-sixth birthday, 1934 (AP Series 3, Box 113, "Honor/Prize Programs, 1930–1939).

47. Ibid.

48. "Success Is Not an Accident" *Avon Outlook* (August 1931): 2.

49. "Will You Help Bring Back Prosperity," *Avon Outlook* (January 1931): 6.

50. "45 Years of Steady Growth," *Avon Outlook* (February 1931): 2.

51. "Success Is Not an Accident" *Avon Outlook* (August 1931): 2.

52. "Our Work Is the Test of Our Value" *Avon Outlook* (September 1931): 2.

53. Historians Susan Porter Benson and Lu Ann Jones both detail the household economies that women built to weather the Depression. While Benson's work focuses on urban working-class women and Jones's on women in the rural South, both note how families relied on neighbors, friends, and family members in a pattern of reciprocal economic exchanges. Sociability mixed with traditions of mutual aid, Benson notes, allowed families to secure basic necessities and some luxury items as women traded, repaired, and borrowed goods from one another. While peddling basic goods and household necessities, CPC women transformed friendship into an economic transaction. See Susan Porter Benson, *Household Accounts: Working-Class Family Economies in the Interwar United States*, (Ithaca, NY: Cornell University Press, 2007), 78. See also Lu Ann Jones, "Gender, Race, and Itinerant Commerce in the Rural New South," *Journal of Southern History*, 66, no. 2 (May 2000): 297–320.

54. Alan Brinkley, *The End of Reform: New Deal Liberalism in Recession and War* (New York, 1995); Ellis W. Hawley, *The New Deal and the Problem of Monopoly* (Princeton, NJ: Princeton University Press, 1965).

55. See Biggart, *Charismatic Capitalism*, 40–41.

56. Avon executives logged the concerns of corporate lawyers in the minutes of the 1940s management conference, but there is little indication of what they believed might happen if they violated the laws. That said, Avon continued to use language that

clearly marked out sales territories, especially prohibited by the FTC in direct sales contracts.

57. The CPC did not inform representatives of their new status. According to Biggart, federal attempts to challenge the "status laws" were modest during the 1940s. Not until 1968 did the IRS begin to vigorously challenge the law and propose to have distributors declared employees. They lost their bid, however, and the Tax Equity and Fiscal Responsibility Act of 1982 defined distributors as independent contractors for federal tax purposes. Many direct sales companies use the "status laws" in their recruiting, pointing out that contractors can qualify for tax-deductible business expenses (see Biggart, *Charismatic Capitalism*, 185, n49).

58. The CPC never used national advertising before the 1930s, a practice that in Peiss's analysis drove the popularity of cosmetics in the 1920s (Peiss, *Hope in a Jar*, 97–134).

Chapter 5

1. August 14, 1935, letter from Wayne Hicklin to Eastman, Los Angeles (AP Series 8, Box 125, Eastman correspondence file).

2. October 1964 interview with Wayne Hicklin, president of Avon Products (AP Series 8, Box 125, Wayne Hicklin, 1964, 1972). The year the Fuller men came to Avon is unclear, and while Hicklin did not specify, the Fuller men may have tried to hire men as city office managers rather than working with the established traveling agents. On Fuller sales management in the Depression and postwar era, see Alfred Fuller, *A Foot in the Door: The Life Appraisal of the Original Fuller Brush Man as Told to Hartzell Spence* (New York: McGraw-Hill, 1960), 199–206.

3. 1942 conference proceedings, 17 (AP Series 7, Box 124, Conferences/Reports). Unfortunately, no specific data about the numbers or districts with Black representatives is available in the archived material.

4. City Sales Manual, c. 1942, 6 (AP Series 5, Box 126).

5. City Sales Manual, c. 1942, 10.

6. City Sales Manual, c. 1942, 5.

7. "Visual Presentation of the Avon Opportunity" accompanied the large format Avon orientation book for new representatives (1940) (AP Series, Box, "Avon Representative Recruitment brochure" file).

8. Ibid.

9. On women's removal from high-wage "men's" jobs following World War II, see Sherna Gluck, *Rosie the Riveter: Women, the War, and Social Change* (New York: Plume, 1988), 15–18, 260–270); Alice Kessler Harris, *Out to Work: A History of Wage Earning Women in the US* (New York: Oxford University Press, 1982).

10. "Visual Presentation of the Avon Opportunity" (1940).

11. On the NADSC and independent contractor legislation, see Chapter 4. See also AP Series 4, Box 120, file "Affiliations/Direct Selling Association, 19211968."

12. Avon Sales and Management Conference, 1942, meeting of branch managers, abstracts, 55.

13. Ibid.

14. Ibid.

15. "Handbook for District Supervisors" (1924) (AP Series 3, Box 113, "Sales System/ Manager's Manual).

16. "Getting the Most Value Out of Your Territory" (1942) and "Avon Wants You to Succeed" (1946) (AP Series 5, Box 120, file Representative/Instruction brochures, 1940–1948).

17. City Sales Guide, c. 1942, pp. 5–6.

18. 1946 New Era Conference proceedings, "City Sales, Cost Analysis" charts, 1945. The figures are not broken down to reflect salary and commission schedules.

19. Lela Eastman interview (1972), p. 6 (AP Series 8, Box 125).

20. Letter from Helen Lathom to Lela Eastman, October 5, 1939 (AP Series 8, Box 125, Eastman correspondence file).

21. Eastman interview (1972).

22. Eastman interview, pp. 33–34.

23. Edward Reis details the aggressive and often intimidating tactics men used with each other to cajole and embarrass one another into procuring more sales. Raymond Edward Ries, "The American Salesman: A Study of a Direct Sales Organization" (PhD dissertation, University of Illinois, Urbana, 1958).

24. August 14, 1935, letter from Wayne Hicklin to Eastman, Los Angeles.

25. Hicklin report, 1942 Avon Sales and Management Conference, 1942 (AP Series 7, Box 124).

26. Ibid.

27. 1942 management conference, 13 (AP Series 7, Box 124, Conferences/Reports).

28. 1942 management conference, 7.

29. 1946 New Era Conference proceedings, "District Sales, 1946 Program" charts. The figures are not broken down to reflect salary and commission schedules.

30. "Manual for Avon Field Managers" (1946), 1–2 (AP Series 5, Box 122).

31. "Avon Round Table: Check of Facts and Figures," 1943, Summary of Discussion and Decisions, 5 (AP Series 7, Box 124). In 1942, city divisions appointed 3,800 fewer new recruits than in 1941, a decrease due directly to a reduction in the number of assistants (AP Series 7, Box 124).

32. City Sales Guide, c. 1942, 41.

33. City Sales Guide, c. 1942, 44.

34. City Sales Guide, c. 1942, 41.

35. 1946 New Era Conference proceedings, "City Sales, Cost Analysis" charts, 1945. The figures are not broken down to reflect salary and commission schedules.

36. Angel Kwolek-Folland, *Engendering Business: Men and Women in the Corporate Office, 1870–1930* (Baltimore: Johns Hopkins University Press, 1994). See also Margery Davies, *Woman's Place Is at the Typewriter: Office Work and Office Workers, 1880–1930* (Philadelphia: Temple University Press, 1982), and Claudia

Goldin, *Understanding the Gender Gap: An Economic History of American Women* (New York: Oxford University Press, 1990).

37. Avon Sales and Management Conference, 1942 (AP Series 7, Box 124). Executive managers, Ewald, Rooks, and Hicklin, monitored the discussion and at the end of the first round summarized key points of each presentation, gave some suggestions to follow up on, then gave each division manager a chance to respond. Abstracted transcripts of each panel were then distributed among the executive and middle management ranks.

38. Avon Sales and Management Conference, 1942, 18 (AP Series 7, Box 124).

39. Ibid., 14.

40. Ibid., 15.

41. Ibid., 15.

42. Ibid., 8.

43. Ibid., 8.

44. Ibid., 9.

45. Ibid., 8.

46. Hicklin interview transcript, 1964, 4.

47. "Avon Round Table: Check of Facts and Figures," 1943, Summary of Discussions and Decisions, 5, 6 (AP Series 7, Box 124).

48. 1947 management conference, Tables "Trend of City Sales Costs" and "Cost of Operations in District Sales" (AP Series 7, Box 124).

49. "Avon Round Table: Check of Facts and Figures," 1943. Summary of Discussions and Decisions: 5, 6 (AP Series 7, Box 124).

50. Ibid. Exact figures are presented in the tables presented in "Avon Round Table" (1943); here I have rounded numbers to the nearest 50 or whole-dollar amount.

51. Hicklin interview transcript, 1964, 5.

52. "Avon Round Table: Check of Facts and Figures," 1943. Summary of Discussions and Decisions: 5, 6.

53. 1947 management conference, Tables "Trend of City Sales Costs" and "Cost of Operations in District Sales".

54. On women and war labor, see Ruth Milkman, *Gender at Work: The Dynamics of Job Segregation by Sex during World War Two* (Champaign: University of Illinois Press, 1982), and Sherna Gluck, *Rosie the Riveter Revisited* (New York: Twayne, 1987)

55. From the "Her Courage Lives Today" advertisement (January 1945) which appeared in *Ladies Home Journal* (AP Series 7a, Box OS-19, Heroines of History campaign, August 1944–March 1946).

56. "Her Courage Lives Today" advertisement, "Heroines of History Campaign" January 1945 (AP Series 7a, Box OS-19) appeared in *Ladies Home Journal* and *Holland's*. The "Heroines" campaign lasted from 1944 to 1946 and featured women who made notable contributions to history. One advertisement honored Deborah Gannett, who fought in the Revolutionary War, was wounded twice, discovered, and given an honorable discharge from the army by George Washington. Her courage "is symbolized by every one of these women in the armed forces and on the home front who desire to be useful to her country, and is determined to be lovely at the same time."

57. 1945 Management conference, Table "Pieces Produced, 1940–1944" (AP Series 7, Box 124).

58. January 1949 conference, Wayne Hicklin, "The Factual Analysis of 'The Mighty Force of Avon'" (AP Series 7, Box 124, Conferences/Reports).

Chapter 6

1. "Help Wanted: Sales," *Fortune* (May 1952): 100–103, 196–204.

2. Ibid.

3. Two important developments in the direct selling industry in the postwar era were the creation of multi-level marketing distribution networks and the growing use and popularity of home parties as a selling technique. Nicole Biggart examines the social and economic structure of multi-level marketing, paying most attention to the post-1970 period in *Charismatic Capitalism: Direct Selling Organizations in America* (Chicago: University of Chicago Press, 1989). Alison Clark examines the dynamics of the Tupperware home-party plan, designed by Tupperware Home Parties president Brownie Wise, in the Cold War era. *Tupperware: The Promise of Plastic in 1950s America* (Washington, DC: Smithsonian Institution Press, 1999).

4. Ironically, although sales work may have been losing its prestige (if indeed it ever really had it), some sales jobs remained "men's" jobs, particularly in durable goods and high commission sales jobs. There was a huge variety, however, within the narrow classifications. Automobile salesmen, for example, could be well paid and have posh offices, if they dealt with new cars, or crass and always scrounging to make a deal if they worked in a used-car lot. On commissioned sales and the masculine culture honored on department store sales floors, see Alice Kessler Harris, "Women's History Goes on Trial: EEOC v. Sears, Roebuck and Company," *Signs* 11 (Summer 1986): 751–779, and Ruth Milkman, "Women's History and the Sears Case," *Feminist Studies* 12 (Summer 1986): 375–400. Joy Parr discusses salesmen's tactics for selling stoves in Canadian stores in "Shopping for a Good Stove: A Parable about Gender, Design, and the Market," in *His and Hers: Gender Consumption and Technology*, ed. Roger Horowitz and Arwen Mohun (Charlottesville: University Press of Virginia, 1998).

5. For analysis of women's postwar domestic lives and the dominant suburban gender ideal, see Elaine Tyler May, *Homeward Bound: American Families in the Cold War Era* (New York: Basic Books, 1988), and Stephanie Coontz, *The Way We Never Were: American Families and the Nostalgia Trap* (New York: Basic Books, 1992).

6. Biggart, *Charismatic Capitalism*, 2. Her reading of National Association of Direct Selling Companies' records for 1936 suggests that women accounted for approximately 10 percent of distributors nationwide in the 1930s.

7. On the literature of suburbanization and consumerism since the nineteenth century, see Kenneth T. Jackson, *Crabgrass Frontier: The Suburbanization of the United States* (New York: Oxford University Press, 1985), and Margaret Marsh, *Suburban Lives* (New Brunswick, NJ: Rutgers University Press, 1990). Suburbanization in

the post–World War II period is discussed in Herbert Gans, *The Levittowners* (New York: Pantheon, 1967), and John Modell, "Suburbanization and Change in the American Family," *Journal of Interdisciplinary Study*, 8 (Spring 1977): 621–646.

8. On consumption patterns and consumers in the postwar era: Lizabeth Cohen, *A Consumers' Republic: The Politics of Mass Consumption in Postwar America* (New York: Knopf, 2008); Liz Cohen, "From Town Center to Shopping Center: The Reconfiguration of Community Marketplaces in Postwar America," in *His and Hers: Gender Consumption and Technology*, ed. Roger Horowitz and Arwen Mohun (Charlottesville: University Press of Virginia, 1998).

9. Proceedings of 1947 conference, opening address, 10–11 (AP Series 7, Box 124).

10. Proceedings of 1950 conference (AP Series 7, Box 124); "Avon Products, Inc.," a study by Hemphill, Noyes, and Co., 1958 (AP Series 1, Box 110, Stock, Shareholder/Official Data, 1946, 1958).

11. Kathy Peiss, *Hope in a Jar: The Making of America's Beauty Culture* (New York: Metropolitan Books, 1998), 245–248; Geoffrey Jones, *Beauty Imagined: A History of the Global Beauty Industry* (New York: Oxford University Press, 2010).

12. See Tables 5.2 and. Statistics from 1942–1949 conference reports (AP Series 7, Box 124).

13. Nowhere in its literature does Avon suggest that the company had trouble in recruiting women during the war who chose instead to work in the higher-paying war industries sector. On women and war labor, see Ruth Milkman, *Gender at Work: The Dynamics of Job Segregation by Sex during World War II* (Chicago: University of Illinois Press, 1987); Sherna Gluck, *Rosie the Riveter Revisited* (New York: Twayne, 1987); and Alice Kessler-Harris, *Out to Work: A History of Wage-Earning Women in the United States* (New York: Oxford University Press, 1982). Avon could have maintained the size of its sales force but instead chose to restrict recruiting in order to focus production efforts on filling military contracts.

14. Memo on Allied Products, 1945 (AP Series 1, Box 110, Allied Products, American Perfumers Laboratories Division, 1944–1945).

15. Proceedings, 1947 conference, opening address, 7 (AP Series 7, Box 124).

16. Ibid., 4.

17. Ibid.

18. Ibid., 7.

19. See Clark Davis, *Company Men and Corporate Cultures in Los Angeles, 1892–1941* (Baltimore: Johns Hopkins University Press, 2001) on the intersection of masculinity and corporate culture.

20. See, for example, the work of Susan Porter Benson, *Counter Cultures: Saleswomen, Managers, and Customers in American Department Stores, 1890–1940* (Chicago: University of Illinois Press, 1986.)

21. Proceedings,1947 conference, opening address, 10–11 (AP Series 7, Box 124).

22. Ibid., 12.

23. January 1949 conference, Wayne Hicklin, "The Factual Analysis of 'The Mighty Force of Avon'" (AP Series 7, Box 124).

24. Ibid. There is no evidence on how Avon assembled the demographic information. It most likely came from representative contracts but could have also come from a poll of sales office managers.

25. January 1949 conference, Tables: "Average Sales Per Representative; by branches; by divisions."

26. A full run of Avon print advertisements is available in AP Series 7-A, Boxes 19–24, complete with a company-sponsored history of advertising collected in a scrapbook. Alison Clark addresses the women's role as "hostess" in the 1940s and argues that it added a new dimension to women's domestic labor. "The term hostess inferred entertainment, conviviality, and increased consumption. . . . [By] opening up the previously private sphere of the home to the brand names and consumer goods of the public sphere, the hostess made the ideal accomplice for the advertisers" (Clark, *Tupperware*, 63–64).

27. Ibid. Quotations from celebrity endorsements are in Box OS (A&B).

28. *Beauty Counselor*, 1954, 2–3.

29. Ibid., 5.

30. Ibid., 56–57.

31. Ibid., 58–59.

32. *Direct Line*, May 1958

33. *Direct Line*, November 1960.

34. Ibid.

35. Ibid.

36. May refers to marriage and the isolated and infantilized role of housewives in *Homeward Bound*, 183–207. According to her reading of the women in the Kelly Longitudinal Study, a long-term psychological study of white married couples in the 1950s, any effort to work outside the home was done in order to shore up a marriage, to contribute to the purchase of household possessions, or otherwise make the home a haven for her husband and children.

37. Cohen, *A Consumer's Republic*. Participation in the marketplace substituted for public engagement.

38. Lindsey Feitz, "Democratizing Beauty: Avon's Global Beauty Ambassadors and the Transnational Marketing of Femininity, 1954–2010" (PhD diss., University of Kansas, 2010).

39. *Avon Direct Line*, June 1957, as quoted in Feitz, "Democratizing Beauty," 25.

40. *Avon Direct Line*, July 1960.

41. Written by Avon Representative Mrs. Dorothy Mizer of Amherst, Ohio. Printed in *The Avon Essence* 2, no. 7 (July 1964).

42. May, *Homeward Bound*; Joanne Meyerowitz, ed., *Not June Cleaver: Women and Gender in Postwar America, 1945–1960* (Philadelphia: Temple University Press, 1994), 4.

43. Report by McDonnell and Co., 1961 Stock valuation (Box 110)

44. Derek A. Newton, "Avon Products, Inc." Case study for the Harvard Business School (1963), p. 8.

45. Lizabeth Cohen, *A Consumer's Republic*, 166–171, shows the intentional limitations placed on African Americans, especially African American veterans, on accessing home ownership in postwar America. Although the GI Bill offered federally subsidized home loans, veterans still had to work through private banks for loans, many of which refused to process loan applications for African Americans they had to broker housing deals through real estate agents who refused to show houses in new suburbs or established middle-class neighborhoods. Real estate practices demarcated neighborhoods according to whether homes were gaining or losing value with red lines, designating homes in urban centers as poor risks and therefore ineligible for federally subsidized loans that could have been used for either purchase or repair. African Americans' lack of access to federal mortgage insurance and loans guaranteed that new developments in the suburbs would remain white only. In some states, Cohen noted, the GI Bill was used for home ownership fewer than eight times by African American veterans.

46. McDonnel and Company, "Financial Analysis of Avon" (1961).

47. Harvard Business School Case Study, 20.

48. Laura Klepacki, *Avon: Building the World's Premier Company for Women* (New York: Wiley, 2005), 94–97.

49. Bud Hastins, *Bud Hastin's Avon Collector's Encyclopedia: Avon and California Perfume Company Products 1886 to Present (The Official Avon Collector's Price Guide)* (Paducah, KY: Collectors Books, Schroeder Publishing, 1979) originally published in 1979 offers trade value advice on CPC and Avon decanters, representative medals and awards, and a variety of other Avon containers and trade catalogs.

50. The "mark" brand of Avon cosmetics, sold by and for teenagers and young adults, was introduced in 2003.

51. "Evaluation of Hidden Customer Program," by Sales Research Department, March 19, 1968 (Box 120—Hidden Customer Program).

52. "Evaluation of Hidden Customer Program" by Sales Research Department, March 19 1968, 4–5.

53. Ibid.

54. Harvard Business School Case Study, 20.

55. Timeline stats are available in Laura Klepacki, *Avon: Building the World's Premier Company for Women* (Hoboken, NJ: John Wiley, 2005), 241–248. Avon's International businesses are explored in a number of new works. The scholarship includes Jessica Chelekis and Suan M. Mudambi, "MNCs and Micro-Entrepreneurship in Emerging Economies: The Case of Avon in the Amazon," *Journal of International Management* 16 (2010): 412–424; Jessica Chelekis, "Direct Sales and Social Relationships in Ponta de Pedras, Para," *Novos Cadernos NAEA* 14, no. 2 (2011): 37–60; Shawn Moura, "Try It at Home: Avon and Gender in Brazil, 1958–1975," *Business History* 57, no. 6 (2015): 800–821; Linda Scott, "Avon in Africa," *Saad Business School Cases*, June 2012.

56. Direct Selling Association "Code of Ethics," 1975.

57. Ibid.

58. Debra A. Valentine, "Pyramid Schemes," International Monetary Fund Seminar on Current Legal Issues Affecting Central Banks, Washington, DC., May 13,

1998. https://www.ftc.gov/public-statements/1998/05/pyramid-schemes   https://pyramidschemealert.org/analysis-amway-accused-of-fraud-pays-150-million-wheres-the-ftc-and-doj/.

59. Thomas Wotruba, *Moral Suasion: Development of the U.S. Direct Selling Association Industry Code of Ethics* (Washington, DC: Direct Selling Education Foundation, 1995).

60. Plans for Progress, April 1968; Avon plan approved by Vice President Hubert Humphrey (Series I, Box 110).

61. Lindsey Feitz, "Democratizing Beauty," discusses Avon's efforts to improve racial and gender diversity in her chapter on Avon's Corporate Social Responsibility efforts, 96–98.

62. Feitz, "Democratizing Beauty," 95. Philip Cochran, "The Evolution of Corporate Social Responsibility," *Business Horizons* 40 (2007): 449–54 charts the development of "corporate social responsibility" and "corporate responsiveness" in the 1960s and 1970s whereby corporations created "pragmatic, codified, action-oriented responses" to social problems.

63. Robert Weems, *Desegregating the Dollar: African American Consumerism in the Twentieth Century* (New York: New York University Press, 1998.

64. Feitz, "Democratizing Beauty," 108.

65. Feitz, "Democratizing Beauty," 110–112; "Personalized Beauty from Avon," RGII Series 4: Selling Methods and Sales Aids, 1972 (Box 118); "Procedural Bulletin: CSR Plan: Field Operations," March 1973 (RGII Series 1, Box 110).

66. Feitz, "Democratizing Beauty," 120.

67. "National Black Advertisements by Uniworld Group and Friends," August 13, 1974 (Avon Archives, Series 7: Advertising, Subseries A: Advertising scrapbook, Box OS-39). As shown in Feitz, "Democratizing Beauty," 116–120.

68. Feitz, "Democratizing Beauty," 101.

69. Ibid.

70. Feitz, "Democratizing Beauty," 125.

71. "Managing a Woman Effectively," no author (RG II, Series I, Admin, Box 110, "Admin: Business Ethics/Policies, 1931–1977").

72. Feitz, "Democratizing Beauty," 148–149.

73. Klepacki, *Avon*, 41–42.

74. Ibid., 42.

75. Feitz, "Democratizing Beauty," 150-151.

76. Klepacki, *Avon*, 43.

77. David F. Larker and Brian Tayan, "Pioneering Women on Boards: The Pathways of the First Female Directors," *Stanford Closer Look Series*, September 13, 2013, analyzed survey results of 2013 Fortune 250 companies and found that, on average, companies named their first female board members in 1985. Avon was not included in this research. Of the seven companies that named women prior to 1960, including Coca-Cola, Pepsi Co., IBM, and Marriott, all chose the wife of the company's founder or chief executive, or in the case of The Gap, the founder herself served. As Larker and Tayan note, companies often chose women with scientific, government, or regulatory

backgrounds. Only 5 percent of companies in their survey chose a woman with an academic background as Avon happened to do.

78. Historian Pamela Laird has researched the gender and class dynamics of corporate networking in *Pull: Networking and Success since Benjamin Franklin* (Cambridge, MA: Harvard University Press, 2007).

79. Joshua L. Kwan, "Leverett's 'Senior' Tutor: House Resident Has a Lifetime of Experience," *Harvard Crimson*, May 14, 1997.

80. Marcia Worthing, "Cecily Selby: First Woman Board Member," *Avon Newsletter* 7, no. 14 (July 14, 1972). According to the *Crimson*, Selby divorced then remarried in 1997.

81. Press Release June 21, 1972, "Dr. Cecily Cannan Selby named to Board to Avon Products, Inc."

82. Marcia Worthing, "Cecily Selby: First Woman Board Member," *Avon Newsletter* 7, no. 14 (July 14, 1972).

83. Procope Clipping File: "Chubb Elects Mrs. Procope," June 18, 1977.

84. "Procope Clipping File: Catalyst Cites 4 Corporation Directors," by Phyllis Lu Simpson in the *New York Amsterdam News*, Saturday April 2, 1977.

85. Ibid.

86. Phyllis Lu Simpson, "Catalyst Cites 4 Corporation Directors," *New York Amsterdam News*, Saturday April 2, 1977.

87. Feitz, "Democratizing Beauty," 120. Avon had "successfully repositioned itself as a racially diverse company that offered employment opportunities, beauty products, and supported philanthropic causes for minority women."

88. Feitz, "Democratizing Beauty," 112.

89. Feitz, "Democratizing Beauty," 118.

90. March 1970 conference, 9.

91. March 1970 conference, 10.

92. "Final Report: Recruitment and Development Focus Groups," submitted by Carol D. Kessler to Distribution, June 19, 1984.

93. Ibid.

94. Ibid.

Chapter 7

1. Avon, Series 7, OS 33, "National Advertising, 1981–1984" Monumental Makeover campaign.

2. *Working Woman* magazine, Smith College Library, Sophia Smith Collection, *Working Woman* Magazine Letters, 1979–1983.

3. Pam Laird, *Pull: Networking and Success since Benjamin Franklin*, Cambridge, MA: Harvard University Press, 2006. Laird's analysis of Avon highlighted Avon's Affirmative Action programs in the 1970s.

4. "The Impact of Restructuring and the Glass Ceiling on Minorities and Women," Lois B. Shaw, Dell P. Champlin, Heidi I. Hartmann, and Roberta M. Spalter-Roth, December 15, 1993; Charlene Marmer-Solomon, "The Corporate Response to Work Force Diversity," *Personnel Journal*, August 1989. Marmer-Solomon was cited in a Department of Labor publication: "The article addresses the changing nature of the workplace and positions the need to embrace differences as a business imperative. It describes programs (including their rationale and impact) that have been developed at a number of large corporations. Among the companies presented are: Xerox, Hewlett Packard, McDonald's, Procter & Gamble, and Avon Products, Inc.," p. 53. Avon's diversity training initiative was also featured alongside DuPont, Apple, and TRW in David Shadovitz, "Special Report: Benchmarking HR: Work Force Diversity," *Human Resource Executive*, June 1992: "Focuses on Gannett's successful Partners in Progress Program, TRW's module for measuring organizational diversity, Avon's exemplary 'Diversity Awareness Training,' US West's 'Promoting Pluralism' program and Apple Computer's Multicultural Diversity Initiative. The results of these measures have included the increase of women and people of color in the organizations."

5. Leslie Wayne and Kenneth N. Gilpin, "Avon Calls on a Man to Lead It; Female Cosmetics Executives Passed over for Top Post," *New York Times*, December 12, 1997.

6. As quoted in Wayne and Gilpin, "Avon Calls on a Man to Lead It."

7. See Felice Schwartz's annual report in the *Catalyst Annual Review*, 1988–89. The report appeared shortly after the publication of her 1989 *Harvard Business Review* article (see note 8 following).

8. Felice Schwartz, "Management Women and the New Facts of Life," *Harvard Business Review* (January/February 1989): 65–76.

9. Schwartz, "Management Women and the New Facts of Life."

10. Susan Yohn, "Cooperation over Confrontation? Working Collectively or Individually? Addressing the Problems of Women in the Corporation," presented at the Business History Conference annual meeting, Frankfurt, Germany, 2014. In author's possession.

11. Schwartz, "Management Women and the New Facts of Life," 70.

12. As quoted in Beverly Beyette, "A New Career Flap: What's a Mommy Track and Why Are So Many Women Upset about It?" *Los Angeles Times*, March 17, 1989.

13. Felice N. Schwartz, *Breaking with Tradition: Women and Work, and the New Facts of Life* (Warner Books: New York, 1992), 98.

14. *Time*, March 27, 1989, as quoted in Schwartz, *Breaking with Tradition*, 106.

15. Schwartz, *Breaking with* Tradition, 106.

16. Susan Yohn, "Cooperation over Confrontation?"

17. *LA Times* 1989.

18. Avon Commercials, "How Good You Look," videocassette, Box 53, Avon Products Inc. photographs and audiovisual materials (Accession 1997.209), Audiovisual Collections and Digital Initiatives Department, Hagley Museum and Library.

19. Avon Commercials, "You Never Looked So Good," videocassettes, Boxes 49 and 51, Avon Products Inc. photographs and audiovisual materials (Accession 1997.209),

Audiovisual Collections and Digital Initiatives Department, Hagley Museum and Library.

20. Ruth Rosen, "Who Said We Could Have It All?" August 2, 2012, on 50:50 Open Democracy   https://www.opendemocracy.net/en/5050/who-said-we-could-have-it-all/.

21. Ibid. See also Natasha Campo, *From Superwomen to Domestic Goddesses: The Rise and Fall of Feminism* (Bern, Switzerland: Peter Lang, 2009), which traces the role of the Australian media in warping the memory of feminism's original goals of liberation to being responsible for advocating the Superwoman. "The memory was of our mothers being 1950s housewives, so the idea of 'having it all' was something quite positive. You'd read articles about Ita Buttrose getting up at 5am to do her exercise and taking her kids off to childcare. Women took pride in how well they could structure their lives."

22. Mary Kay Ash, *Mary Kay: You Can Have it All – Lifetime Wisdom from America's Foremost Woman Entrepreneur by Mary Kay Ash* (Prima Publishing, 1996), 68.

23. Ibid., 73.

24. Ibid., 79

25. Ibid., 82.

26. Ibid., 84.

27. "Mary Kay Cosmetics May Make Avon Bid," *New York Times*, D4, May 26, 1989.

28. 1987 Women of Enterprise, Awards Program Strategic Plan (c. 1986), p. 4, Box 15 Series V, Public Relations.

29. On the growing number of female proprietors and CEOs in American business in the 1970s and '80s, see Angel Kwolek-Folland, *Incorporating Women: A History of Women and Business in the United States* (New York: Palgrave, 1998), 189–209.

30. Ibid., 3.

31. Sharing the Dream, Women of Enterprise Awards, 1991, 6.

32. Ibid., 5.

33. 1987 Women of Enterprise, Publicity Files, Box 15, Series V, Public Relations.

34. 1987 Women of Enterprise, Awards Program Strategic Plan (c. 1986), p. 8, Box 15, Series V, Public Relations, Mission Statement, 3.

35. 1987 Women of Enterprise, Awards Program Strategic Plan (c. 1986), p. 8, Box 15, Series V, Public Relations, "Objectives," 2.

36. 1987 Women of Enterprise, Awards Program Strategic Plan (c. 1986), p. 2, Box 15, Series V, Public Relations. Program Description: The Avon archives offer an insight into the range of applications that the program received. Files for the top ten finalists in 1987 and 1988, for example, show that Avon welcomed the diverse voices of women who made clear that sexism and racism hobbled their opportunities. Later in the 1990s, Avon highlighted women whose remarks hewed closer to language of sexual discrimination. After the first two years, Avon kept application materials from only the top five candidates making it difficult to know how many applicants continued to voice their experience of racial discrimination and whether or not Avon intentionally weeded them out.

37. Avon Archives, Box 15, Women of Enterprise, Finalist Applications, Jackson-Randolph file.

38. Avon Archives, Box 15, Women of Enterprise, Finalist Applications, Padilla file. Parentheses in original.

39. Avon Archives, Box 15, 1987 Women of Enterprise, Finalist Applications, Padilla file.

40. Avon Archives, Box 15, Women of Enterprise, Finalist Applications, Thurlow file.

41. Avon Archives, Box 15, Women of Enterprise, Finalist Applications, Yue file.

42. Application files for the non-winners were not preserved.

43. National Attitude Survey, New World Decisions, 31.

44. Women's lack of access to credit has functioned to limit women's financial independence throughout the nineteenth and twentieth centuries. See Susan Yohn, "Crippled Capitalists: The Inscription of Economic Dependence and the Challenge of Women's Entrepreneurship in the Nineteenth Century," *Feminist Economics* 12 , no. 1–2 (January/April 2006): 85–109. Debra Michals writes about the significance of the 1974 Equal Credit Opportunity Act in *title*.

45. National Attitude Survey, New World Decisions, 31.

46. National Attitude Survey, New World Decisions, Tables 15, 16a, and 16b.

47. Avon Foundation, 2020. https://www.avon.com/blog/avon-insider/avon-foundation-for-women-billion.

48. Avon corporate website https://www.avonworldwide.com/supporting-women/violence-against-women-and-girls.

49. Dana Canedy, "Opportunity Re-Knocks at Avon; Passed Over Before, A Woman is Named Chief Executive," New York Times, Section C, p 1, November 5, 1999. Profile of Jung, References for Business, https://www.referenceforbusiness.com/businesses/A-F/Jung-Andrea.html.

50. Ibid.

51. Avon TV Creative Stealsmatick, Box 53, Avon Products, Inc., photographs and audio-visual materials (Accession 1997.209), Audiovisual Collections and Digital Initiatives Department, Hagley Museum and Library,

52. Robin Finn, "Spearheading a Marketing Makeover at Avon," *New York Times*, Section B, p. 2, May 10, 2001.

53. Courtney Kane, "Using Real Women and Believable Promises, Avon Tries a New Way of Advertising Beauty Products," *New York Times*, February 22, 2002, C-4 .

54. Avon: Great Brand, Messy Business and Seemingly Undervalued Shares," *Forbes*, January 29, 2011.

55. SEC press release, "SEC Charges Avon with FCPA Violations," December 2014.

56. "Avon: Great Brand, Messy Business and Seemingly Undervalued Shares," *Forbes*, January 29, 2011.

57. Janet Morrissey, "Wall St. Is Pounding on Avon's Door," *New York Times,* Section BU, p. 1, February 2, 2013.

58. Andrew Martin, "New Chief Selected at Avon," *New York Times*, April 9, 2012.

59. Jenna Goudreau, "New Avon CEO Vows to Restore the 126-Year-Old Beauty Company to Former Glory," *Forbes*, February 27, 2013.

Index

For the benefit of digital users, indexed terms that span two pages (e.g., 52–53) may, on occasion, appear on only one of those pages.

Figures are indicated by an italic f following the page number.

"A Delicate Question" (essay), 54–55
Absent husband, 58, 181, 182
Adams, Dennis J., 70
Advertising, 118–20, 150–51
    "Avon Calling!" slogan, 173–75
    career opportunity approach, 206–7
    celebrity endorsements, 172–73
    as demonstrating company's public
        image, 237–38
    domestic ideology of, 186
    focus groups, 207–8
    having it all theme, 218–19
    magazine, 29, 166–67, 172,
        190, 196
    for minority customers, 196–97, 199f
    national campaign, 29, 118, 129–
        32, 134–35
    "Pink Ribbon Touch," 171–72
    postwar themes, 172–78
    pre-selling through, 172
    recruitment, 176–77, 178, 206–7
    selling Avon as business
        opportunity, 173–75
    storyboard, 119f
    submissive language, 178
    television commercials, 166–67,
        173–75, 190, 205–6, 233–34
    truth in, 193–94
    women pioneers' achievements
        featured, 158–59
    "You never looked so good"
        catchphrase, 218
Affirmative action, 166, 192–93,
    195, 196–97
African Americans, 54
    bias against, 116–17

on board of directors, 204–5
    entrepreneurship, 22, 116–17
    intentional limitations on, 267n.45
    in management, 205–6
    markets, 21–22, 116–17, 137–38, 195–
        97, 199f
    representatives, 137–38, 195–97,
        199f, 205–6
Agents Credit Association, 127–28,
    244n.12, 245n.21. See also Direct
    Selling Association; National
    Association of Direct Selling
    Companies (NADSC)
Agnew, Mrs. R. W., 41–42, 43
A.L. Williams Life Insurance, 9
Albee, Mrs. Persus Foster Eames, 18–19,
    75–76, 246n.27
Albee figurine, 19
Allen, Mrs. George, 63–64
Allen, Mrs. J. R., 68–69
Alley, W. J., 109
Allied Products, 6
Alvarado, Linda, 230
American Ideal label, 5
Amsterdam News, 204–5
Amway, 6–7, 9, 192–93, 194, 211–12, 221
Anderson, Katherine, 56–57
Armand cosmetics company, 114
Arruiti, Mrs. M., 91
Ash, Mary Kay, 6–7, 8, 9, 219–21
Attack of the Mary Kay
    Commandos, 220–21
Automobiles, 34, 91–92, 255n.32
Avon-Allied, 167–68
Avon Anew brand, 235–36
Avon Army, 155–62

"Avon Cares" program, 194–95
Avon Color brand, 235–36
Avon Essence (magazine), 185
Avon Foundation, 10, 232–33
Avon Lady, 1. *See also* representatives
  dual identity, 237–38
  as economic actor and domestic
    woman, 165
  fame of, 1, 240
  as icon of white suburban America, 165
  poem, 185–86
  portrayal in advertising, 172–78
Avon Maid, 112, 113*f*
"Avon Opportunity, The," 138–39
Avon Outlook, 121, 125
Avon Products, Incorporated. *See also*
    California Perfume Company
  affiliated brands, 6, 167–68
  Amway's takeover bid, 11, 221
  annual sales figures, 155, 156, 208
  beauty advice, 178–80
  brand name origin, 1–2, 112
  bribes paid to China, 234–35
  career ladder for women in, 147–48
  challenges to philosophy, 192–93
  closure of US facilities, 236
  as company for women, 10–11,
    166, 209–10, 213–14, 232–33,
    234, 236
  competition for women's labor, 206–8
  conservative gender role view, 181
  cosmetic lines, 113*f*, 121, 129–32, 131*f*
  Coty's takeover offer, 235
  digital marketplace
    competition, 235–36
  direct selling industry support, 194–95
  dual-marketing formula, 8, 192–93
  first female chief executive, 233, 234
  as following beauty trends, 167
  Fortune 250 company status, 212
  Government and Public Relations
    Department created, 195
  hobby sales, 165–66
  100th anniversary, 209
  in-home sales commitment, 187, 206
  information sharing by
    management, 153–54
  as largest direct sales company, 166–67

management conferences, 151–52
management style, 135–36
Mary Kay's takeover bid, 11, 221
as mass producer, 167–68
middle management layer, 133–34
military contracts, 155, 159–61, 167–68
move to London, 235–36
paternalistic management philosophy,
  166, 170, 197–98, 239
personalized service commitment,
  172, 187
post-World War II growth, 6
private contracts, 167–68
product line expansion, 189
racially inclusive corporate identity, 197
rebranding, 212, 234
relationship with African American
  organizations, 196–97
representative tenure and sales, 171
restricted territories, 140–42
retail availability, 190, 234
rural market focus, 4
sales philosophy, 9–10
segregated city sales offices, 137–38
shift in emphasis, 129
sixtieth anniversary, 166–67
stocks, 187, 188–89, 235
as successful direct selling organization
  model, 129
Summer Olympics sponsorship, 233–34
woman-to-woman sales method as
  advantage, 169
women's issues focus, 165, 209–10, 211
workplace selling, 206
Avon Promise to End Violence Against
  Women and Girls, 231–32
"Avon Salutes Its Representatives," 158*f*
Avon Walk for Breast Cancer, 231–32
"Avon Wants You to Succeed" (1946), 141

Baarman, Fanny, 70
Bachler, Henry, 87–88, 90–92, 114–15
Balverde-Sanchez, Laura, 223
"Be Hostess to Loveliness" campaign, 160*f*,
  161*f*, 162*f*, 172
Beauty consultants. *See* representatives
Beauty Counselor, 178–80
Beauty Counselors company, 189

Beauty culturalists, 22
"Becoming" line, 234
Bell, Mr., 152–53
"Better Way" sales campaign, 187–92
Beveridge, Frank Stanley, 5–6, 109
Blattler, O. E., 121, 153
Board of directors, 201–6, 213–14
Bond, Mrs. Ella Bacon, 104*f*
Bowman Company, 204–5
Branch management system, 134–36, 154
Breast Cancer Crusade, 231–32
Breathed, Berke, 220–21
Breedlove, Sarah, 22
Brockman, Philip, 114–15
Brown, Helen Gurley, 10, 217–18
Brown, Mrs. S. M. E., 103*f*
Broyles, Viola, 91
Brush Runabout contest, 34, 35*f*
Buell, Victor, 163, 169–70,
    188–89
Bulletin. See CPC Bulletin
Bunker, Addie, 56–57
Bush, George, 212–13
Business strategy, 19, 36, 37, 108–9,
    123–24, 129. *See also* positive
    thinking
Buster, Emma, 79–80, 92
Butts, Miss Elizabeth, 99*f*
Buying clubs, 69–71

California Perfume Company, 1, 3–5,
    12–40. *See also* Avon Products,
    Incorporated
  as alternative business
    organization, 20–21
  Avon brand products, 112, 113*f*, 131*f*
  catalogs, 23–27
  celebrity-endorsed lines, 111–12
  closing of original facilities, 236
  color cosmetics, 111–12, 129–32
  competitors, 69–70
  as contemporary firm, 71–72
  contract with representatives, 38–39
  correspondence department, 29–30
  customer location, 54
  Daphne fragrance line, 111–12
  direct selling format mastery, 39–40
  executive staff changes, 114–16

  expenses, 72
  growth of, 23
  high turnover, 39–40
  hiring policy, 77–79
  increase in sales force, 107–8
  Kardex system, 28–29
  launch of Avon cosmetics brand, 112
  manufacturing facilities, 23, 247n.34
  name origin, 12–13
  nepotism, 258n.25
  new payment system, 121–22
  peddler tradition impact on, 13–14
  products, 5, 13, 23–25
  profits, 107–8
  regional sales offices, 23
  representatives' earnings, 106, 107–8
  rural market focus, 16–17, 21
  sales method, 13
  sample cases, 25–27
  scientific management, 28
  selling success ethic, 123–24
  shipping expenses, 27–28
  short term part-time sales corps, 20
  Suffern lab, 23, 24*f*, 236
  trends resulting from female sales
    corps, 20–21
  warehouses, 23
  women's magazines promotion, 21
Callahan, Willard, 147–48, 153
Calling, concept of work as, 4
"Career for Women" ad series, 176–
    77, 179*f*
Catalogs, 23–27. *See also* company
    literature
  color plate, 25–27, 26*f*
  "CP Book, The," 23–25
  as CPC's only promotional material, 25
  "For Beauty, Health, and Home," 23–25
  leave, 62–63
  money-back guarantee, 25
  recruiting pitch, 25
Catalyst organization, 209–10, 213–14
Chadwick, Norman, 155, 171, 172
Charles of the Ritz, 167–68
Chats, 82–84, 87–88, 97–98
City markets, 5–6, 116–22
  career advancement for women
    in, 147–49

City markets (*cont.*)
    characteristics creating difficulty
       with, 116
    CPC as lagging behind in, 117–18
    group recognition, 145
    initial test markets, 117
    limitations, 5–6, 191–92
    locating "good population," 116–17
    other management styles *vs.*
       Avon's, 135–36
    postwar era development, 166–67
    recruiting in, 116–17, 137–40
    reorganization, 129–32
    sales meetings, 142–45, 151
    territories, 137–38, 140–42
    training for, 146
    turnover rate, 141, 171
City sales office managers
    assistant managers and, 148–49
    compensation, 135, 142, 156
    corporate expectations, 161–62
    discontinued contracts
       survey, 260n.43
    Eastman as first, 133
    ideal, 149
    manual for, 150–51
    McConnell Jr.'s vision for, 135
    mobility, 149–50
    motivating representatives, 144–45
    office space, 143–44
    recruiting as main task, 138
    standardization of role, 150–51
    territory mapping, 137–38
    tracking of successful, 145–46
    turnover rate, 171
    women as, 133–34
Civil rights movement, 166, 192–208
Clark, Edna McConnell, 201
Clark, Hays, 201
Clark, Van Alan, 201, 258n.25
Clean Piles of Coin, 44–45
Clyde, Mrs. E. Earle, 98–100
Coffin, Mrs. Cora, 125–26
Cohen, Lizabeth, 257n.8
Colbert, Claudette, 172–73, 174*f*
Cold calling, 190–91
Cole, Mrs. H. B., 66
Colgate-Palmolive, 167–68

Commercial travelers' organizations, 96,
    256n.53
Company literature, 20, 37–38, 39. *See*
    also catalogs; instruction manuals;
    recruiting manuals
    absent husband, 58, 181, 182
    advice for traveling agents, 92
    business as social network
       substitute, 126–27
    city sales meeting bulletins, 145–46
    conquer and overcome theme, 129–32
    exotic stories from representatives, 126
    female pronoun use, 37–38
    fishing story, 37–38
    image of representatives in, 42, 182
    independent nature of work
       emphasized, 124
    male anecdotes in, 37–38
    managerial skills of women promoted
       in, 187
    as motivational, 108–9, 122–27
    neutrality on women's issues, 46–47
    as primary communication with
       representatives, 73–74
    purposes, 122–23
    representatives' voices in, 125–26, 127
    wars and battles referenced in, 38
Consumer rights, 193–95
Consumption patterns, 241n.6
Contests, 34–35, 144–45
Cooling-off periods, 193–95
Cooper, Mason, 152, 153
Corporate culture, 9–10
    communication as creating uniform, 80
    female friendly, 213–14, 217–18
    outdated, 216
    popular trend in women's, 224
    separation of male and female managers
       in, 154
    shifts needed in, 9–10, 214
    social movement impacts on,
       166, 196–97
Corporate domesticity, 42–43, 46, 47
Corporate Responsibility Statement,
    198–200
Corporate structure, 2, 6, 9, 16, 39–40
Cosmetics
    bias against "painted ladies," 21

color, 111–14, 157–58
demand by women of color for, 116–17
evolving attitudes toward, 5, 21
increasing demand for, 21
postwar expansion of industry, 167
rural women's use of, 112–14
training for representatives, 178–79
as volatile trade, 114
Cover Girl cosmetics brand, 167
"CP Book, The" (catalog), 23–25
CPC Bulletin, 27
CPC Outlook, 27, 31–32
"Our General Agents" column, 97
rhetorical strategies, 125
seasonal products highlighted, 62–63
testimonials, 68–69
top-selling representatives listed
in, 50–51
walking articles, 63
"You Can't Keep a Good Representative
Down," 126
Creason, Mark, 153–54
Creed, Mrs. G. B., 66
Crowley, Mary, 6–7, 9

D. H. McConnell and Co., 248n.56
Daphne fragrance line, 111–12
Davis, Brian, 59
Denny, Riley, 156
Depression era
company literature, 108–9, 122–27
cosmetic companies during, 114
direct selling as supplemental
income, 127–28
explanations for Avon's survival during,
109, 129–32
household economies during, 260n.53
increased sales force, 107–8
market-wide beauty product sales,
111, 112
merchandising strategies, 121
profits, 107–8
recruiting goals increased, 120–21
representatives' earnings, 106, 107–8
turnover rate, 120–21
Detwiler, Paul, 153
DeVos, Richard, 7–8
Dillon, Annette, 56–57

"Ding Dong! Avon Calling" advertising
campaign, 166–67, 173–75, 190
Direct Line (newsletter), 184–85
Direct Sales Association, 6–7, 195
Direct sales business model, 2–4, 6–7, 9
advantages, 14–15
Avon's devotion to, 240
commission structures, 183–84
defined, 2
during Depression, 107, 109–
10, 127–28
disadvantages, 14–15
feminization of, 9, 164
franchises vs., 243n.11
hallmarks of, 239
home parties, 7–8
independent contractor classification,
2, 128–29
inefficiency, 16
mail-order sales vs., 14–15, 16–17
multi-level marketing as
competition, 211–12
operating costs, 110–11
operating structure, 127–28
postwar era, 164, 264n.3
public distrust of, 17–18, 21–22
recruiting expenses, 110–11
reputation of salesmen, 15, 16
retail as competition, 14–15
as thriving on representatives' morality
tales, 126
traditional businesses vs., 109–10
worker solidarity avoidance, 73–74
Direct Selling Association, 192–95,
244n.12. See also Agents Credit
Association; National Association of
Direct Selling Companies (NADSC)
Discrimination, 55, 198–200, 211, 213–14,
216, 224–25, 228–29, 236
District managers, 146–47
African American, 196–97
compensation, 147–48, 156
corporate expectations, 161–62
Manual for, 147
District Sales Division, 146–47, 196–97
Diversity, 166, 196–98, 200–3, 223, 224–25
"Does It Pay?" (booklet), 68–69
Donahue, Phil, 223–24

Door-to-door sales representatives. *See* representatives
Downline, 7–8, 211–12
Dr. Zabrieskie's Soap, 180
Dreher, Monroe, 118, 172–75
DSOW (District Supervisor On Way), 81–82
Dual-marketing formula, 8
Dunn, Irene, 172–73
Durkee, Mrs. L. E., 66
Dyroen-Lancer, Becky, 233–34

Eastman, Lela, 86–87, 88, 90–92, 118–20
    automobile, 91–92, 133
    on Avon as new company name, 118
    on boarding houses as home like, 94
    as city sales office manager, 133, 136, 142–44, 148–49
    contests, 144–45
    first radio advertising, 120
    as suited to life on road, 93–94, 97–98
    as traveling agent, 88
Elizabeth Arden, 6, 167
Ellis, Mrs. Emma, 65–66
Emotional logic, 61, 150, 259–60n.42
Encyclopedia Britannica, 109, 127–28, 144–45
Ethical Code of Conduct, DSA, 193–95
Ewald, John, 3–4, 114–15, 121
    appointed McConnell Jr.'s successor, 159
    approach to managing women, 153–54
    "Better Business" keynote address, 167, 168
    corporate impersonality challenges, 168–69
    creation of brotherhood among management staff, 169
    on hard luck, 126
    management conferences, 152
    national advertising, 120
    on needs of representatives, 166–67, 169–70
    retirement, 190
    retrospective of McConnell Sr.'s ideals and practices, 168–69
    selling campaigns, 121, 129–32
    "Success Is Not An Accident," 125–26

Feeley, Robert, 145–46, 171
Feiler, Mrs. Mabel, 41, 43
Feitz, Lindsey, 184–85, 195, 196, 197
Feminine Mystique, The (Friedan), 184–85, 216–17
Feminist movement, 10–11, 166, 192–208, 211
    antifeminist position countering, 218–19
    efforts to embrace language of, 197–200
    referenced in advertising, 198*f*
    rural, 52–53
    second wave, 239
    stereotypes, 218–19
    Superwoman image, 218–19
    women separating themselves from, 218–19
    workplace equality as goal, 217–18
Fiddler, Anna, 57
Field managers. *See* district managers
Field Sales Division. *See* District Sales Division
Figsbee, Anna, 246n.23
Findley, Mrs. F. M., 86–88
Fogartie, Louise, 82, 85–86, 89, 92, 93–96, 106–7, 136
"For Beauty, Health, and Home" (catalog), 23–25
Franklin, Mrs. R. J., 41–42, 43
Friedan, Betty, 184–85, 216–17
Fuller, Alfred, 3–4, 5–6
Fuller, Evelyn, 3–4
Fuller Brush Company, 3–4, 9, 17–18, 109, 122, 127–28, 136, 144–45, 159, 189, 194
Fusee, Free, 190

Gannett, Deborah, 263n.56
Gender
    as central to Avon business model, 237
    glass ceiling at Avon, 149–50
    management strategies and assumptions about, 122
    networks based on, 71
    role in management standardization, 151–52
    wage-earning potential, 71

"Getting the Most Value Out of Your Territory" (1942), 141
Gideons travelers association, 15, 127–28
Gilbert, Mrs. G. M., 90–91
Ginthner, Mrs. Nelle, 173, 176*f*
Glass ceiling, 10, 149–50, 212–13, 237, 239
Glenn, Mrs. Roy, 66
Godey's Lady's Book, 21
Gold, Christina, 213–14
Gold Aluminum Flatware, 248n.56
Goodman, Ellen, 215
Goss, Mrs. Hattie, 101*f*
"Great Oak, The" (McConnell), 168–69
Green, Hetty, 44–45
Green River Ordinance, 245n.21
Gregory, Paul, 153
Guest, Mrs. William, 31–32

H. M. Rogers Company, 34
Harvey, Mrs. Byron, Jr., 172–73
Hassan, Fred, 235
Having It All: Love, Sex, Money Even if You're Starting from Nothing (Brown), 10, 217–18
"Having it all" phrase, 217–19
Henderson, A. D., Sr., 258n.25
Henderson, Alexander, Jr., 258n.25
"Her Courage Lives Today" advertisement, 263n.56
Hicklin, Wayne, 114–15, 117, 133, 153
  on city markets, 146, 155
  on failure of Fuller Brush men, 136
  on guaranteed salaries, 121–22
  ideal Avon sales representative, 171
  on national advertising, 120
  on representatives during wartime, 156
  television advertising, 190
  on three-week selling cycle, 121
  tracking successful managers, 145–46
"Hidden Customer" sales campaign, 190–91
Holland Furnace, 194
Holt, Miss Myrtle, 78*f*
Home Interiors and Gifts, 6–7, 9, 194
Home party sales system, 5–8, 264n.3

"Honoring a WAVE," 160*f*
"How Good You Look" campaign, 218
Hughs, Mrs. Will, 65–66
Hunter, Miss Fannie, 49*f*
Husbands, 58–61, 104–5, 181, 182

"I Bring Beauty Wherever I Go" ad series, 177*f*, 178–81
"If You're Serious, You're Avon" campaign, 206–8
Immigrants, 53–55, 116–17, 224–26
"In Praise of Cadet Nurses," 161*f*
Instruction manuals, 25–27, 36, 44, 54–55, 56, 57, 79–80, 83–84, 147, 196. *See also* company literature
International Federation of Commercial Travelers, 96
International markets, 9–10, 192, 232–35
Internet platforms, 233, 234

J. R. Watkins, 69
Jackson-Randolph, Marie, 225
Jobbers, 16
Johannes, Connie, 173–75, 176–77
Joyner-Kersee, Jackie, 233–34
Jung, Andrea, 10–11, 213–14, 232*f*, 233–35
"Just Another Avon Lady" television commercial, 233–34

King, Albert, 64–65
King, Mrs. Albert, 64–65, 66–67
Kropf, Susan, 213–14, 232*f*
Kruvant, M. Charito, 223
Kwolek-Folland, Angel, 246n.26

Larkin Soap Company, 69–70
Lathom, Gladys, 142–43, 146, 148–49
Leatherbury, Mrs. Margaret, 85*f*
Linnell, Mrs. Amy, 34
Little Mrs. Smith, 170–71, 198–200
Loden, Marilyn, 212–13
Low income markets, 196
Lyman's Limited, 167–68

Madame C. J. Walker's Manufacturing Company, 22, 54

Madden, Paul, 137–38, 153
Mail-order sales, 14–15, 16–17
Malone, Annie Turnbo, 22, 54
"Management Women and the New Facts of Life" (Schwartz), 214
"Managing a Woman Effectively," 198–200
Mark cosmetics line, 11
Marketing, 10
    to African Americans, 195, 197, 199f, 204–6
    Avon brand, 168
    catalogs, 25
    conservative strategy, 167
    consumers as potential representatives, 172
    increased costs of, 234
    internet, 11, 233, 240
    money-back guarantees, 16–17
    multicultural approach, 205–6
    reports, 188
    sales spiel as venue for, 25, 29
    women's work pattern changes and, 206
Mary Kay Cosmetics, 3, 6–7, 8–9
    as addressing different market from Avon, 192–93
    author's experience with, 238
    commission structure, 211–12
    as competition for Avon, 211–12, 219–20
    earnings for independent contractors, 211–12
    emotional logic, 150
    hobby sales, 211–12
    recruiting philosophy, 8
    sales meetings, 192–93
    sales structure, 8
    Seminar, 238
Mary Kay on People Management (Ash), 221
Mass-consumer society, 257n.8
Mathews, Mrs. Claire, 174f
Max Factor cosmetics company, 3, 6, 114, 167
May, Elaine Tyler, 186
Maybelline cosmetics company, 114, 167–68
McConnell, David, Jr., 3–4, 115f
    branch management system, 134–35

company name change, 5
corporate culture influence, 114–15
death, 159
national advertising campaign, 120
as skillful manager, 159
as successor to McConnell Sr., 114
McConnell, David H., Sr., 3–4, 14f
    on canvassing, 63
    conservative business practices, 17
    CPC as fitting into women's domestic role, 61
    death, 129
    on Depression-era business, 107–8
    "Great Oak, The," 168–69
    inventory calculation, 30
    letters to representatives, 29–30
    move to background in decision making, 114
    new payment system, 121–22
    "peculiar method" of sales, 13
    perfume line, 12–13
    positive thinking, 124
    reasons for hiring women, 19–20
    relationship of company and representatives, 31–32
    tableware line, 248n.56
    three-week selling cycle, 121
    Union Publishing Company, 12–13
    on women as doing most of spending, 124
McConnell, George, 247n.34
McCoy, Sherilyn S., 235–36
McDonel and Company, 187, 188–89
McGoovan, Hattie, 126
McNutt, Mrs. Charles, 125–26
"Medallion of Honor for Women of Achievement," 160f, 161f, 162f
Megargel, Pauline, 56–57
Men
    as bestowing economic opportunity on women, 198–200
    exclusive hold on corporate power, 161–62
    as executive staff, 6, 133–34, 149–50, 153
    grooming products for, 180
    perceived knowledge of women, 200–1

postwar increase in college-
   educated, 164–65
professional jobs *vs.* sales, 163
reluctance to address sexism, 200–1
sales as job for, 242n.10, 264n.4
training of new, 169
Menard, Miss Lillian, 67–68
Metcalfe, Mrs. Marie, 84*f*
Meyerowitz, Joanne, 186
Miller, Effie, 34, 35*f*
Miller, Mrs. W., 91
MINN-WE Foundation, 228
"Mirror Mirror on the Wall" panel, 212–13
Mitchell, David, 190, 193, 195, 197
Mizer, Dorothy, 185
"Mommy track," 10, 216–17
Monumental Makeover, 209, 210*f*
Moore, Mrs. Mary Ella, 98*f*
Motivation, 29–35. *See also* company
   literature
   contests, 34–35, 144–45
   encouragement letters, 28, 29–30, 41–42
   monthly newsletter, 31–32
   personalization of letters, 29–30
   prizes as sales incentives, 32–35, 33*f*
   sales reports, 31–32
   warning letters, 28, 31
Multi-level marketing, 6–8, 21–22,
   183–84, 192–93, 211–12, 219–
   20, 264n.3

Napper, Lottie, 57
National Association of Direct
   Selling Companies (NADSC),
   127–29, 140
National Labor Relations Act of 1935,
   127–28, 129–32
National Recovery Act, 127–28
Natura Group, 235–36
Neighbors, Patricia, 180–81, 200
New Avon, 235–36
New Deal, 127–32
Nixon, Richard, 193–94
Norris, Mrs. Zada, 147–48
"Now You Are In Business For Yourself,"
   129, 130*f*
Nunemaker, Irene, 153–54, 178–79
Nutrilite Company, 7–8

Order of United Commercial Travelers, 96
"Our General Agents" (newsletter
   column), 89
Outlook. See Avon Outlook; CPC Outlook

Packaging, 5, 23–25, 112, 172, 189
Padilla, Mary Ann, 225–26
Pedrick, Mrs. A. L., 58
Perrin, Charles, 213–14
"Pink Ribbon Touch" plan, 171–73
"Plans for Progress" bulletin, 195
Ponds skin care company, 114
Poro cosmetics company, 22
Positive thinking, 29, 36–40, 76, 123–24,
   126. *See also* business strategy
Postwar era
   Avon as business leader for
      women, 164
   changes in business during, 163–64
   city sales office development, 166–67
   conservatism, 166–78
   cosmetics industry statistics, 187
   cultural constraints for women, 186
   direct selling, 164, 184–85, 264n.3
   gender ideology contradictions, 187
   hobby sales, 165–66
   increased representative
      recruitment, 167
   management style, 169
   national advertising campaign, 166–
      67, 171
   pre-selling focus, 172
   representative demographics, 164–65
   sales management standardized, 166–67
   shift in priorities, 166
   suburban markets penetration, 166–67
   survey of direct sales cosmetic
      purchases, 189
   view of salesmanship, 163
Powell, Sharlyne, 226–27
Preston, James, 193–94, 200–1, 213–14
Prevey, Jennie, 56–57
Prince Matchabelli, 167–68
Princess House, 9
Procope, Ernesta, 204–5
Procope, John, 204–5
Product safety, 193–94
Prout, Miss Flora A., 98–100

Public relations, 194–95, 196–97, 209, 221–22, 224, 231–32
PUSH (People United to Save Humanity), 196–97, 204–5

Quality Bonus, 88, 90, 107

R. G. Dun credit organization, 252n.40
Racism, 198–200, 224–26, 228–29
Rader, Sarah, 56–57
Reagan, Ronald, 226
Real Silk (hosiery company), 4, 86
Ream, Mrs. S., 70
Recordon, Gertrude, 111–12
Recruiting manuals, 46–47, 63–64, 181–82. *See also* company literature
Recruitment
    biases in, 53–55
    in city markets, 116–17, 137–40
    married representatives, 51, 58
    multicultural approach, 205–6
    quotas, 88, 106–7
    rural women, 51–52
    scripted pitch for, 138–39
    town classifications, 51–52
    working women, 206–7
"Rediscovering the American Dream" program, 222
Regal company, 194
Reich, Robert, 212–13
Reichard, Paul, 152–53
Representatives, 1, 18. *See also* Avon Lady
    advancement to traveling agent, 56–57
    age of, 55, 171, 188
    as ambassadors of beauty, 127
    average sales per, 171
    black, 54–55
    canceling of contract, 66
    categories, 43–44
    census occupation titles, 55–56
    contract with CPC, 38–39
    cosmetics and beauty training, 178–79, 180–81
    CPC as support network, 72–73
    credit, letter of, 27–28, 59–60
    delinquent, 30, 31
    demographic profile, 4, 164–65

department store sales agents *vs.* direct selling, 249n.5
deposit, 59–60
as directors and participants in consumption, 42–43
earnings, 41–42, 89, 157, 181, 183–84
encouragement letters, 28, 29–30, 41–42
expenses, 27, 59–60, 72, 183–84
familiarity with sales work, 68–69
family mobility, 53–54
full-time *vs.* part-time, 63–65
image as preserve for whiteness, 53–54
imagining experience of, 238
inactive, 81–82
as independent contractors, 2, 20–21, 128–29, 260–61n.56, 261n.57
isolation of, 73–74
legal status, 140
letters from, 41–42
limitations in describing, 49–50
listed in newsletters, 50
married *vs.* single, 51, 58
as morally bound to company, 31–32, 248n.51
new, 146
old, 140–41, 142–43
on-site supervision as absent, 122–23
as owning business, 72
prize-winning, 50–51, 52
productivity increase during wartime, 157
profiles of, 44, 48–67, 171, 188, 210–11
racially inclusive corps of, 166
ratio of men to women, 51
rights, 194–95
sales records, 28–29
sample cases, 25–27
self-confidence required by job, 123
serving only own family needs, 66
as short term part-time labor, 20
situation reports, 65–66
social interactions as rewarding, 239
social network reliance, 53–54
stories in company literature, 106–26
tenure, 67, 171
territories, 140–42
title changes, 246n.22
training, 61–64, 123, 146, 151, 183*f*

warning letters, 28, 31, 81–82
women hired as, 1–2
Revlon cosmetics company, 3,
    114, 167
Ries, Raymond, 110–11, 257–58n.14
Robinson, Miss Susie, 126
Rooks, Russel, 117, 135, 140, 146–47,
    153, 190
Rural feminism, 52–53
Rural markets, 4, 16–17, 67–71, 112–14,
    146–47

Sales leaders, 62–63, 151
Sales meetings, 142–45, 146, 147, 151,
    165–66, 184–85
Sales reports, in newsletters, 31–32
Salesman Americanus, 164, 169–70
Salesmen, 15–16, 17–18, 96, 163
"Salute to an Army Nurse," 162f
Sample cases, 18–19, 25–27, 55, 59–60
Sanford, Mrs. Ed, 67–68
Scheele, William, 25–27, 29–30
Schwartz, Felice, 214–17, 222
Sears, R. W., 16–17
Sears and Roebuck, 14–15, 16–17
Selby, Cecily, 201–4
Selling cycles
    three-week, 121, 150–51, 189
    two-week, 189
"Selling in Today's Economy" (Buell), 163
Setter, Mrs. A. M., 90–91
Shaklee, 9
Situation reports, 65–66, 81
Skin-So-Soft product line, 189, 235–36
Sklar, Stuart, 234
Snow, Eugene, 65, 66–67, 77–79, 79f
Social networks, 4, 7, 8, 9, 16–18, 53–54,
    67–71, 117–18, 126–27
Sorenson, Mrs. Robert, 66
Sothern, Ann, 175f
Speak Out initiative, 231–32
Sproule, Jane, 55–56, 57
Stanley Home Products, 5–7, 109, 189,
    241–42n.9
"Statement on Corporate
    Responsibility," 195
Statue of Liberty, 209
Steih, Marie, 64f

Stoeppelwerth, Sydney, 223
"Story of Avon, The," 181–82
Studebaker, Veral, 59
Suburban markets, 5–7, 134–35, 164–
    65, 166–67
Superwoman, image of feminist as, 218–19

Tangee cosmetics company, 114
Taylor, Mark, 31–32, 114–15, 140, 153–54
"Teen-agers' Beauty Care," 180
"Teenage Good Grooming" educational
    campaign, 189
Teenage market, 180, 189
Territory system, 18, 128–29, 137–38,
    140–42, 145
Them, Mrs. Fred, 125–26
Thurlow, Heida, 227–28
"Tiebolt" company, 110–11, 144–45,
    257–58n.14
Tober, Barbara, 227
Training, 61, 83–88
    black representatives, 137–38
    city markets, 146, 148, 191–92
    company literature, 61–63
    consumers, 171
    cosmetics, 178–79, 180–81
    Manual of Instruction (1915), 83–84
    payment collection, 110–11
    professional, 206–7
    representative/customer scenarios, 151
    rural markets, 146
    sales meetings and, 143–44, 151
    by traveling agents, 61–62, 84–87
    "Women in Management Awareness
        Training Program," 198–200
"Travel Talks," 75, 98–100
Travelers Protective Association, 256n.53
Traveling agents, 4, 18–19, 239. See also
    city sales office managers; district
    managers
    addressing husbands' objections, 59
    age of, 98–100
    appearance, 79–80
    business personality, 76, 77
    communication with home office
        managers, 80
    community event attendance, 92–93
    company reliance on, 77

Traveling agents (*cont.*)
  criteria for hiring, 77–80
  culture of, 77–79
  earnings, 88–92, 106–7
  expenses, 89–90
  family obligations, 100–2, 104–5
  as historically important, 76
  independence, 83, 92
  instruction manuals, 25–27, 44, 54–55, 56, 58
  interaction with men, 93–94
  lack of professional associations, 96–97
  life on road, 92–96
  lodging while traveling, 94–96
  marital status, 98–100
  nature of job, 77
  performance records, 28–29
  personal profiles, 98–105
  previous work experience, 100–3
  recruiting materials, 82
  recruitment resistance anecdotes, 58–59
  representative profiles, 28
  requirements, 76–77
  routes, 81
  safety of, 93–94
  schedule, 95
  sisterhood of, 96–98
  situation reports, 65–66, 81
  start as successful representatives, 76–77
  success of company as hinging on, 75
  tracking, 80–83
  training, 83–88
  traveling trunk, 82
  women employed as, 75–76
  work as calling, 76
Tupperware, 3, 6–7, 9, 194
Turlington, Mrs. Mary, 85–86, 88
Tussy, 167–68

Uniworld Group, 196–97, 205–6

Van Andel, Jay, 7–8

W. T. Rawleigh Company, 69
Wagner Act. *See* National Labor Relations Act of 1935
Walker, Madame C. J., 22, 54n.28, 54, 116–17
Walker Method, 22
Wearever Aluminum Cookware, 4, 5–6, 127–28, 144–45
Weirich, Miss Mary, 66
Wellington, Sheila, 213–14
Wesley, Mrs. Mary A., 70
Whiteness
  as associated with business and respectability, 54
  Avon Lady as white suburban America icon, 165
  beauty standards of, 205–6
  board of directors, 204–5
  in national advertising campaigns, 173
  representative image as preserve for, 53–54
  television commercials, 218
Williams, Alphonse, 114–15
Williams, Miss Sara, 91
Williams, Mrs. Hetty, 91
Winston, Mary, 223
Wise, Brownie, 6–7, 9
Women
  as active economic agents, 44–46
  on board of directors, 201–5
  business *vs.* non-profit image of, 44–46
  career-first *vs.* career and family, 215–17
  changing societal roles of, 46–47
  corporate culture participation, 154
  costs of employing in management, 215
  early direct selling recruitment, 3–4, 6
  as emasculating workplace, 217–18
  empowerment by CPC business strategy, 36–40
  entrepreneurship, 1, 10, 38–39, 44–45, 68, 72, 173–75, 187, 211, 221–32, 237–38
  exclusive hiring as Avon representatives, 1–2
  farm *vs.* non-farm, 52–53
  gendered notions of appropriate behavior, 47–48
  glass ceiling at Avon, 149–50
  growth of sales jobs for, 164–65
  hostess role, 266n.26
  lack of business support system for, 222

in management, 2, 6, 10–11, 133–34,
149–50, 202*f*, 212–15, 237–38, 239
married, as representatives, 51, 58
maternal role in corporations, 18–19,
246n.26
motivations for starting business,
229, 230–31
obstacles to business success, 229–30
personal approach to managing, 153–54
presence in business
environments, 143–44
as responsible for economic security,
124, 129
retaining in management, 214–16
as salaried employees, 2
sales work as familiar to, 68–69
as shoppers, 241n.6
stereotype of masculine, 216
under-representation in
management, 212
wartime industrial work *vs.* direct
selling, 157–58
work patterns, 206
working outside home, 249–50n.10,
266n.36
"Women Hold Key Avon Management
Positions," 202*f*
"Women in Management Awareness
Training Program," 198–200
Women of Enterprise Award program, 10,
211, 221–32, 236
analysis of applicants, 229–30
applications, 224–25, 228–29
awards gala, 223–24
barriers to business goals, 228–29
criteria for, 223
diversity of, 223–25
honorary award winners, 231

irony of, 231–32
language of, 223
non-Avon women prioritized, 231
personal hardship prioritized, 224–
25, 230–31
as public relations strategy, 221–22, 224
publicity as main reward, 223–24
role model status, 223–24, 226–27
SBA Office of Women's Business
Ownership as partner, 222
Tiffany crystal trophy, 223–24
winners, 223, 225–28, 230
Women's liberation movement. *See*
feminist movement
Women's rights, 46, 165
Women's suffrage, 46
Women's trades, 68
Wood, Mrs. C. A., 75, 100–2
Working Woman magazine, 209–10
World Gift Corporation, 8
World War II era
city markets focus, 155–56
cosmetic sales during, 158–59
drafting of upper management
staff, 155
increased sales during, 155, 156
industrial work for women *vs.* direct
selling, 157–58
military contracts for toiletries kits, 155,
159–61, 167–68
productivity increase of
representatives, 157
reduction in number of representatives,
155, 159–61

Yardley of London, 167–68
Young, Loretta, 172–73
Yue, May, 228